1996 Edition

The Definitive Guide to Buying a Truck

by Jack Gillis

with

Karen Fierst
and
Scott Beatty

HarperPerennial
A Division of HarperCollins*Publishers*

Publisher's Note

Every attempt has been made to ensure that the ratings, statistics, and other data found in this book were current and accurate when this book went to press. Because of occasional changes by automobile manufacturers in their vehicles' design and performance, however, some of this data may change. During the year, new information released by the government, manufacturers or private sources may affect the data in the book.

About the Author

Jack Gillis spent three years as a marketing analyst with the U.S. Department of Transportation's National Highway Traffic Safety Administration. While at NHTSA, he prepared the first edition of *The Car Book* and in 1981 he began developing the guide independently. Since its introduction, nearly 3 million consumers have received copies of his *Car Books*.

Gillis is a Contributing Correspondent for NBC's "Today Show" and a Contributing Editor at *Good Housekeeping*. He has appeared on all three network evening news programs as well as local and national talk shows, including "Donahue," "Nightline," "The Oprah Winfrey Show," "Good Morning America," and "The Larry King Show." He is frequently quoted in *The Wall Street Journal*, *The New York Times*, *Business Week*, *Money* magazine, *The Washington Post*, and *USA Today*.

Gillis was cited by the National Press Club as one of the best in consumer journalism. Two of his books were among *Money* magazine's "10 Best Personal Finance Books of 1988," and *Sylvia Porter's Personal Finance Magazine* selected him as one of America's personal finance heroes. He is Director of Public Affairs for the Consumer Federation of America, the nation's largest consumer advocacy organization, and Executive Director of the Certified Automotive Parts Association—a non-profit, quality standards organization.

He received his MBA from The George Washington University and BA from the University of Notre Dame. Gillis is married to Marilyn Mohrman–Gillis, and they have four children, Katie, John, Brian, and Brennan.

Also by Jack Gillis

The Car Book
The Used Car Book
The Car Repair Book
The Social Security Book for Women
The Childwise Catalog (coauthor)
How to Make Your Car Last Almost Forever
The Armchair Mechanic (coauthor)
How to Fly (coauthor)
The Bank Book (editor)
The Product Safety Book (editor)
Money in the Bank (editor)

HarperCollins books may be purchased for educational, business, or sales promotional use. For information, please write: Special Markets Department, HarperCollins Publishers, Inc., 10 East 53rd Street, New York, NY 10022.

ISSN: 1062-2578

ISBN 0-06-273281-1

96 97 98 CW 5 4 3 2 1

Cover design by © Gillis and Associates

Photo credits: Chrysler Corporation; Chevrolet Motor Division, General Motors Corporation; GMC Truck Division, General Motors Corporation; Oldsmobile Division, General Motors Corporation.

Back Cover Photo of Jack Gillis: Donna Cantor-MacLean

Contents

Acknowledgments

As is the case each year, many talented individuals have contributed to this *sixth* edition of *The Truck, Van and 4x4 Book*. This year a new name appears as co-author—Scott Beatty. Under his direction, the staff collected, analyzed, and tabulated many thousands of bits of information about today's new vehicles. Because of his incredible project management skills and organizational ability, this amazingly complex project was carried out with grace and competence under extreme deadline pressure. Amy Burch, the other half of the leadership team, assembled the best designed and most seamlessly produced *Truck, Van and 4x4 Book* to date. As always, calm and cool under pressure, Amy developed the expertise necessary to deliver, for the first time, an extraordinarily complex cover and page design completely on disk. And she did so singlehandedly! Also, the experience and institutional knowledge of 11 year *Car Book* veteran Karen Fierst were key elements in this successful effort.

Scott and Amy were able to accomplish great feats due, in particular, to the tremendous assistance of Ashley Cheng, who jumped in with both feet the day he arrived. In addition, Kaz Hickok contributed terrific proofing and copy editing skills, and the gold dust twins, Marshall Einhorn and Ben Becker, were the best summer interns money could buy! Underlying this effort was the excellent foundation provided by last year's co-author, Jay Einhorn, who left our ranks to become a Graduate Fellow at MIT.

This year's edition would not have been possible without essential contributions from many other talented individuals including: Clarence Ditlow and the staff of the Center for AutoSafety; John Noettl, president of Vehicle Support Systems, and his staff; legal expert Phil Nowicki; Carolyn Gorman of the Insurance Information Institute; Susan Cole, color maven; and Amy Shock, who kept everything else in the office going. Very special thanks go to my friend, fellow entrepreneur and terrific literary agent, Stuart Krichevsky.

As always, the most important factor in being able to bring this information to the American car buyer for sixteen years is the encouragement, support, and love from my brilliant and beautiful wife, Marilyn Mohrman–Gillis.

-J.G.

As Always,

for Marilyn &
Katie, John, Brian, and Brennan

Introduction

The best-selling vehicle in America is not a car—it's a truck! In fact, the fastest growing vehicle types continue to be pickups, 4x4s, and minivans. This once limited vehicle class with few options has grown into a new generation of vehicles that are diverse, versatile, and as luxurious and comfortable as any sedan—but, a little short on safety.

The safety criteria that consumers use to evaluate passenger cars are equally important for truck and van buyers. However, trucks, vans, and 4x4s are not required to have all the life-saving safety features which are becoming standard on passenger cars. In addition, because of their unique designs, trucks, vans, and 4x4s have distinct features that aren't available on passenger cars—hence, *The Truck, Van & 4x4 Book.*

Like our other annual consumer references, *The Car Book* and *The Used Car Book*, our goal with *The Truck, Van & 4x4 Book* is to guide you through the various criteria used in selecting the very best vehicle. This sixth edition of the book includes over twice the amount of data included in the first edition—all at your fingertips. This year we've continued our full page, easy-to-understand, vehicle rating pages which detail the information you need to make a smart and safe choice. We've also completely updated the "Buying Guide" which allows you to easily compare individual vehicles with others in their size class.

Minivans are popular because very few station wagons are large enough to hold growing families. Pickups are well-liked because many are priced in the $9,000 to $12,000 range. If you are interested in buying one of these vehicles, be warned: *They do not have to meet many of the same safety standards applied to passenger cars.*

While thousands of Americans buy these vehicles for family and non-commercial use, these vehicles are not required to adhere to the same safety standards as cars. For example, bumpers need not meet any strength requirements. Thanks to pressure from safety advocates and consumers, the government will be requiring all minivans, trucks, and sport utilities to meet the 1997 standards imposed on cars, but not until 1999. A new standard on roof strength is also being adopted. However, it does not go far enough to effectively protect occupants in a rollover situation.

Recently, Americans have learned about incredible accidents from which drivers have simply walked away—all because a simple bag inflated to cushion the impact. But what about the buyers of trucks and sport utility vehicles? Tragically, too many companies have chosen not to offer life-saving protection like airbags.

So how does today's consumer buy safety? Many people mistakenly believe that handling and performance are the key elements in a vehicles' safety. While an extremely unresponsive vehicle could cause an accident, most new vehicles meet basic handling requirements. In fact, many people actually feel uncomfortable driving high-performance vehicles because the responsive steering, acceleration, and suspension systems can be difficult to get used to. But the main reason handling is overrated as a safety measure is that automobile collisions are, by nature, accidents. Once they've begun, they are beyond human capacity to prevent, no matter how

TIP

Typical Operating Costs

The table below shows the operating costs of some popular vehicles. For this comparison, these costs include operating expenses (fuel, oil, maintenance and tires) and ownership expenses (insurance, depreciation, financing, taxes and licensing) and were based on keeping the vehicle for three years and driving 20,000 miles per year.

	Annual Costs		
	Operating	**Ownership**	**Total**
Ford Club Wagon Custom	$2,790	$6,056	$8,846
Chevy Blazer	$2,320	$6,101	$8,421
Chevrolet Lumina Minivan	$2.120	$6,031	$8,151
Jeep Cherokee	$2,510	$6,017	$8,527
Chevy Fleetside Pickup	$2,470	$5,512	$7,982
Ford Ranger	$2,180	$5,502	$7,682

Source: Runzheimer International, Rochester, Wisconsin.

well your vehicle handles. Since accidents are, unfortunately, statistically inevitable, the key to protecting yourself is to purchase a vehicle that offers good crash protection.

Consumer concern for safety has influenced auto makers attitudes, as have our demands for quality—U.S. vehicles are better built than ever. And because we're demanding that companies stand behind their products, we're seeing better warranties, too. Since we began providing comparative warranty information a few years ago, a number of auto makers have told us that they've been forced to offer better warranties now that consumers can tell the difference.

There is no question that buyers of pickups, minivans, and 4x4s need help, and that's what *The Truck, Van and 4x4 Book* is all about—information on a very important and expensive purchase. Consumers are learning that they can get better-performing and safer choices by buying vehicles with good safety records, low maintenance costs, long warranties, and insurance discounts. These and many other features are summarized in "The Buying Guide," which includes more information than ever before—all at your fingertips. Then you can read the individual chapters to learn more about each model.

"The Safety Chapter" presents crash test results, as well as lists of special features. Consumers can look for these features, such as anti-lock brakes and air bags, to compensate for the fact that these vehicles do not have to meet the same safety standards as passenger cars. We also discuss the new 1999 side impact standards for trucks, vans and 4x4s and inform you of which vehicles already meet these standards. Finally, we include tips for safe towing and off-roading.

"The Fuel Economy Chapter," in addition to describing special gas-saving devices, provides fuel economy tips for truck and van owners, as well as the complete EPA mileage ratings for trucks, vans, and sport utility vehicles.

"The Maintenance Chapter" allows you to compare maintenance costs, offers advice on service contracts, and tips for dealing with a mechanic.

"The Warranty Chapter" offers a critical comparison of the new warranties and lets you know the best and worst before you get into trouble down the road. It will also tip you off to secret warranties.

"The Insurance Chapter" will help you save money on an expense that is often forgotten in the showroom.

Because most of us can't tell one tire from another, we've included "The Tire Chapter" to help you select the best.

"The Complaint Chapter" provides a road map to resolving inevitable problems quickly and efficiently. We provide consumers with their only access to the hundreds of thousands of vehicle complaints on file with the U.S. Government. Thanks to the efforts of the Center for Auto Safety, we continue to include this otherwise unavailable information—and it's all-new and updated for 1996.

Review "The Showroom Strategy Chapter" for tips on getting the best price—for many of us, one of the hardest and most distasteful aspects of car buying.

Finally, our all new "Ratings Chapter" provides a detailed review of each 1996 model. These pages provide, at a glance, an overview of all the criteria you need to make a good choice. You'll be able to quickly assess key features and see how the vehicle stacks up against its competition so you can make sure your selection is the best vehicle for you. Prices have more than doubled since 1980, so we've also included the percent of *dealer* mark-up to help you negotiate the very best price.

The information in *The Truck, Van & 4x4 Book* is based on data collected and developed by our staff, private automobile engineering firms, the U.S. Department of Transportation, and the Center for Auto Safety. With all of this data in hand, you'll find some great choices for 1996. *The Truck, Van & 4x4 Book* will guide you through the trade-offs, claims, promises, facts, and myths to the vehicle that will best meet your needs.

—Jack Gillis

Buying Guide

The Buying Guide provides an overall comparison of 1996 vehicles in terms of safety, fuel economy, maintenance, insurance costs, warranty, complaint ratings, and other key items.

Based on these comparisons, this chapter also offers a list of Best Bets—the 1996 minivans, sport utility vehicles, and pickups that rated tops when all of these categories were considered.

Also included is summary information on towing, cargo space, and average prices. You can find more detailed information on these categories throughout the book. In general, there are five key steps to buying a vehicle.

1 Narrow your choice down to a particular class of vehicle—sport utility, pickup, minivan, or van. These are general classifications and some vehicles may fit into more than one category. In most cases, *The Truck, Van & 4x4 Book* presents the vehicles by size class.

2 Determine what features are really important to you. Most buyers consider safety on the top of their list, which is why "The Safety Chapter" is right up front in *The Truck, Van & 4x4 Book*. Airbags, power options, ABS, the number of doors and passengers, as well as "hidden" elements such as maintenance and insurance costs, should be considered at this stage in your selection process.

3 Find 3 or 4 vehicles that meet the needs you outlined above *and* your pocketbook. It's important not to narrow your choice down to one vehicle because then you lose all your bargaining power in the showroom. In fact, because vehicles today are more similar than dissimilar, it's not hard to keep three or four choices in mind. On the rating pages in the back of the book, we suggest some competitive choices for your consideration. For example, if you are interested in the Jeep Cherokee, you should also consider the Ford Explorer.

4 Make sure you take a good long test drive. The biggest buying mistake most of us make is to overlook those nagging problems that seem to surface only after we've brought the vehicle home. Spend at least an hour driving the vehicle. This includes time on the highway, parking, taking it in and out of your driveway or garage, sitting in the back seat, and using the storage area. Whatever you do, *don't talk price until you're ready to buy!*

5 This is the stage most of us dread—negotiating the price. While price negotiation is a buying tradition, a few car makers and dealers are trying to break tradition by offering so-called "no-haggle pricing." Because they're still in the minority, and because it's almost impossible to establish true competition between dealers as individuals, we offer a new means to avoid negotiating altogether by using the non-profit CarBargains pricing service.

Now that you have a quick guide to the necessary steps in making a good choice, use the tables that follow to quickly review the new vehicles and the pages in the back for a detailed critique of each model. See "The Showroom Strategy Chapter" for more details on getting the best price.

In This Chapter...

Using the Buying Guide

The "Buying Guide" will allow you to quickly compare the 1996 models.

To fully understand these summary charts, it is important to read the appropriate section of the book. You will note that here and throughout the book, some of the charts contain empty boxes. This indicates that the data was unavailable at the time of printing.

Here's how to understand what's included in "The Buying Guide."

Page Reference: The page in the back of the book where you'll find all the details for this vehicle.

Overall Rating: This is the "bottom line." It shows how well this vehicle stacks up on a scale of 1 to 10 when compared to all others on the market. The overall rating considers safety, maintenance, fuel economy, warranty, insurance costs, and complaints. Due to the importance of crash tests, vehicles with no crash test results as of our publication date cannot be given an overall rating. More recent results may be available from the Auto Safety Hotline at 1-800-424-9393 (see page 73).

Crash Test Rating: This indicates how well the vehicle performed in the U.S. Government's 35-mph frontal crash test program. We have analyzed the 1996 models, compared them to all the government tests ever performed, and given them a rating from *very good* to *very poor*. These ratings allow you to compare the test results of one vehicle with another, relative to all of your choices.

Airbags: Hidden in the steering wheel hub and, in some cases, the passenger side of the dashboard, airbags inflate instantly in frontal crashes to prevent the occupant from violently hitting the dashboard, windshield, or steering wheel. An asterisk indicates that the feature is optional, whereas "driver" or "dual" (on both driver and passenger sides) indicates that airbags are standard.

Anti-lock Brake System (ABS): These keep your wheels from locking up by automatically "pumping" the brakes up to five times per second. ABS decreases braking distance, prevents skidding, and allows more control in a sudden stop. Although ABS is typically connected to all four wheels, in many sport utility vehicles it is connected to only the rear wheels. Two-wheel anti-lock

Best Bets for 1996

Based on information in the *Buying Guide*, this list shows the highest-rated vans, sport utility, and pickup trucks in each of the size categories. Ratings are based on expected performance in six important categories (crash tests, fuel economy, repair costs, warranties, insurance costs, and complaints), with the heaviest emphasis on crash test performance. In some of the weight classes, not many vehicles (or none at all) were deemed worthy of selection as a "best bet."

Minivans
Ford Windstar (10)
Oldsmobile Silhouette (9)
Pontiac Trans Sport (9)

Large Sport Utility
Ford Bronco (7)
Chevrolet Tahoe (5)

Mid-Size Sport Utility
Ford Explorer (10)
Mitsubishi Montero (6)

Compact Pickups
Dodge Dakota (9)
Ford Ranger (7)

Standard Pickups
Chevrolet C/K Series (10)
GMC Sierra (10)
Ford F-Series Pickup (9)

brakes are not as effective as four-wheel.

Side Impact Protection: By 1999, light trucks, vans and sport utility vehicles must have increased side impact protection built in, and starting this year, some vehicles do. Find out which vehicles have this much needed protection. A *strong* rating means that the vehicle meets the 1999 requirement, a *weak* rating means it does not.

Fuel Economy: This is the EPA-rated fuel economy for city and highway driving measured in miles per gallon. A single model may have a number of fuel economy ratings because of different engine and transmission options. We have included the figure for what is expected to be the most popular model.

Repair Rating: This rating is based on nine typical repairs after the warranty expires and the cost of following the manufacturer's preventive maintenance schedule during the warranty period.

Warranty Rating: This is an overall assessment of the vehicle's warranty when compared to all other warranties. The rating considers the important features of each warranty, with emphasis on the length of the basic and powertrain warranties.

Complaint Index: This rating is based on the number of complaints about that vehicle on file at the U.S. Department of Transportation. The complaint index will give you a general idea of experiences others have had with models which are essentially unchanged for this model year. An empty box means that the vehicle is entirely new for 1996 or that we had insufficient data to calculate a rating.

Insurance Cost: Many automobile insurance companies use ratings based on the vehicle's accident and occupant injury history to determine whether or not the insurance premium of a vehicle should be a *discount* or a *surcharge*. (Your insurance company may or may not participate in a rating program.) If the vehicle is likely to receive neither, we label it *regular*.

Typical Price: This price range will give you a general idea of the "sticker," or asking price of a vehicle. It is based on the lowest to highest retail price of the various models, and it does not include options or the discount that you should be able to negotiate using a service such as CarBargains (see page 90).

Other Specifications: Most people buy a truck, van, or sport utility vehicle because they have some special needs—carrying lumber, towing, off-roading, or carpooling. In order to help you narrow down your choice to those vehicles which best meet your requirements, we've included a variety of key specifications on each page in *The Ratings* section at the end of the book.

Trucks Are Hot!

The U.S. truck population has grown to over 60 million vehicles—over three times the number of trucks that were on the road 20 years ago. Twenty-eight percent of all trucks are 12 years old or over and 23 percent are under three years old. The average truck age is over eight years old.

Vehicle	See Pg.	Overall Rating■ Poor ⇔ Good	Crash Test	Air Bags	Anti-Lock Brakes	Side Impact Protection	Fuel Economy
Minivans							
Chevrolet Astro	99		No Test	Dual	4-wheel	Weak	16/21
Chevrolet Lumina	103		Good	Driver	4-wheel	Weak	19/26
Chrysler T & C	107		No Test	Dual	4-wheel	Strong	17/24
Dodge Caravan	108		No Test	Dual	4-wheel	Strong	20/26
Ford Aerostar	112		Average	Driver	2-wheel	Weak	18/24
Ford Windstar	118		Very Good	Dual	4-wheel	Strong	17/23
GMC Safari	120		No Test	Dual	4-wheel	Weak	16/21
Honda Odyssey	127		Good	Dual	4-wheel	Strong	20/24
Isuzu Oasis	130		No Test	Dual	4-wheel	Weak	20/24
Mazda MPV	140		No Test	Dual	4-wheel	Weak	16/22
Mercury Villager	141		No Test	Dual	4-wheel	Weak	17/23
Nissan Quest	146		No Test	Dual	4-wheel*	Weak	17/23
Olds Silhouette	148		Good	Driver	4-wheel	Weak	19/26
Plymouth Voyager	149		No Test	Dual	4-wheel	Strong	20/26
Pontiac Trans Sport	150		Good	Driver	4-wheel	Weak	19/26
Toyota Previa	155		Average	Dual	4-wheel*	Strong	18/22
Full Size Vans							
Chevy Van/Express	101		No Test	Dual	4-wheel	Weak	15/19
Dodge Ram Vn/Wgn.	111		No Test	Driver	2-wheel**	Weak	15/17
Ford Econ./Clb Wgn.	114		Average	Driver	4-wheel	Weak	14/15
GMC Savana	121		No Test	Dual	4-wheel	Weak	13/17

■ Due to the importance of crash tests, vehicles with no crash test results as of publication date cannot be given an overall rating.

Warranty	Complaint Rating	Insurance Rating	Repair Rating	Typical Price $	Overall Rating■ Poor ⇔ Good	See Pg	Vehicle
							Minivans
Very Poor	Good	Discount	Good	$18-19,000		99	Chevrolet Astro
Very Poor	Poor	Discount	Very Good	$19-20,000		103	Chevrolet Lumina
Very Poor		Regular	Very Good	$24-29,500		107	Chrysler T & C
Very Poor		Regular	Very Good	$16-24,000		108	Dodge Caravan
Very Poor	Average	Discount	Very Good	$17-23,500		112	Ford Aerostar
Very Poor		Regular	Good	$18-24,500		118	Ford Windstar
Very Poor	Average	Discount	Good	$18-19,000		120	GMC Safari
Very Poor		Regular	Poor	$23-25,000•		127	Honda Odyssey
Good		Regular	Poor	$25-28,000		130	Isuzu Oasis
Poor	Poor	Regular	Poor	$21-28,000•		140	Mazda MPV
Very Poor	Poor	Discount	Good	$19-26,500		141	Mercury Villager
Poor	Very Poor	Discount	Good	$21-26,000		146	Nissan Quest
Poor	Average	Discount	Very Good	$21-23,000		148	Olds Silhouette
Very Poor		Regular	Very Good	$16-19,500		149	Plymouth Voyager
Very Poor	Average	Discount	Very Good	$17-18,000•		150	Pontiac Trans Sport
Very Poor	Good	Discount	Poor	$24-32,000		155	Toyota Previa
							Full Size Vans
Very Poor		Regular	Good	$19-23,000		101	Chevy Van/Express
Very Poor	Very Good	Discount	Good	$16-22,000		111	Dodge Ram Vn/Wgn.
Very Poor	Good	Discount	Good	$17-26,000		114	Ford Econ./Clb Wgn.
Very Poor		Regular	Good	$19-23,000		121	GMC Savana

*Optional; **4-wheel optional; •Based on 1995 data.

Vehicle	See Pg.	Overall Rating ■ Poor ⇔ Good	Crash Test	Air Bags	Anti-Lock Brakes	Side Impact Protection	Fuel Economy
Small Sport Utilities							
Geo Tracker	126		Poor	Dual	4-wheel*	Weak	24/26
Jeep Wrangler	135		No Test	Driver	4-wheel*	Weak	19/20
Kia Sportage	136		No Test	Driver	2-wheel	Weak	19/23
Suzuki Sidekick	151		No Test	Dual	2-wheel**	Weak	23/26
Suzuki X-90	152		No Test	Dual	4-wheel	Weak	25/28
Toyota RAV4	156		No Test	Dual	4-wheel*	Weak	24/29
Mid-Size Sport Utilities							
Chevrolet Blazer	100		Very Poor	Driver	4-wheel	Weak	18/24
Ford Explorer	115		Good	Dual	4-wheel	Weak	18/23
GMC Jimmy	119		Very Poor	Driver	4-wheel	Weak	17/22
Honda Passport	128		No Test	Dual	2-wheel**	Weak	16/19
Isuzu Rodeo	131		No Test	Dual	2-wheel**	Weak	15/18
Isuzu Trooper	132		No Test	Dual	4-wheel	Weak	16/18
Jeep Cherokee	133		Good	Driver	4-wheel*	Weak	19/23
Jeep Gr. Cherokee	134		No Test	Dual	4-wheel	Strong	15/21
Land Rover Discovery	137		No Test	Dual	4-wheel	Strong	13/16
Mitsubishi Montero	143		Very Good	Dual	4-wheel*	Weak	15/18
Nissan Pathfinder	144		No Test	Dual	2-wheel	Weak	17/20
Oldsmobile Bravada	147		Very Poor	Driver	4-wheel	Strong	16/21
Toyota 4Runner	153		No Test	Driver	2-wheel**	Weak	19/21
Large Sport Utilities							
Chevrolet Suburban	105		Very Good	Driver	4-wheel	Weak	13/18
Chevrolet Tahoe	106		Average	Driver	4-wheel	Weak	14/17
Ford Bronco	113		Very Good	Driver	4-wheel	Strong	14/17
GMC Suburban	124		Very Good	Driver	4-wheel	Weak	13/18
GMC Yukon	125		Average	Driver	4-wheel	Weak	14/17
Land Rover Rng. Rvr.	138		No Test	Dual	4-wheel	Strong	12/15
Toyota Land Cruiser	154		No Test	Dual	4-wheel	Weak	13/15

■ Due to the importance of crash tests, vehicles with no crash test results as of publication date cannot be given an overall rating.

Warranty	Complaint Rating	Insurance Rating	Repair Rating	Typical Price $	Overall Rating■ Poor ⇔ Good	See Pg	Vehicle
							Small Sport Utilities
Very Poor	Very Good	Surcharge	Average	$14-15,000		126	Geo Tracker
Very Poor	Poor	Surcharge	Very Good	$12-16,000		135	Jeep Wrangler
Average		Regular	Good	$14-16,000		136	Kia Sportage
Very Poor	Good	Regular	Average	$13-19,000		151	Suzuki Sidekick
Very Poor		Regular	Average	$13-16,000		152	Suzuki X-90
Very Poor		Regular	Poor	$16-18,000		156	Toyota RAV4
							Mid-Size Sport Utilities
Very Poor		Surcharge	Good	$19-23,000		100	Chevrolet Blazer
Very Poor		Discount	Very Good	$20-30,000		115	Ford Explorer
Very Poor		Surcharge	Good	$19-23,500		119	GMC Jimmy
Very Poor	Poor	Regular	Good	$17-26,000•		128	Honda Passport
Good	Average	Regular	Good	$17-26,000		131	Isuzu Rodeo
Good	Good	Discount	Average	$24-33,500•		132	Isuzu Trooper
Very Poor	Poor	Regular	Very Good	$15-22,000		133	Jeep Cherokee
Very Poor	Very Poor	Regular	Very Good	$25-33,000		134	Jeep Gr. Cherokee
Poor		Regular	Very Poor	$29-30,000		137	Land Rover Discovery
Average	Good	Surcharge	Poor	$28-38,000		143	Mitsubishi Montero
Poor		Regular	Good	$21-31,000		144	Nissan Pathfinder
Poor		Regular	Good	$29-30,000		147	Oldsmobile Bravada
Very Poor	Good	Surcharge	Average	$22-25,000		153	Toyota 4Runner
							Large Sport Utilities
Very Poor	Very Poor	Discount	Good	$24-28,000		105	Chevrolet Suburban
Very Poor		Discount	Good	$23-31,000		106	Chevrolet Tahoe
Very Poor	Average	Discount	Average	$23-28,500		113	Ford Bronco
Very Poor	Very Poor	Discount	Good	$24-27,500		124	GMC Suburban
Very Poor	Very Poor	Discount	Good	$19-23,500		125	GMC Yukon
Poor	Poor	Regular	Very Poor	$55-56,000		138	Land Rover Rng. Rvr.
Very Poor	Poor	Surcharge	Average	$40-41,000		154	Toyota Land Cruiser

*Optional; **4-wheel optional; •Based on 1995 data.

Vehicle	See Pg.	Overall Rating ■ Poor ⇔ Good	Crash Test	Air Bags	Anti-Lock Brakes	Side Impact Protection	Fuel Economy
Compact Pickups							
Chevrolet S-Series	104		Poor	Driver	4-wheel	Weak	23/30
Dodge Dakota	109		Very Good	Driver	2-wheel**	Weak	21/25
Ford Ranger	117		Good	Dual*	2-wheel**	Weak	22/27
GMC Sonoma	123		Poor	Driver	4-wheel	Weak	18/25
Isuzu Hombre	129		No Test	Driver	4-wheel*	Weak	23/30
Mazda B-Series PU	139		Good	Driver	2-wheel**	Weak	22/27
Mitsu. Mighty Max	142		No Test	None	None	Weak	21/25
Nissan Pickup	145		No Test	Driver	2-wheel	Weak	18/20
Toyota Tacoma	158		No Test	Driver	4-wheel*	Weak	23/28
Standard Pickups							
Chevrolet C/K Series	102		Very Good	Driver	4-wheel	Weak	17/22
Dodge Ram Pickup	110		No Test	Driver	2-wheel**	Weak	16/20
Ford F-Series Pickup	116		Very Good	Driver	2-wheel	Strong	15/19
GMC Sierra	122		Very Good	Driver	4-wheel	Weak	17/22
Toyota T100	157		Very Good	Driver	4-wheel*	Weak	17/21

■ Due to the importance of crash tests, vehicles with no crash test results as of publication date cannot be given an overall rating.

Warranty	Complaint Rating	Insurance Rating	Repair Rating	Typical Price $	Overall Rating▪ Poor ⇔ Good	See Pg	Vehicle
							Compact Pickups
Very Poor	Very Good	Regular	Good	$11-18,000		104	Chevrolet S-Series
Very Poor	Average	Regular	Good	$11-20,000		109	Dodge Dakota
Very Poor	Good	Surcharge	Good	$10-19,000		117	Ford Ranger
Very Poor	Very Poor	Regular	Good	$11-18,500		123	GMC Sonoma
Good		Regular	Good	$10-16,000		129	Isuzu Hombre
Poor	Poor	Surcharge	Good	$10-20,500		139	Mazda B-Series PU
Average	Very Good	Surcharge	Poor	$10-12,000		142	Mitsu. Mighty Max
Poor	Very Good	Surcharge	Good	$10-18,500		145	Nissan Pickup
Very Poor		Regular	Poor	$12-19,500		158	Toyota Tacoma
							Standard Pickups
Very Poor	Very Good	Regular	Good	$14-24,000		102	Chevrolet C/K Series
Very Poor	Good	Regular	Good	$14-25,000		110	Dodge Ram Pickup
Very Poor	Very Good	Discount	Good	$14-21,000		116	Ford F-Series Pickup
Very Poor	Very Good	Regular	Good	$14-21,000		122	GMC Sierra
Very Poor	Very Good	Surcharge	Poor	$14-22,000		157	Toyota T100

*Optional; ** 4-wheel optional; ▪ Based on 1995 data.

Corporate Twins

"Corporate twin" is a term for similar vehicles sold under different names. In many cases, the vehicles are virtually identical, such as the Chevrolet Lumina Minivan, the Oldsmobile Silhouette, and the Pontiac Trans Sport. Sometimes the difference is in body style and luxury options, as with the Chrysler Town and Country and the Dodge Grand Caravan. Generally, twins have the same mechanics, engine, drive train, size, weight, and internal workings. In the past, this was mainly an American phenomenon. Recently, U.S. manufacturers have been selling Asian imports marketed under a U.S. name. In most cases, the only difference is the name plate and the price, sometimes, you will find differences in style. We call these "Asian Cousins."

Twins

General Motors

Chevrolet Lumina Minivan
Oldsmobile Silhouette
Pontiac Trans Sport

Chevrolet Astro
GMC Safari

Chevy Van/Chevy Express
GMC Savana

Chevrolet Blazer
GMC Jimmy
Oldsmobile Bravada

Chevrolet Suburban
GMC Suburban

Chevrolet S-Series Pickup
GMC Sonoma

Chevrolet C/K Series Pickup
GMC Sierra

Chevrolet Tahoe
GMC Yukon

Chrysler

Chrysler Town & Country
Dodge Grand Caravan
Plymouth Grand Voyager

Dodge Caravan
Plymouth Voyager

Isuzu

Honda Passport
Isuzu Rodeo

Honda Odyssey
Isuzu Oasis

Asian Cousins

Ford Ranger—*Mazda B-Series*
Geo Tracker—*Suzuki Sidekick*
Mercury Villager—*Nissan Quest*
Chevrolet S10—*Isuzu Hombre*

SAFETY

For most of us, safety is one of the most important factors in choosing a new vehicle, yet it is also one of the most difficult items to evaluate. To give the greatest possible protection to its occupants, a vehicle should offer a wide variety of safety features including dual airbags and anti-lock brakes (ABS). While these features are becoming more common, they are not yet found on all models.

Another key factor in occupant protection is how well a vehicle performs in a crash test. In order for you to use the crash test information to evaluate your new vehicle choices, we have analyzed and presented the results of the U. S. Department of Transportation crash test program in this chapter. The crash tests measure how well each vehicle protects the driver and front-seat passenger in a frontal crash.

Also described in this chapter are current options and safety features available in this year's models. Additionally, we've included a state-by-state list of the safety belt laws and a detailed discussion of an important, and too often overlooked, safety feature—the child safety seat.

Crash Test Program: In 1979, the U.S. Department of Transportation began an experimental program to compare the occupant protection of one vehicle to that of another. These crash tests show significant differences in the abilities of various automobiles to protect belted occupants during frontal crashes.

In the test, an automobile is sent into a concrete barrier at 35-mph, causing an impact similar to that of two identical vehicles crashing head on at 35-mph. The test vehicle contains electronically monitored dummies in the driver and passenger seats. These data are analyzed to determine the impact of such a collision on a human being.

The government releases an incomplete and confusing array of numbers that are very difficult to understand and almost impossible to use in comparing vehicles.

We have analyzed the data and presented the results using our own *Crash Test Index*. This Index provides an overall means of comparing the results. The following tables allow you to compare the crash test performances of today's vehicles.

It is best to compare the results within weight class, such as compacts to compacts. Do not compare vehicles with differing weights. For example, a small sport utility that is rated *Good* may not be as safe as a full size van with the same rating.

The results evaluate performance in frontal crashes only, which account for about 50 percent of auto-related deaths and serious injuries. Even though the tested vehicle may have airbags, the dummies are also belted.

We rate the crash test results of each vehicle relative to all of the vehicles ever crash tested. This method of rating the vehicles gives you a better idea of the true top performers among the '96 models and identifies those which have substantial room to improve their occupant protection.

The Truck, Van & 4x4 Book wants to stimulate competition, and that's what this new rating program is intended to do. You, the buyer, now know which are truly the best performers. Manufacturers who have chosen to build better performing vehicles will likely be rewarded with your decision to purchase their models.

In This Chapter ...

Crash Tests: How the Vehicles Are Rated

A vehicle's ability to protect you in a crash depends on its ability to absorb the force of impact rather than transfer it to you, the occupant. This is a function of the vehicle's size, weight, and, most importantly, design. The crash tests measure how much of the crash force is transferred to the head, chest, and thighs of the occupants in a 35-mph crash into a barrier.

The vehicles are listed here by weight class, then alphabetically by manufacturer. The first column provides our overall Crash Test Index. This Index is a number which describes all the forces measured by the test. Lower index numbers are better. The Index is best used to compare vehicles within the same size and weight class.

The second column provides an overall rating of *Very Good, Good, Average, Poor* or *Very Poor*. These results reflect the vehicle's performance in relation to all other models ever tested. This exclusive **Truck, Van & 4x4 Book Crash Test Rating** lets you compare, at a glance, the overall performance of the vehicles you'll find in the showroom this year.

The next two columns indicate the likelihood of each occupant sustaining a life-threatening injury, based on the dummies' head and chest scores. Lower percentages mean a lower likelihood of being seriously injured. This information is taken directly from government analysis of the crash test results.

The last two columns indicate how the dummies' legs fared. Legs labeled *Poor* did not meet the government's standards. Those that did meet the standards are rated *Average*, *Good* and *Very Good,* reflecting performance relative to all other vehicles ever tested. These leg injury ratings are not weighted as heavily as head and chest results in determining overall performance.

Results on the following pages indicate how this year's vehicles can be expected to perform in the tests. They are included here only when the design has not changed enough to dramatically alter results. It is expected that, with more crash protection, the current model should produce similar or better results.

Crash test results may vary due to differences in the way vehicles are manufactured, in how models are equipped, and in test conditions. There is no absolute guarantee that a vehicle that passed the test will adequately protect you in an accident. "Corporate twins" that are structurally the same, such as the Dodge Caravan and Plymouth Voyager, can be expected to perform similarly. Keep in mind that some two-door models may not perform exactly like their four-door counterparts and pickups with different-sized cabs or beds may perform differently.

Crash Test Performance: The Best

Here is a list of the best crash test performers (among the 1996 vehicles for which crash test information is available). Lower Crash Test Index numbers indicate better performance. See the following tables for more results.

Minivans
Ford Windstar (1911)
Honda Odyssey (2889)
Chevy Lumina Minivan (3263)
Oldsmobile Silhouette (3263)
Pontiac Trans Sport (3263)

Mid-Size Sport Utility
Ford Explorer 4 dr. 4x4 (2595)
Jeep Cherokee 4 dr. (3330)

Compact Pickup
Dodge Dakota 2 dr. (2302)
Ford Ranger (2771)
Mazda B-Series (2771)

Standard Pickup
Ford F-Series (1590)
Chevrolet C/K Series (2131)
GMC Sierra (2306)
Toyota T100 (2316)

Large Sport Utility
Ford Bronco 2 dr. 4x4 (1505)
Mitsu. Montero 4 dr. 4x4 (2387)
Chev. Suburban 4 dr. 4x4 (2388)
GMC Suburban 4 dr. 4x4 (2388)

Crash Test Performance	Injury Index	Truck Book Rating	Likelihood of Life Threatening Injury		Leg Injury Rating	
			Driver	Passngr	Driver	Passngr
Minivan						
Chevy Lumina (Tr. Sport)	3263	Good	10%	23%	Moderate	Moderate
Ford Aerostar	3544	Average	15%	23%	Moderate	Good
Ford Windstar	1911	*Vry. Gd.*	10%	8%	Good	Good
Honda Odyssey	2889	Good	16%	15%	Moderate	Vry. Gd.
Olds. Silhouette (Tr. Sport)	3263	Good	10%	23%	Moderate	Moderate
Pontiac Trans Sport	3263	Good	10%	23%	Moderate	Moderate
Toyota Previa	3858	Average	20%	23%	Moderate	Good
Full Size Van						
Ford Econoline/Club Wgn.	4098	Average	19%	29%	Moderate	Vry. Gd.
Small Sport Utility						
Geo Tracker (Sidekick) 4X4	5995	**Poor**	44%	30%	Moderate	Moderate
Mid-Size Sport Utility						
Chevrolet Blazer 4dr. 4x4	8348	**Vry. Pr.**	23%	84%	Moderate	Vry. Gd.
Ford Explorer 4dr. 4x4	2595	Good	14%	13%	Good	Good
GMC Jimmy (Blazer) 4dr. 4x4	8348	**Vry. Pr.**	23%	84%	Moderate	Vry. Gd.
Jeep Cherokee 4dr.	3330	Good	16%	20%	Moderate	Moderate
Olds Bravada (Blazer) 4dr.	8348	**Vry. Pr.**	23%	84%	Moderate	Vry. Gd.
Large Sport Utility						
Chev. Suburban 4dr. 4X4[1]	2388	*Vry. Gd.*	13%	11%	Good	Good
Chevrolet Tahoe	3792	Average	14%	26%	Moderate	Moderate
Ford Bronco 2dr. 4X4[1]	1505	*Vry. Gd.*	9%	6%	Vry. Gd.	Vry. Gd.
GMC Suburban 4dr. 4X4[1]	2388	*Vry. Gd.*	13%	11%	Good	Good

HOW TO READ THE CHARTS:

1234 **Injury Index**

The overall numerical injury rating for front seat occupants in a frontal crash. *Lower numbers mean better performance.*

Very Good **Truck Book Rating**

How the vehicle compares among all government test results to date. The range includes very good, good, average, poor and very poor.

00% **Likelihood of Life Threatening Injury**

The chance of life threatening injury to the driver/passenger in a frontal 35 mph crash. *Lower percentages mean better performance.*

Good **Leg Injury Rating**

Injury rating for driver and passenger legs in a frontal crash, when compared to all government test results to date.

Crash Test Performance	Injury Index	Truck Book Rating	Likelihood of Life Threatening Injury		Leg Injury Rating	
			Driver	Passngr	Driver	Passngr
GMC Yukon	3792	Average	14%	26%	Moderate	Moderate
Mitsu. Montero 4dr. 4x4	2387	*Vry. Gd.*	13%	12%	Moderate	Vry. Gd.
Compact Pickup						
Chevrolet S-Series	6275	**Poor**	34%	50%	Moderate	Vry. Gd.
Dodge Dakota	2302	*Vry. Gd.*	7%	18%	Vry. Gd.	Vry. Gd.
Ford Ranger	2771	Good	14%	13%	Moderate	Moderate
GMC Sonoma (S-10)	6275	**Poor**	34%	50%	Moderate	Vry. Gd.
Mazda B-Series (Ranger)	2771	Good	14%	13%	Moderate	Moderate
Standard Pickup						
Chevrolet C/K Series	2131	*Vry. Gd.*	9%	11%	Moderate	Good
Dodge Ram	---	---	---	10%	Vry. Gd.	---
Ford F-Series	1590	*Vry. Gd.*	9%	6%	Good	Vry. Gd.
GMC Sierra (C/K Series)	2306	*Vry. Gd.*	15%	8%	Moderate	Good
Toyota T100	2316	*Vry. Gd.*	14%	10%	Good	Vry. Gd.

[1]Vehicle tested with fewer air bags than now available. Similar or better results should occur with 1996 air bag offering.

HOW TO READ THE CHARTS:

1234 **Injury Index**

The overall numerical injury rating for front seat occupants in a frontal crash. *Lower numbers mean better performance.*

Very Good **Truck Book Rating**

How the vehicle compares among all government test results to date. The range includes very good, good, average, poor and very poor.

00% **Likelihood of Life Threatening Injury**

The chance of life threatening injury to the driver/passenger in a frontal 35 mph crash. *Lower percentages mean better performance.*

Good **Leg Injury Rating**

Injury rating for driver and passenger legs in a frontal crash, when compared to all government test results to date.

Even though thousands of Americans buy minivans, pickups, and 4x4s for family and non-commercial use, the National Highway Traffic Safety Administration has only recently taken steps to improve their safety, and it will take years to fully implement these rules.

As of 1992, trucks and vans must have head restraints in order to reduce the frequency and severity of head and neck injuries, and they are required to have rear-seat lap and shoulder belts in order to prevent injury to passengers in the back seat of a vehicle. There are also new testing rules for manual belt systems to ensure their strength and reliability, and new limitations on the rearward displacement of the steering column will lower the chances of chest, neck, or head injuries.

Missing Safety: While these are steps in the right direction, here are some key safety standards that will not be required for at least two years:

1. Automatic crash protection—requirement phase-in (began in 1995) with full implementation in 1998.
2. Side crash protection—required in cars by 1997, not required in trucks until 1999.

Automatic Crash Protection: One safety feature that many trucks, vans, and 4x4s are missing is automatic crash protection. Over a decade ago, in cooperation with the federal government, the automobile industry developed two forms of automatic crash protection: airbags and automatic safety belts. While these devices will not prevent all deaths, they will cut in half your chances of being killed or seriously injured in a car.

Federal law requires all new *passenger* cars to be equipped with automatic crash protection that will protect the driver and front-seat passenger in a 30-mph collision into a fixed barrier. But this protection is not required in all pickups, vans, or 4x4s until 1998.

Unfortunately, because they are not required by the government, many of this year's light trucks do not have full airbag protection. Here's what the buyer's of those vehicles are missing because the government dragged its feet on this lifesaving requirement:

Hidden in the steering wheel hub and the right side of the dashboard, airbags provide unobtrusive and effective protection in frontal crashes. By spreading crash forces over the head and chest, airbags protect the body from contact with hard surfaces.

Studies of the actual operation of the airbags in 10,000 test vehicles reported no cases of failure in deployment or malfunction of the inflator. This reliability rate (99.995 percent) is far higher than that of such safety features as brakes, tires, steering, and lights, which show failure rates of up to 10 percent.

Here are some answers to typical questions asked about airbags.

Is the gas that inflates airbags dangerous? Nitrogen, which makes up 79.8 percent of the air we breathe, is the gas that inflates the bags. A solid chemical, sodium azide, generates this nitrogen gas. Sodium azide presents no hazard in normal driving, in crashes or in disposal.

Will airbags inflate by mistake? Airbags will inflate only in frontal impacts equivalent to hitting a solid wall at about 10-mph or higher. They will not inflate when you go over bumps or potholes or when you hit something at low speed.

In the unlikely event of an inadvertent airbag deployment, you would not lose control of the vehicle. Airbags are designed to deploy and then deflate in fractions of a second.

A Note for Pregnant Women:

The American College of Obstetricians and Gynecologists strongly urges pregnant women to always wear a safety belt, including on the ride to the hospital to deliver the baby! In a car crash, the most serious risk to an unborn baby is that the mother may be injured. Obstetricians recommend that the lap and shoulder belts be used, with the lap belt as low as possible on the hips, under the baby. And remember, when bring your baby home from the hospital, "Make the first ride a safe ride!"

Will airbag systems last very long? Airbags are reliable and require no maintenance. Because they have only one moving part, the device that senses impact, there is nothing to wear out. Although they work throughout the life of the vehicle, some manufacturers suggest inspections at anywhere from two to ten years.

Will airbags protect children? Studies of actual crashes indicate that children are protected by airbags. However, most vehicles do not offer airbags on the passenger side, where children often sit. In addition, rear-facing child safety seats should not be used in the front seat of a vehicle with a passenger airbag.

Will airbags protect occupants without seat belts? Airbags are designed to protect unbelted front-seat occupants in 30-mph frontal crashes into a wall. Equipping vehicles with airbags reduced the average injury severity in serious frontal crashes by 64-percent, even though over 80-percent of the occupants were unbelted. Airbags do not protect you in a side or rear crash. The best protection is provided by a combination of airbags and lap and shoulder safety belts. With airbags and seat belts, you'll be protected in the event of side impact and rollover crashes, as well as in frontal crashes.

The following list indicates which front seat passengers will be unprotected by airbags this year.

Who's NOT Offering Airbags?

Vehicle	Which Front Occupant Unprotected
Minivan	
Chevrolet Astro/Lumina Minivan	Passenger Unprotected
Ford Aerostar	Passenger Unprotected
Oldsmobile Silhouette	Passenger Unprotected
Pontiac Trans Sport	Passenger Unprotected
Full Size Van	
Dodge Ram Wagon/Van	Passenger Unprotected
Ford Econoline	Passenger Unprotected
Small Sport Utility	
Jeep Wrangler	Passenger Unprotected
Kia Sportage	Passenger Unprotected
Mid-Size/Large Sport Utility	
Chevrolet Blazer/Tahoe/Suburban	Passenger Unprotected
Ford Bronco	Passenger Unprotected
GMC Jimmy/Suburban/Yukon	Passenger Unprotected
Jeep Cherokee	Passenger Unprotected
Oldsmobile Bravada	Passenger Unprotected
Toyota 4Runner	Passenger Unprotected
Compact Pickup	
Chevrolet S-Series Pickup	Passenger Unprotected
Dodge Dakota	Passenger Unprotected
Ford Ranger	Passenger Unprotected*
GMC Sonoma	Passenger Unprotected
Isuzu Hombre	Passenger Unprotected
Mazda B-Series	Passenger Unprotected
Mitsubishi Mighty Max	**Both Unprotected**
Nissan Pickup	Passenger Unprotected
Toyota Tacoma	Passenger Unprotected
Standard Pickup	
Chevrolet C/K Series	Passenger Unprotected
Dodge Ram	Passenger Unprotected
Ford F-Series	Passenger Unprotected
GMC Sierra	Passenger Unprotected
Toyota T100	Passenger Unprotected

* Passenger airbag optional

Anti-Lock Brakes

Almost all manufacturers are now offering anti-lock braking systems (ABS). ABS shortens stopping distance on dry, wet, even icy roads. It works by sensing the speed of each wheel. If a wheel begins to lock up or skid, it automatically releases the wheel's brakes, allowing the wheel to roll normally again and thus stopping the skid. When the wheel stops skidding, the brakes are instantly reapplied. This cycle can be repeated many times per second. Remember—don't pump your brakes in a skid, the ABS does it for you.

All truck, van and 4x4 manufacturers offer some form of ABS with the exception of the Mitsubishi Mighty Max. The best systems work on all four wheels. Many truck manufacturers have chosen to only offer it on the rear wheels. Two-wheel ABS is not as effective as four-wheel. The following table indicates what the various manufacturers are offering.

Vehicle	ABS
Chevy Astro	4-Wheel
Chevy Blazer	4-Wheel
Chevy C/K Series	4-Wheel
Chevy Van/Express	4-Wheel
Chevy Lumina MV	4-Wheel
Chevy S-Series	4-Wheel
Chevy Suburban	4-Wheel
Chevy Tahoe	4-Wheel
Chrys. T & C	4-Wheel
Dodge Caravan	4-Wheel
Dodge Dakota	4-Wheel*
Dodge Ram	4-Wheel*
Dodge Ram Van/Wgn	4-Wheel*
Ford Aerostar	2-Wheel
Ford Bronco	4-Wheel
Ford Econ./Club Wgn	4-Wheel
Ford Explorer	4-Wheel
Ford F-Series	2-Wheel
Ford Ranger	4-Wheel*
Ford Windstar	4-Wheel

Vehicle	ABS
GMC Jimmy	4-Wheel
GMC Safari	4-Wheel
GMC Savana	4-Wheel
GMC Sierra	4-Wheel
GMC Sonoma	4-Wheel
GMC Suburban	4-Wheel
GMC Yukon	4-Wheel
Geo Tracker	4-Wheel*
Honda Odyssey	4-Wheel
Honda Passport	4-Wheel*
Isuzu Hombre	4-Wheel*
Isuzu Oasis	4-Wheel
Isuzu Rodeo	4-Wheel*
Isuzu Trooper	4-Wheel
Jeep Cherokee	4-Wheel*
Jeep Grand Cherokee	4-Wheel
Jeep Wrangler	4-Wheel*
Kia Sportage	2-Wheel
Lnd Rvr Discovery	4-Wheel
Lnd Rvr Range Rvr	4-Wheel

Vehicle	ABS
Mazda B-Series	4-Wheel*
Mazda MPV	4-Wheel
Mercury Villager	4-Wheel
Mitsu. Mighty Max	None
Mitsu. Montero	4-Wheel*
Nissan Pathfinder	2-Wheel
Nissan Pickup	2-Wheel
Nissan Quest	4-Wheel*
Olds Bravada	4-Wheel
Olds Silhouette	4-Wheel
Plymouth Voyager	4-Wheel
Pontiac Trans Sport	4-Wheel
Suzuki Sidekick	4-Wheel*
Suzuki X-90	4-Wheel
Toyota 4Runner	4-Wheel*
Toyota Land Cruiser	4-Wheel
Toyota Previa	4-Wheel*
Toyota RAV4	4-Wheel*
Toyota T100	4-Wheel*
Toyota Tacoma	4-Wheel*

* Optional

Rollover

The risk of rollover is a significant safety issue especially with sport utility vehicles. Because of their relatively high center of gravity, they don't hug the road like smaller, lower automobiles and trucks. As a result, they are more likely to turn over on sharp turns or corners. Not only does a rollover increase the likelihood of injuries, but it also increases the risk of the occupant being thrown from the vehicle. In fact, the danger of rollover with sport utilities is so severe that manufacturers are now required to place a sticker, shown below, where it can be seen by the driver every time the vehicle is used.

To understand the concept behind these vehicles' propensity to roll over, consider this: Place a section of 2x4 lumber on its 2-inch side. It is easily tipped over by a force pushing against the side. But if you place it on its 4-inch side, the same force will cause it to slide rather than tip over. Similarly, in a moving vehicle, the forces generated by a turn can cause a narrow, tall vehicle to roll over.

Ironically, even though sport utility vehicles have a higher tendency to roll over than passenger cars, the government does not require these vehicles to have the same side impact or roof protection.

When the government itself looked into this problem, they reported that some sport utility vehicles were nearly 20 times more likely than a passenger car to experience a fatal rollover. One way to prevent the rollover problem is to widen the distance between the center of the tires (called the track). Thankfully, some manufacturers have begun to do just that. But can vehicles already in use be modified to reduce rollover risk? One possibility is to use smaller-diameter tires, which would reduce the height of the vehicle and lower its center of gravity. Another alternative is to weld weights underneath the vehicle to make it more stable. Be careful, however—neither of these alternatives has been fully tested. *You should not attempt any modifications without checking with the manufacturer.* Most importantly, don't increase your vehicle's probability of rollover by adding larger tires and wheels or a higher suspension system.

As the trend of buying light trucks, minivans, and sport utility vehicles for private passenger use grows, the Center for Auto Safety is fighting to require safety standards for vehicle stability. If you experience a problem with your sport utility vehicle, contact the Center for Auto Safety (page 79) and the Auto Safety Hotline, 800-424-9393 (202-366-0123 in Washington, DC).

In order to alert consumers to the problem of rollover, the government requires the following warning on certain vehicles.

This is a multipurpose passenger vehicle which will handle and maneuver differently from an ordinary passenger car, in driving conditions which may occur on streets and highways and off road. As with other vehicles of this type, if you make sharp turns or abrupt maneuvers, the vehicle may roll over or may go out of control and crash. You should read driving guidelines and instructions in the Owner's Manual, and wear your seat belt at all times.

Side Crash Protection

Each year, an estimated 240 people die and another 1,000 are seriously injured in side collisions. To better protect drivers and passengers, the government is requiring auto makers to gradually improve the side impact protection of their passenger cars. By 1997, all cars must meet this new standard which includes stronger steel beams in the doors, more interior padding, and the ability to resist intrusion from other vehicles.

When it comes to trucks, 4x4s, and minivans, auto makers have been slow to implement improvements in side protection. The government is not requiring these popular vehicles to have increased side impact protection until 1999. Fortunately, some auto makers have already begun to add this safety feature to their 1996 vehicles.

To let you know which manufacturers are offering better side protection, we have rated the 1996 trucks, minivans and 4x4s as either *Strong* or *Weak.* A *Strong* rating means the vehicle *already* meets the 1999 side impact protection standards. A *Weak* rating means that the vehicle does not yet meet side impact protection standards.

Vehicle	Side Impact Protection
Minivans	
Chevy Astro	Weak
Chevy Lumina Minivan	Weak
Chrys. Town and Country	Strong
Dodge Caravan	Strong
Ford Aerostar	Weak
Ford Windstar	Strong
GMC Safari	Weak
Honda Odyssey	Strong
Isuzu Oasis	Weak
Mazda MPV	Weak
Mercury Villager	Weak
Nissan Quest	Weak
Oldsmobile Silhouette	Weak
Plymouth Voyager	Strong
Pontiac Trans Sport	Weak
Toyota Previa	Strong

Vehicle	Side Impact Protection
Full Size Vans	
Chevy Van/Chevy Express	Weak
Dodge Ram Van/Ram Wgn	Weak
Ford Econoline/Club Wgn	Weak
GMC Savana	Weak
Small Sport Utilities	
Geo Tracker	Weak
Jeep Wrangler	Weak
Kia Sportage	Weak
Suzuki Sidekick	Weak
Suzuki X-90	Weak
Toyota RAV4	Weak
Mid-Size Sport Utilities	
Chevrolet Blazer	Weak
Ford Explorer	Weak
GMC Jimmy	Weak
Honda Passport	Weak

Vehicle	Side Impact Protection
Mid-Size Sport Utilities (cont.)	
Isuzu Rodeo	Weak
Isuzu Trooper	Weak
Jeep Cherokee	Weak
Jeep Grand Cherokee	Strong
Land Rover Discovery	Strong
Mitsubishi Montero	Weak
Nissan Pathfinder	Weak
Oldsmobile Bravada	Strong
Toyota 4Runner	Weak
Large Sport Utilities	
Chevrolet Suburban	Weak
Chevrolet Tahoe	Weak
Ford Bronco	Strong
GMC Suburban	Weak
GMC Yukon	Weak
Land Rover Range Rover	Strong
Toyota Land Cruiser	Weak

Vehicle	Side Impact Protection
Compact Pickups	
Chevrolet S-Series Pickup	Weak
Dodge Dakota	Weak
Ford Ranger	Weak
GMC Sonoma	Weak
Isuzu Hombre	Weak
Mazda B-Series Pickup	Weak
Mitsubishi Mighty Max	Weak
Nissan Pickup	Weak
Toyota Tacoma	Weak
Standard Pickups	
Chevy C/K Series Pickup	Weak
Dodge Ram Pickup	Weak
Ford F-Series Pickup	Strong
GMC Sierra	Weak
Toyota T100	Weak

Off-Road Driving

One reason to buy an off-road vehicle is the ability to take advantage of some of our country's more remote areas. But off-roading also presents some unique hazards. The best way to ensure your safety is to understand the dangers, and to be prepared.

Before going out, be sure your vehicle is in top shape. Fill up the tank, and check the spare tire and the fluid levels. Also, find out about the local laws that apply to off-roading through the law enforcement people in the area.

Loading up: It is important to load your vehicle carefully and safely. The heaviest items should be on the floor as far forward of the rear axle as possible. Be sure you secure the load so that loose objects can't hit someone or fall out of the vehicle. And remember, heavy loads on the roof or piled high in the cargo area will raise the vehicle's center of gravity and increase your chances of rolling over.

Controlling your vehicle: On an unpaved surface, the best way to control your vehicle is to control your speed—at a higher speed, you have less time to look for and react to obstacles. Off the road, your vehicle will bounce more and your wheels may leave the ground, so keep a firm grip on the steering wheel. You'll also need more distance for braking.

Off-roading can take you over a wide variety of surfaces, including rocks, grass, sand, mud, snow, and ice. Each of these surfaces affects the control of your vehicle in different ways.

Driving in mud reduces your traction and increases your braking distance. It is best to use a low gear and keep your vehicle moving so you don't get stuck. Driving on sand, snow, and ice severely reduces tire traction.

Before driving through water, make sure that it isn't too deep, or your vehicle may be damaged. If you decide to go ahead, drive slowly—otherwise water can splash your ignition system or tailpipe, causing you to stall. *Caution:* Rushing water is especially dangerous and should be avoided. It can sweep your vehicle away. Even at low speeds, it can wash away the ground from under your tires, and you could lose control.

Driving on hills: Off-road terrain often requires you to drive up, down, or across a hill, each of which presents its own safety hazards. There are some hills that can't be driven—they are simply too steep for any vehicle. If you have any doubt about the steepness, don't drive the hill. Here are some things to keep in mind as you approach a hill:

- Is there a constant incline, or does the hill get sharply steeper in places?
- Is there good traction on the hillside, or will the surface cause you to slip?
- Is there a straight path up or down the hill?
- Are there trees or rocks on the hill that block your path?
- What's beyond the hill? Walk it first if you don't know—it's the smart way to see if you'll find a cliff, a fence, or another steep hill.
- Is the hill simply too rough? Steep hills often have ruts, gullies, and exposed rocks because they are more susceptible to erosion.

Driving uphill: If you decide you can safely drive up a hill, use a low gear and get a smooth start up the hill. Try to maintain your speed. If you use more power than you need, the wheels may start to spin or slide. Avoid twists and turns, if possible, and drive as straight a route as you can. Always slow down as you approach the top of the hill. If your vehicle stalls on the hill, quickly brake to prevent yourself from rolling backwards. Then restart your engine, shift into reverse, and slowly back down the hill. Never shift into neutral to "rev up" the engine and go forward. Your vehicle will roll backwards quickly, and you may

Environmental Concerns

Off-road vehicles can damage and erode soil, disturb wildlife and its habitat, pollute natural areas, and endanger other land users. The U.S. Forest Service has developed a code of conduct for off-roaders called "Tread Lightly." This program provides tips on how to enjoy off-roading responsibly, without damaging the environment.

For information about the "Tread Lightly" program, or if you have any questions about off-roading and the environment, write to the U.S. Department of Agriculture, U.S. Forest Service, P.O. Box 96090, 14th and Independence Ave, SW, Washington, DC 20090-6090, or call the U.S. Forest Service at 202-205-1706.

Towing Safety

lose control. And never attempt to turn around. If the hill is steep enough to stall your vehicle, it is certainly steep enough to make you roll over.

Driving downhill: If you decide you can go down a hill safely, keep your vehicle headed straight down and use a low gear. The engine drag will help your brakes. Never drive downhill with your transmission in neutral, because your brakes will have to do all the work and could overheat and fade. Drive slowly, and avoid turns that take you across the hill. Avoid braking so hard that you lock the wheels or you won't be able to steer your vehicle. If your wheels lock up during downhill braking and the vehicle starts to slide, just ease off the brakes quickly and you should straighten out.

Driving across a hill: Even a hill that's not too steep to drive straight up or down can be a problem to drive across. Since your vehicle is not as wide as it is long, driving across a steep hill can cause your vehicle to roll over. Watch out for loose gravel and wet grass which can cause your tires to slip downhill. If the vehicle does slip sideways, it could hit something that will trip it and make it roll. If you feel your vehicle starting to slide sideways, turn downhill. This should help you straighten out and stop your slipping.

If your vehicle stalls when you're crossing a hill, be sure that you and your passengers get out on the uphill side, even though that door is harder to open. If you get out on the downhill side and the vehicle starts to roll over, you'll be right in its path.

Safe Towing

If you regularly tow a camper, boat, or other trailer, it is important that your vehicle be capable of safely towing the load. Towing a trailer puts considerable strain on a vehicle, making every system work harder. The tires, brakes, and engine all experience extra stress, with the most strain on the automatic transmission. Power from the engine is transmitted to the wheels through a fluid coupling (called a torque converter) that can become extremely hot when towing. If the fluid is burned from overheating, the transmission can be severely damaged.

If you do a great deal of towing over long distances, installing an *auxiliary transmission cooler* will reduce the operating temperature of the fluid and help prevent damage to your transmission. You can also prolong the life of your vehicle by towing in drive rather than overdrive, except on long stretches of road. Towing in drive provides more power, and it places less stress on the entire vehicle than does overdrive.

The vehicle rating pages in the back of the book include the weight rating that a vehicle can safely tow. Many of these vehicles can pull more; however, they will need special modification.

1. Never pull more than the maximum allowable trailer weight listed in your owner's manual.
2. Never attempt to tow if your engine is not running smoothly.
3. Check tire inflation regularly and keep a spare trailer tire in your truck when towing.
4. Service your cooling system regularly.
5. Replace tires, brakes, and shock absorbers well before you normally would. They need to be kept in above average condition to tow safely.
6. Use overload shocks if the hitch weight requires it.
7. Be especially cautious when towing a boat because tires can be damaged on a ramp.
8. If you tow regularly, change your automatic transmission fluid at *half* the recommended mileage. If your owner's manual suggests 30,000 miles, change it every 15,000 miles, or if it is discolored or smells burnt.
9. Install an auxiliary transmission cooler to protect the transmission. Typical costs range from $20 to $100.

Safety Belts

About 60 percent of occupants killed or injured in vehicle crashes would have been saved from serious harm had they been wearing safety belts. Yet many Americans do not use these life-saving devices.

Safety belts are particularly important in minivans, 4x4s and pickups because there is a greater chance of being killed or seriously injured in a rollover accident. The simple precaution of wearing your belt greatly improves your odds of survival.

Why don't people wear their belts? Sometimes they simply don't know the facts. Once you know the facts, you should be willing to buckle up.

While most safety advocates welcome the passage of safety belt usage laws, the ones passed to date are weak and generally unenforced. In addition, most of the laws are based on "secondary" enforcement—meaning that you cannot be stopped for failing to wear your belt. If you are stopped for another reason and the officer notices you don't have your belt on by the time he or she reaches the vehicle, you may be fined. In states with "primary" enforcement, you can be stopped for not wearing a safety belt. Yet, in many cases the fines are less than a parking ticket. In Arkansas, however, you can get a $10 credit toward a primary violation if you are wearing a seat belt and in Wyoming, a $5 credit.

Another unusual feature of these laws is that most of them allow drivers to avoid buckling up if they have a doctor's permission. This loophole was inserted to appease those who were not really in favor of the law. However, many doctors are wondering if they will be held responsible for the injuries of unbuckled patients. In fact, the State of New York Medical Society cautions doctors never to give medical dispensation from the law because "no medical condition has yet been found to warrant a medical exemption for seat belt use."

Even though most state laws are weak, they have heightened awareness and raised the level of usage. Belt use in states that have passed a safety belt law tends to rise sharply after the law is enacted. However, after the law has been on the books a few months, safety belt use drops.

The tables on the following pages describe the current safety belt laws. In some cases, the driver is responsible for all or some of the passengers as noted; otherwise, occupants are responsible for themselves. All states are listed, even those that do not yet have safety belt laws. We hope that the blanks following Maine and New Hampshire will soon be filled with new laws.

Safety Belt Myths and Facts

Myth: *"I don't want to be trapped by a seat belt. It's better to be thrown free in an accident."*

Fact: The chance of being killed is 25 times greater if you're ejected. A safety belt will keep you from plunging through the windshield, smashing into trees, rocks, or other cars, scraping along the ground, or getting run over by your own or another's vehicle. If you are wearing your belt, you're far more likely to be conscious after an accident to free yourself and other passengers.

Myth: *"Pregnant women should not wear safety belts."*

Fact: According to the American Medical Association, "Both the pregnant mother and the fetus are safer, provided the lap belt is worn as low on the pelvis as possible."

Myth: *"I don't need it. In case of an accident, I can brace myself with my hands."*

Fact: At 35 mph, the impact of a crash on you and your passengers is brutal. There's no way your arms and legs can brace you against that kind of collision; the speed and force are just too great. The force of impact at only 10 mph is roughly equivalent to the force of catching a 200-pound bag of cement dropped from a first floor window.

Safety Belt Laws

	Law Applies To:	Driver Fined For:	Enforcement	Max. Fine 1st Offense
Alabama	Front seat only	Self only	Secondary	$25
Alaska*	All occupants	0 to 15 year olds	Secondary	$15
Arizona	Front seat only	5 to 16 year olds	Secondary	$10
Arkansas	Front seat only	Self only	Secondary	$25[1]
California*	All occupants	4 to 16 year olds	Primary	$20
Colorado	Front seat only	4 to 16 year olds	Secondary	$15
Connecticut	Front seat only	4 to 16 year olds	Primary	$15
Delaware	Front seat only	All occupants	Secondary	$20
Dist. of Columbia	Front seat only	Self only	Secondary	$15
Florida	Front seat only	0 to 15 year olds	Secondary	$27
Georgia	All occupants	4 to 18 year olds	Secondary[2]	$15[2]
Hawaii	Front seat only	4 to 15 year olds	Primary	$20
Idaho	Front seat only	Self only	Secondary	$5
Illinois	Front seat only	6 to 16 year olds	Secondary	$25
Indiana	Front seat only	Self only	Secondary	$25
Iowa	Front seat only	Self only	Primary	$10
Kansas	Front seat only	Self only	Secondary	$10
Kentucky*	All occupants	Over 40 inches	Secondary	$25
Louisiana	Front seat only	Self only	Primary	$25[1]
Maine	No law			
Maryland	Front seat only	0 to 15 year olds	Secondary	$25
Massachusetts*	All occupants	12 to 16 year olds	Secondary	$25
Michigan	All occupants	4 to 16 year olds	Secondary	$25
Minnesota	All occupants	4 to 11 year olds[3]	Secondary	$25
Mississippi	Front seat only	Self only	Secondary	$25
Missouri	Front seat only	4 to 16 year olds	Secondary	$10

* In these states driver can be held liable in court for *all* passengers.
See next page for footnotes.

Safety Belt Laws

	Law Applies To:	Driver Fined For:	Enforcement	Max. Fine 1st Offense
Montana*	All occupants	Over 4 years old	Secondary	$20
Nebraska	Front seat	Over 5 years old	Secondary	$25
Nevada*	All occupants	5 to 18 year olds	Secondary	$25
New Hampshire	No law			
New Jersey	Front seat only	5 to 18 year olds	Secondary	$20
New Mexico	Front seat only	Self only	Primary	$25
New York	Front seat[4]	4 to 16 year olds	Primary	$50
North Carolina	Front seat only	6 to 16 year olds	Primary	$25
North Dakota	Front seat	Over 11 years old	Secondary	$20
Ohio	Front seat only	Over 4 years old	Secondary	$25
Oklahoma	Front seat only	Self only	Secondary	$25
Oregon*	All Occupants	0 to 15 year olds	Primary	$95
Pennsylvania	Front seat only	4 to 18 year olds	Secondary	$10
Rhode Island*	All Occupants	Over 12 years old	Secondary	None
South Carolina	All Occupants[5]	6 to 17 year olds	Secondary	$10
South Dakota	Front seat	5 to 18 year olds	Secondary	$20
Tennessee	Front seat only	Over 4 years old	Secondary	$10
Texas	Front seat only	4 to 15 year olds	Primary	$50
Utah	Front seat only	2 to 18 year olds	Secondary	$10
Vermont*	All occupants	Over 13 years old	Secondary	$10
Virginia	Front seat only	4 to 16 year olds	Secondary	$25
Washington*	All occupants	0 to 15 year olds	Secondary	$47
West Virginia	Front seat[6]	All occupants	Secondary	$25
Wisconsin	All occupants[5]	4 to 15 year olds	Secondary	$10
Wyoming	Front seat only	Over 3 years old	Secondary	None[1]

* In these states driver can be held liable in court for *all* passengers.
[1] In Arkansas, reward for buckling up is a $10 reduction in primary violation fine; in Wyoming, a $5 reduction. In Louisiana, 10% reduction in fine for moving violation.
[2] Primary for 14 to 18 year olds; $25 fine if driver is a minor.
[3] Parent driver is responsible for 11 to 15 year olds in front seat.
[4] Driver responsible for 4 to 10 year olds riding in rear seat.
[5] Covers rear seat occupants where shoulder belts are available.
[6] Driver responsible for occupants 0 to 17 years old in rear seat.

Child Safety Seats

How many times have you gone out of your way to prevent your children from being injured, taken care to keep household poisons out of reach, or watched carefully while they swam? Probably quite often. Yet, despite these efforts, many parents let their children sleep, unrestrained in the back of a minivan or roam around in a moving vehicle.

Ironically, of all hazards, the automobile poses the greatest threat to your children's health. After the first weeks of an infant's life, vehicle crashes are the single leading cause of death and serious injury for children. Yet nearly 80 percent of the children who have died in vehicles could have been saved by proper use of child safety seats or safety belts.

Being a safe driver is no excuse for not having everyone in your vehicle buckled up. Quite often crashes or sudden swerves are caused by the recklessness of others. Even at low speeds, a child can be hurled violently against the inside of a vehicle.

At 30-mph, a crash or sudden braking can wrench your child from your arms with a tremendous force. At this speed, even a ten-pound infant would be ripped from your arms with a force of nearly 300 pounds. If you aren't wearing a safety belt, your own body will be an additional hazard to a child in your lap. You will be thrown forward with enough force to crush your child against the dashboard or the back of the front seat.

The best and only reliable way to protect your child in a vehicle is to use a safety seat. In an emergency, if no seat is available and the child can sit upright, buckle up the child in the back seat. But there really is no alternative for an infant.

By using a child safety seat on every ride, you will help to establish the habit of regular safety belt use when your children get older. As a lifelong wearer of safety belts, your child reduces his or her chances of being killed or seriously injured in a crash by 50 percent.

Buying Tips: Most consumers find that seats with an automatic retracting harness and a shield are the easiest to use. Here are some important, additional tips for correct use:

☑ Make sure the seat you buy can be properly installed in your vehicle. You will find that some car seats cannot be properly buckled into certain vehicles.

☑ Determine how many straps or buckles must be fastened to use the seat. The easy-to-use seats require only one, once the seat is buckled into vehicle.

☑ Make sure the seat is wide enough for growth and bulky winter clothes.

☑ Make sure your child is comfortable. Can your child move his or her arms freely, sleep in the seat, and, if older, see out the window?

Locking Clips

Children are safest if they are restrained in the middle of the back seat of your vehicle. If you put the safety seat somewhere other than the middle, you may need a locking clip. This clip is necessary if the latchplate on the safety belt slides freely along the belt; without it, the safety seat can move or tip over. You should always remove the clip when it is not being used with a safety seat.

Register Your Child Seat

Last year, the U.S. Department of Transportation recalled millions of child safety seats for serious safety defects. Tragically, most parents never heard about these recalls and the majority of these problem seats are still being used. You can do two things to protect your children—first, call the Auto Safety Hotline at 800-424-9393 and find out if your seat has been recalled. If so, they will tell you how to contact the manufacturer for a resolution. Second, make sure you fill out the registration card that must come with all new seats. This will enable the company to contact you should there be a recall. If you currently own a seat, ask the Hotline for the address of your seat's manufacturer and send them your name, address and seat model, asking them to keep it on file for recall notices.

Seat Types

There are six types of child seats: *infant-only, convertible, toddler-only, child/booster, booster* and *built-in*.

Infant-Only Seats: Infant-only seats can be used from birth until your baby reaches a weight of 17-20 pounds. This type of seat must be installed facing the rear in a semi-reclined position. In a collision, the crash forces are spread over the baby's back, the strongest body surface. The seat's harness should come from below the child's shoulders in the rear-facing position.

One benefit of an infant-only seat is that you can easily install and remove the seat with the baby in place. Most infant car seats can also be used as household baby seats. Caution: Some household baby seats look remarkably similar to infant safety seats. These are not crash worthy and should *never* be used as car safety seats.

Convertible Seats: Buying a convertible seat can save you the expense of buying both an infant and a toddler seat. Most convertible seats can be used from birth until the child reaches four years and 40 pounds. When used for an infant, the seat faces rearward in a semi-reclined position. When the child is at least a year old and 20 pounds or more, the frame can be adjusted upright and the seat turned to face forward.

As with any safety seat, it is extremely important that the straps fit snugly over the child's shoulders. A good way to ensure that the straps are adjusted correctly is to buy a seat with an automatically adjusting harness. Like a car safety belt, these models automatically adjust to fit snugly on your child.

Convertible seats come in three basic types:

The *five-point harness* consists of two shoulder and two lap straps that converge at a buckle connected to a crotch strap. These straps are adjustable, allowing for growth and comfort.

The *T-shield* has a small pad joining the shoulder belts. With only one buckle, many parents find this the simplest and easiest-to-use type of convertible seat; but, it will not fit newborns properly.

The *tray shield* is another convenient model, since the safety harness is attached to the shield. As the shield comes down in front of the child, the harness comes over the child's shoulders. The shield is an important part of the restraint system, but like the T-shield, it will not fit small infants.

Toddler-Only Seats: These are really booster child seats and they may take the place of convertible seats when a child is between 20 and 30 pounds. Weight and size limits vary greatly among seats.

Child/Booster Seats: Some manufacturers are now making a variety of combination child/booster seats. For example, one model can be converted from a 5-point harness to a high-backed, belt-positioning booster seat. They can be used for children ranging from 20 to 40 pounds, making them a very economical choice.

Booster Seats: Booster seats are used when your child is too big for a convertible seat, but too small to use safety belts. Most car lap/shoulder belts do not adequately fit children with a seating height less than 28". Booster seats can be used for children over 30 pounds and come in three types:

Belt-positioning booster seats raise the child for a better fit with the vehicle's safety belts. If your child is under 3 years old, do not use belt-positioning booster seats because your child may be able to unbuckle him or herself.

The *removable-shield booster seat* can be used with a lap/shoulder belt with the shield removed, or with a lap belt with the shield on. This seat can be adapted to different vehicles and seating positions, making it a good choice.

The *shield-type booster seat* has a small plastic shield with no straps and can be used only with lap belts. Typically, the safety belt fastens in front of the shield, anchoring it to the vehicle. Most safety experts recommend using these seats until a child is 4 years old and 40 pounds.

Built-In: Chrysler, Ford, GM, and Volvo offer the option of a fold-out toddler seat on some of their models. These seats are only for children older than one and can come as either a five-point harness or a booster with 3-point belt; however, the 3-point booster is not recommended for children under 3 years old. This built-in seat is an excellent feature because it is always in the car and does not pose the problem of compatibility that often occurs with separate child seats.

Name of Seat	Price	Harness Type/Comments
Infant Safety Seats		
Century 565	$40-50	3-pt.; tilt-indicator
Century 590	$60-65	3-pt.; tilt indicator; separate base stays in car; can be used in second car without base
Cosco Arriva	$40-80	3-pt.; detachable base, can use without base, correct recline indicator
Cosco Dream Ride	$60	3-pt.; to 17-20 lbs. (depending on mfg date); use flat as carbed side facing; use as car seat rear facing
Cosco TLC	$25-35	3-pt.
Evenflo Dyn-O-Mite	$25-35	3-pt.; shoulder belt can wrap around back of seat to provide added support
Evenflo Joy Ride	$25-45	3-pt.; shoulder belt wraps around front of seat
Evenflo On My Way	$35-65	3-pt.; detachable base, can use without base
Evenflo Travel Tandem	$35-65	3-pt.; separate base stays in car; can be used in second car without base
Gerry Guard with Glide	$50-70	3-pt.; use as glider in house; must be converted to in-car position
Gerry Secure Ride	$40-50	3-pt.; tilt-indicator
Kolcraft Infant Rider	$60-70	3-pt.; to 18 lbs. only
Kolcraft Rock 'N Ride	$30-50	3-pt.; up to 18 lbs; no harness height adjustment; separate base stays in car; can be used in second car without base
Convertible Safety Seats		
Babyhood Baby Sitter	$90	5-pt.
Century 1000 STE	$50-75	5-pt.; adjustable crotch strap positions
Century 2000 STE	$60-85	T-shield; adjustable crotch strap positions
Century 3000 STE	$70-85	Tray shield; adjustable crotch strap positions
Century 5000 STE	$90-100	Tray shield; adjustable crotch strap positions
Century Smart Move	$120-130	5-pt.; tray shield; adjustable shield grows with child
Cosco Touriva 5-pt.	$50-80	5-pt.
Cosco Touriva Overhead	$60-100	Tray-shield; adjustable shield in luxury model
Cosco Touriva Soft Shield	$70-100	T-shield
Evenflo Champion	$50-70	Tray shield; optional tether available

Based on data collected by the American Academy of Pediatrics.

Name of Seat	Price	Harness Type/Comments
Convertible Safety Seats cont'd.		
Evenflo Scout	$40-60	T-shield/5-pt.; optional tether available
Evenflo Trooper	$40-70	5-pt or Tray shield, optional tether available
Evenflo Ultra I, Premier	$60-110	Tray shield; adjustable shield
Evenflo Ultra V, Premier	$65-110	5-pt.; optional tether available
Gerry Guard SecureLock	$80-90	Tray shield/Automatic/harness adjustment
Gerry Pro-Tech	$70	5-pt.; automatic harness adjustment
Kolcraft Auto-Mate	$50-70	5-pt.; requires 2-handed operation
Kolcraft Traveler 700	$80-90	Tray shield; requires 2-handed operation
Safeline Sit 'N Stroll	$150-170	5-pt.; converts to stroller
Toddler-Only Vests and Built-In Seats		
Chrysler Built-In Seat	$100-200	5-pt. (20-40 lbs.); built in option in Minivans; one converts; to belt-positioning booster (40 lbs.); in sedan, adjust to fit child (20-65 lbs.)
E-Z-On Vest	$60	4-pt. (25+ lbs.); tether strap must be installed in vehicle
Ford Built-In	$225	5-pt. (20-60 lbs.); in minivan
GM Built-In	$125-225	5-pt. (20-40 lbs., Booster 40-60 lbs.); manual harness adjustment
Little Cargo Travel Vest	$40-50	5-pt.; (25-40 lbs.); simplified strap-buckle system;auto lap belt attached through padded stress plate
Booster		
Name of Seat	**Price**	**Belt Position/Comments**
Century Breverra	$60-70	Belt through base when used with shield; belt positioning booster seat with lap/shoulder belt
Cosco Explorer	$25-30	Wrap-around/seat has high back to support child's neck and head.
Fisher-Price T-Shield	$45-50	Wrap-around /Belt positioning booster for hip/shoulder belt (30-60 lbs.); shield with crotch post for lap belt (40-60 lbs.)
Gerry Double Guard	$50-55	Wrap-around/Belt through base with shield for lap belt; belt positioning booster for lap shoulder use; internal lap strap
Kolcraft Tot Rider II	$30-40	Wrap-around/Belt positioning booster seat with lap/shoulder belt; shield with crotch post for lap belt

Based on data collected by the American Academy of Pediatrics.

Tips for Using Your Child Safety Seat

The incorrect use of child safety seats has reached epidemic proportions. Problems fall into two categories: incorrect installation of the seat and incorrect use of the seat's straps to secure the child. Over 75 percent of seats in a national survey were incorrectly installed. In the vast majority of these, the vehicle's safety belt was improperly routed through the seat.

The incorrect use of a child safety seat can deny a child lifesaving protection and may even contribute to further injury. In addition to following your seat's installation instructions, here are some important usage tips:

☑ The safest place for the seat is the center of the back seat.

☑ Use a locking clip when needed. Check the instructions in both your child seat manual and your owner's manual.

☑ Keep your child rear-facing for at least a year.

☑ Never place a rear-facing child seat in a seat protected by an airbag.

☑ Regularly check the seat's safety harness and the vehicle's seat belt for a tight, secure fit because the straps will stretch on impact.

☑ Don't leave sharp or heavy objects or groceries loose in the vehicle. Anything loose can be deadly in a crash.

☑ In the winter, dress your baby in a legged suit to allow proper attachment of the harness. If necessary, drape an extra blanket over the seat after your baby is buckled.

☑ Be sure all doors are locked.

☑ Do not give your child lollipops or ice cream on a stick while riding. A bump or swerve could jam the stick into his or her throat.

Buckled Up = Better Behavior: Medical researchers have concluded that belted children are better behaved. When not buckled up, children squirm, stand up, complain, fight, and pull at the steering wheel. When buckled into safety seats, however, they displayed 95 percent fewer incidents of bad behavior.

Children behave better when buckled up because they feel secure. In addition, being in a seat can be more fun because most safety seats are high enough to allow children to see out the window. Also, children are less likely to feel carsick and more likely to fall asleep in a car seat.

Make the car seat your child's own special place, so he or she will enjoy being in it. Pick out some special soft toys or books that can be used only in the car seat to make using the seat a positive experience.

Set a good example for your child by using your own safety belt every time you get in a vehicle.

Safety Belts for Kids: Normally, children under 40 pounds should always be in a child safety seat. If no seat is available, use a safety belt if the child is able to sit up unsupported.

When your child outgrows the safety seat, he or she should always use the vehicle's safety belt. The belt should be snug and as low on the hips as possible. If the shoulder belt crosses the face or neck, it is best to use a belt-positioning booster; otherwise, place the shoulder strap behind the child's back. Never use pillows or cushions to boost your child. In an accident, they may let the child slide under the lap belt or allow the child's head to strike the vehicle's interior.

Never put a belt around yourself with a child in your lap. In an accident or sudden stop, both your weight and the child's would be forced into the belt, with the child absorbing a much greater share of the crash force. The pressure could push the belt deep into the child's body, causing severe injury or death.

Strapping two children into one belt can also be very dangerous—it makes proper fit impossible.

Rear-facing Child Safety Seats

Never use a rear-facing child safety seat in a seating position that has an airbag. To deploy fast enough to protect adult occupants, an airbag inflates with enough force to potentially cause serious head and chest injuries to a child in a rear-facing safety seat. And remember, airbags do not take the place of child safety seats.

Child Restraint Laws

Every state now requires children to be in safety seats or buckled up when riding in vehicles. The following table provides an overview of the requirements and penalties in each state. You will note that most states use the child's age to define the law, although some states have height or weight requirements as well. Also, in most states, the laws are not limited to children riding with their parents, but require that any driver with child passengers makes sure those children in the vehicle are buckled up.

	Law Applies To:	Children Covered Through:	Max. Fine 1st Offense	Safety Belt OK:
Alabama	All drivers	5 yrs.	$10	4-5 yrs.
Alaska	All drivers	15 yrs.	$50	4-15 yrs.
Arizona	All drivers	4 yrs. or 40 lbs.	$50	No
Arkansas	All drivers	4 yrs. or 40 lbs.	$25	4 yrs.
California	All drivers	15 yrs.	$100	4-15 yrs.
Colorado	All drivers	15 yrs.	$50	4-15 yrs., over 40 lbs.
Connecticut	All drivers	3 yrs. or 40 lbs.	$90	40 lbs.+
Delaware	All drivers	15 yrs..	$29	4-15 yrs.
Dist. of Columbia	All drivers	15 yrs.	$55	3-15 yrs.
Florida	All drivers	5 yrs.	$155	4-5 yrs.
Georgia	All drivers	4 yrs.	$25	3-4 yrs.
Hawaii	All drivers	3 yrs.	$100	3 yrs. only
Idaho	All drivers	3 yrs. or 40 lbs.	$52	No
Illinois	All drivers	5 yrs.	$25	4-5 yrs.
Indiana	All drivers	4 yrs.	$500	3-4 yrs.
Iowa	All drivers	5 yrs.	$10	3-5 yrs.
Kansas	All drivers	13 yrs.	$20	4-13 yrs.
Kentucky	All drivers	Under 40 inches	$50	No
Louisiana	Resident drivers	4 yrs.	$50	3-4 yrs. in rear
Maine	All drivers	18 yrs.	$55	4-18 yrs.
Maryland	All drivers	9 yrs.	$25	4-9 yrs.,over 40 lbs.
Massachusetts	All drivers	11 yrs.	$25	All ages
Michigan	All drivers	3 yrs.	$10	1-3 yrs. in rear
Minnesota	All drivers	3 yrs.	$50	No
Mississippi	All drivers	3 yrs.	$25	No

Child Restraint Laws

	Law Applies To:	Children Covered Through:	Max. Fine 1st Offense	Safety Belt OK:
Missouri	All drivers	3 yrs.	$25	All ages in rear
Montana	Resident Parent/Guardian[1]	3 yrs. or 40 lbs.	$25	2-3 yrs.
Nebraska	Resident drivers	4 yrs.	$25	4 yrs., over 40 lbs.
Nevada	All drivers	4 yrs. or 40 lbs.	$100	No
New Hampshire	All drivers	11 yrs.	$43	4-11 yrs.
New Jersey	All drivers	4 yrs.	$25	11/2-4 yrs. in rear
New Mexico	All drivers	10 yrs.	$25	1-4 yrs. in rear[2]
New York	All drivers	15 yrs.[3]	$100	4-10 yrs. in rear
North Carolina	All drivers	11 yrs.	$25	4-11 yrs.
North Dakota	All drivers	10 yrs.	$20	3-10 yrs.
Ohio	All drivers	3 yrs. or 40 lbs.	$100	No
Oklahoma	Resident drivers	5 yrs.	$25	4-5 yrs.
Oregon	All drivers	15 yrs.	$95	4-15 yrs.
Pennsylvania	All drivers	3 yrs.	$25	No
Rhode Island	All drivers	12 yrs.	$30	3-12 yrs.
South Carolina	All drivers	5 yrs.	$25	1-5 yrs. in rear[4]
South Dakota	All drivers	4 yrs.	$20	2-4 yrs.
Tennessee	All drivers	12 yrs.	$10	4-12 yrs.
Texas	All drivers	3 yrs.	$50	2-3 yrs.
Utah	All drivers	7 yrs.	$20	2-7 yrs.
Vermont	All drivers	12 yrs.	$25	5-12 yrs.
Virginia	Parent/Guardian	3 yrs.	$50	No
Washington	All drivers	9 yrs.	$47	3-9 yrs.
West Virginia	All drivers	8 yrs.	$20	3-8 yrs.
Wisconsin	All drivers	7 yrs.	$75	4-7 yrs.
Wyoming	Parent/Guardian[1]	2 yrs.[5]	$25	1-2 yrs.

[1] In own vehicle only.
[2] 5-10 year olds in all seats
[3] 9 year olds in rear
[4] 4-5 year olds in front seat
[5] 3 yrs. if less than 40 lbs.

FUEL ECONOMY

A vehicle's fuel efficiency affects both our environment and our wallets—which is why comparative mileage ratings are an important factor to most consumers. To save money and the environment, the first and most obvious step is to select a vehicle that gets high mileage, so we've included the Environmental Protection Agency's fuel economy ratings for all 1996 vehicles. We also discuss numerous factors that affect your vehicle's fuel efficiency, and caution you against the many products that falsely promise more gas mileage.

Using EPA ratings is an excellent way to incorporate fuel efficiency in selecting a new vehicle. By comparing these ratings, even among vehicles of the same size, you'll find that fuel efficiency varies greatly. One sport utility might get 29 miles per gallon (mpg) while another gets only 15 mpg. If you drive 15,000 miles a year and you pay $1.20 per gallon for fuel, the 29 mpg vehicle will save you $319 a year over the "gas guzzler."

Octane Ratings: Once you've purchased your vehicle, you'll be faced with choosing the right gasoline. Oil companies spend millions of dollars trying to get you to buy so-called higher performance or high octane fuels. Because high octane fuel can add considerably to your gas bill, it is important that you know what you're buying.

The octane rating of a gasoline is *not* a measure of power or quality. It is simply a measure of the gas's resistance to engine knock, which is the pinging sound you hear when the air and fuel mixture in your engine ignites prematurely during acceleration.

The octane rating appears on a yellow label on the fuel pump. Octane ratings vary with different types of gas (premium or regular), in different parts of the country (higher altitudes require lower octane ratings), and even between brands (Texaco's gasolines may have a different rating than Exxon's).

In This Chapter . . .

Determining the Right Octane Rating for Your Vehicle: Using a lower-rated gasoline saves money. Most vehicles are designed to run on a posted octane rating of 87. The following procedure can help you select the lowest octane level for your vehicle.

1 Have your engine tuned to exact factory specifications by a competent mechanic, and make sure it is in good working condition.

2 When the gas in your tank is very low, fill it up with your usual gasoline. After driving 10 to 15 miles, find a safe place to come to a complete stop and then accelerate rapidly. If your engine knocks during acceleration, switch to a higher octane rating. If there is no knocking sound, wait until your tank is very low and fill up with a lower rated gasoline. Repeat the test. When you determine the level of octane that causes your engine to knock during the test, use gasoline with the next highest rating.

Note: Your engine may knock when accelerating a heavily loaded vehicle uphill or when the humidity is low. This is normal and does not call for a higher-octane gasoline.

Factors Affecting Fuel Economy

Fuel economy is affected by a number of factors that you can consider before you buy.

Transmission: Manual transmissions are generally more fuel-efficient than automatic transmissions. In fact, a four-speed manual transmission can add up to 6.5 miles per gallon over a three-speed automatic. However, the incorrect use of a manual transmission wastes gas, so choose a transmission that matches your preference. Many transmissions now feature an overdrive gear, which can improve a vehicle's fuel economy by as much as 9 percent for an automatic transmission and 3 percent for a manual transmission.

Engine: The size of your vehicle's engine greatly affects your fuel economy. The smaller your engine, the better your fuel efficiency. A 10-percent increase in the size of an engine can increase fuel consumption by 6 percent.

Cruise Control: Cruise control can save fuel because driving at a constant speed uses less fuel than changing speeds frequently.

Air Conditioning: Auto air conditioners add weight and require additional horsepower to operate. They can cost up to 3 miles per gallon in city driving. At highway speeds, however, an air conditioner has about the same effect on fuel economy as the air resistance created by opening the windows.

Trim Package: Upgrading a vehicle's trim, installing soundproofing, and adding undercoating can increase the weight of a typical vehicle by 150 pounds. For each 10 percent increase in weight, fuel economy drops 4 percent.

Power Options: Power steering, brakes, seats, windows, and roofs reduce your mileage by adding weight. Power steering alone can cause a 1-percent drop in fuel economy.

Here are some tips for after you buy:

Tune-Up: If you have a 2 to 3 mpg drop over several fill-ups that is not due to a change of driving pattern or vehicle load, first check tire pressure, then consider a tune-up. A properly tuned engine is a fuel saver.

Tire Inflation: For maximum fuel efficiency, tires should be inflated to the top of the pressure range stamped on the sidewall. Check tire pressure when the tires are cold—before you've driven a long distance.

Short Trips: Short trips can be expensive because they usually involve a "cold" vehicle. For the first mile or two, a cold vehicle gets 30- to 40-percent of the mileage it gets when fully warm.

Using Oxyfuels

Today's gasoline contains a bewildering array of ingredients touted as octane boosters or pollution fighters. Some urban areas with carbon monoxide pollution problems are requiring the use of oxygen-containing components (called oxyfuels) such as ethanol and MTBE (methyl-tertiary-butylether). The use of these compounds is controversial. Some auto companies recommend their use; others caution against them. Most companies approve the use of gasoline with up to 10-percent ethanol, and all approve the use of MTBE up to 15-percent. Many companies recommend against using gasoline with methanol, alleging that it will cause poorer driveability, deterioration of fuel system parts, and reduced fuel economy. These companies may not cover the cost of warranty repairs if these additives are used, so check your owner's manual and warranty to determine what additives are covered. Also check the gas pump, as many states now require the pump to display the percentage of methanol and ethanol in the gasoline.

Checking Your MPG

Once you make your purchase, you'll want to keep track of your fuel economy. Here's an easy way to do it:

Step One

The next time you fill your tank, note the mileage on the odometer.

Step Two

When your tank is nearly empty, fill it up completely, and write down the mileage and the number of gallons of gas that you buy.

Step Three

Subtract the current odometer reading from the previous reading and divide the result by the number of gallons of gas you bought. This gives your miles per gallon.

Current Mileage	25,601
Previous Mileage	-25,301
	300

300÷10 = **30 MPG**

You will get the best estimate of your vehicle's gas mileage by keeping a record over several tankfuls. There may be small differences each time because of changes in weather, where you drive, the vehicle's condition, and whether your driving is primarily city or highway.

TIP

Estimating Your Fuel Costs

The table below will help you estimate annual fuel costs. First, find a vehicle's estimated mpg from the list at the end of this chapter. Next, find the mileage rating on the table below and read across until you reach the column of the amount you typically pay for gas. This price estimates what you can expect to pay for gas during an average year. Multiply this price by the number of years you expect to keep the vehicle. By calculating this number for the vehicles you are considering, you will see how differences in gas mileage will affect your pocketbook.

	Price per Gallon					
MPG	1.60	1.50	1.40	1.30	1.20	1.10
50	480	450	420	390	360	330
48	500	469	438	406	375	344
46	522	489	457	424	391	359
44	545	511	477	443	409	375
42	571	536	500	464	429	393
40	600	563	525	488	450	413
38	632	592	553	513	474	434
36	667	625	583	542	500	458
34	706	662	618	574	529	485
32	750	703	656	609	563	516
30	800	750	700	650	600	550
28	857	804	750	696	643	589
26	923	865	808	750	692	635
24	1000	938	875	813	750	688
22	1091	1023	955	886	818	750
20	1200	1125	1050	975	900	825
18	1333	1250	1167	1083	1000	917
16	1500	1406	1313	1219	1125	1031
14	1714	1607	1500	1393	1286	1179
12	2000	1875	1750	1625	1500	1375
10	2400	2250	2100	1950	1800	1650
8	3000	2813	2625	2438	2250	2063

Based on driving 15,000 miles per year.

Products That Don't Work

Hundreds of products on the market claim to improve fuel economy. Not only are most of these products ineffective, some may even damage your engine.

Sometimes the name or promotional material associated with these products implies they were endorsed by the federal government. In fact, no government agency endorses *any* gas saving products. Many of the products, however, *have* been tested by the U.S. EPA.

Of the hundreds of so-called gas saving devices on the market, only five tested by the EPA have been shown to *slightly* improve your fuel economy without increasing harmful emissions. Even these, however, offer limited savings because of their cost. They are the Pass Master Vehicle Air Conditioner P.A.S.S. Kit, Idalert, Morse Constant Speed Accessory Drive, Autotherm, and Kamei Spoilers. We don't recommend these products because the increase in fuel economy is not worth the investment in the product.

Do NOT Buy These Devices

Purported gas-saving devices come in many forms. Listed below are the types of products on the market. Under each category are the names of devices actually reviewed or tested by the EPA for which there was *no evidence of any improvement in fuel economy.*

AIR BLEED DEVICES
- ADAKS Vacuum Breaker
- Air Bleed
- Air-Jet Air Bleed
- Aquablast Wyman Valve Air Bleed
- Auto Miser
- Ball-Matic Air Bleed
- Berg Air Bleed
- Brisko PCV
- Cyclone - Z
- Econo Needle Air Bleed
- Econo-Jet Air Bleed Idle Screws
- Fuel Max
- Gas Saving Device
- Grancor Air Computer
- Hot Tip
- Landrum Mini-Carb
- Landrum Retrofit Air Bleed
- Mini Turbocharger Air Bleed*
- Monocar HC Control Air Bleed
- Peterman Air Bleed*
- Pollution Master Air Bleed
- Ram-Jet
- Turbo-Dyne G.R. Valve

DRIVING HABIT MODIFIERS
- Fuel Conservation Device
- Gastell

FUEL LINE DEVICES
- Fuel Xpander
- Gas Meiser I
- Greer Fuel Preheater
- Jacona Fuel System
- Malpassi Filter King
- Moleculetor
- Optimizer
- Petro-Mizer
- Polarion-X
- Russell Fuelmiser
- Super-Mag Fuel Extender
- Wickliff Polarizer

FUELS AND FUEL ADDITIVES
- Bycosin*
- EI-5 Fuel Additive*
- Fuelon Power Gasoline Fuel Additive
- Johnson Fuel Additive*
- NRG #1 Fuel Additive
- QEI 400 Fuel Additive*
- Rolfite Upgrade Fuel Additive
- Sta-Power Fuel Additive
- Stargas Fuel Additive
- SYNeRGy-1
- Technol G Fuel Additive
- ULX-15/ULX-15D
- Vareb 10 Fuel Additive*
- XRG #1 Fuel Additive

IGNITION DEVICES
- Autosaver
- Baur Condenser*
- BIAP Electronic Ignition Unit
- Fuel Economizer
- Magna Flash Ignition Ctrl. Sys.
- Paser Magnum/Paser 500/ Paser 500 HEI
- Special Formula Ignition Advance Springs*

INTERNAL ENGINE MODIFICATIONS
- ACDS Auto. Cyl. Deactivation Sys.
- Dresser Economizer*
- MSU Cylinder Deactivation*

LIQUID INJECTION
- Goodman Engine Sys. Model 1800*
- Waag-Injection System*

MIXTURE ENHANCERS
- Basko Enginecoat
- Dresser Economizer
- Electro-Dyne Superchoke*
- Energy Gas Saver*
- Environmental Fuel Saver*
- Filtron Urethane Foam Filter*
- Gas Saving and Emission Control Improvement Device
- Glynn-50*
- Hydro-Catalyst Pre-Combustion System
- Lamkin Fuel Metering Device
- Petromizer System
- Sav-A-Mile
- Smith Power and Deceleration Governor Spritzer*
- Turbo-Carb
- Turbocarb

OILS AND OIL ADDITIVES
- Analube Synthetic Lubricant
- Tephguard*

VAPOR BLEED DEVICES
- Atomized Vapor Injector
- Econo-Mist Vacuum Vapor Injection System
- Frantz Vapor Injection System*
- Hydro-Vac
- Mark II Vapor Injection System*
- Platinum Gasaver
- POWER FUeL
- Scatpac Vacuum Vapor Induction System
- Turbo Vapor Injection System*
- V-70 Vapor Injector

MISCELLANEOUS
- Brake-Ez*
- Dynamix
- Fuel Maximiser
- Gyroscopic Wheel Cover
- Kat's Engine Heater
- Lee Exhaust and Fuel Gasification EGR*
- Mesco Moisture Extraction Sys.
- P.S.C.U. 01 Device
- Treis Emulsifier

* For copies of reports on these products, write Test and Evaluation Branch, U.S. EPA, 2565 Plymouth Rd., Ann Arbor, MI 48105. For the other products, contact the National Technical Information Service, Springfield, VA 22161. (703-487-4650).

Fuel Economy Ratings

Every year the Department of Energy publishes the results of the Environmental Protection Agency's fuel economy tests in a comparative guide. In the past, millions of these booklets have been distributed to consumers who are eager to purchase fuel-efficient vehicles. However, the government has recently limited the availability of the guide. Because the success of the EPA program depends on consumers' ability to compare the fuel economy ratings easily, we have reprinted the EPA mileage figures for this year's vehicles.

The mileage estimates below and on the next few pages are the EPA city and highway figures.

A Note about the Ratings: When the EPA figures were first released, they were best used to compare fuel efficiency among vehicles—not to predict expected mileage. Because of changes in how the EPA presents the mileage ratings, these figures should better predict your expected mileage. When buying a vehicle, however, it's still best to use the EPA mileage estimates on a relative basis: if one vehicle is rated at 20 mpg and another at 25, the 25 mpg vehicle will nearly always perform better than the 20 mpg vehicle.

1996 Truck, Van and 4x4 Fuel Economy Winners and Losers

The Misers	MPG City /Highway	Annual Fuel Cost[1]
Toyota RAV4 2WD (2.0L/4/M5)	24/30	$666
Chevrolet S10 Pickup 2WD (2.2L/4/M5)*	23/30	$693
GMC Sonoma 2WD (2.2L/4/M5)*	23/30	$693
Isuzu Hombre Pickup 2WD (2.2L/4/M5)*	23/30	$693
Toyota RAV4 2WD (2.0L/4/L4)	24/29	$693
Geo Tracker Conv. 2WD (1.6L/4/M5)	24/26	$720
Geo Tracker Conv. 4x4 (1.6L/4/M5)	24/26	$720
Geo Tracker Van 2WD (1.6L/4/M5)	24/26	$720
Geo Tracker Van 4x4 (1.6L/4/M5)	24/26	$720
Toyota Tacoma 2WD (2.4L/4/M5)	23/28	$720
The Guzzlers		
Dodge Ram Wagon B3500 2WD (5.9L/8/L4)	11/14	$1499
Dodge Ram Pickup 2500 4WD (5.9L/8/L4)	11/15	$1384
Dodge Ram Pickup 1500 4WD (5.9L/8/L4)	11/15	$1384
Dodge Ram Wagon B1500/B2500 2WD (5.2L/8/A3)	12/14	$1384
Ford Econoline E250 2WD (4.9L/8/A3)	12/14	$1384
Dodge Ram Pickup 2500 4WD (5.2L/8/M5)	12/15	$1384
Dodge Ram Pickup 2500 4WD (5.9L/8/M5)	12/16	$1285

Based on 1996 EPA figures. (Engine size/number of cylinders/transmission type)

[1] Based on driving 15,000 miles per year.

* These models have "shift indicator" lights.

1996 EPA Figures

The following pages contain the EPA mileage ratings and the average annual fuel cost for most of the vehicles sold in the United States. We have arranged the list in alphabetical order. After the vehicle name, we have listed the engine size in liters, the number of cylinders, and some other identifiers: A = automatic transmission; L = lockup transmission; M = manual transmission.

The table includes the EPA city (first) and highway (second) fuel economy ratings. The city numbers will most closely resemble your expected mileage for everyday driving. The third column presents your average annual fuel cost. Reviewing this number will give you a better idea of how differences in fuel economy can affect your pocketbook. The amount is based on driving the vehicle 15,000 miles per year.

Vehicle (eng./trans.)	City	Hwy	Cost
Chevy Astro (4.3L/6/L4)	17	22	$ 947
Chevy Astro (4.3L/6/L4)	16	21	$1001
Chevy Astro (4.3L/6/L4)	16	20	$1001
Chevy Astro (4.3L/6/L4)	15	19	$1058
Chevy Blazer 2wd (4.3L/6/L4)	17	22	$ 947
Chevy Blazer 2wd (4.3L/6/M5)	18	24	$ 900
Chevy Blazer 4wd (4.3L/6/L4)	16	21	$1001
Chevy Blazer 4wd (4.3L/6/M5)	17	22	$ 947
Chevy Blazer AWD (4.3L/6/L4)	16	21	$1001
Chevy Lumina MV 2wd (3.4L/5/L4)	19	26	$ 857
Chevy PU (4.3L/6/L4)	17	22	$ 947
Chevy PU C1500 (4.3L/6/M5)	17	22	$ 947
Chevy PU C1500 (5.0L/8/L4)	15	19	$1058
Chevy PU C1500 (5.0L/8/M5)	15	20	$1058
Chevy PU C1500 (5.7L/8/L4)	15	19	$1125
Chevy PU C1500 (5.7L/8/M5)	14	20	$1125
Chevy PU C1500 (6.5L/8/L4)	16	21	$1001
Chevy PU C2500 (5.0L/8/L4)	15	19	$1125
Chevy PU C2500 (5.0L/8/M5)	15	20	$1058
Chevy PU C2500 (5.7L/8/L4)	14	18	$1125
Chevy PU C2500 (5.7L/8/M5)	13	17	$1285
Chevy PU C2500 (6.5L/8/L4)	16	20	$1058
Chevy PU K1500 (4.3L/6/L4)	16	20	$1001
Chevy PU K1500 (4.3L/6/M5)	15	21	$1058
Chevy PU K1500 (5.0L/8/L4)	14	18	$1125
Chevy PU K1500 (5.0L/8/M5)	14	19	$1125
Chevy PU K1500 (5.7L/8/L4)	13	17	$1201
Chevy PU K1500 (5.7L/8/M5)	13	18	$1201
Chevy PU K1500 (6.5L/8/L4)	15	19	$1125
Chevy S-10 PU (2.2L/4/M5)	23	30	$ 693
Chevy S-10 PU (4.3L/6/L4)	16	21	$1001
Chevy S-10 PU (4.3L/6/L4)	20	24	$ 857
Chevy S-10 PU (4.3L/6/M5)	17	22	$ 947
Chevy S-10 PU (4.3L/6/M5)	18	25	$ 900
Chevy S-10 PU 2wd (2.2L/4/L4)	20	27	$ 783
Chevy Suburban C1500 (5.7L/8/L4)	13	18	$1201
Chevy Suburban K1500 (5.7L/8/L4)	13	17	$1285
Chevy Tahoe C1500 (5.7L/8/L4)	14	17	$1201
Chevy Tahoe K1500 (5.7L/8/L4)	13	17	$1201
Chevy Tahoe K1500 (6.5L/8/L4)	15	18	$1125
Chevy Van G1500/G250 (4.3L/6/L4)	15	19	$1125
Chevy Van G1500/G250 (4.3L/6/L4)	15	19	$1125
Chevy Van G1500/G250 (5.0L/8/L4)	14	18	$1201
Chevy Van G1500/G250 (5.0L/8/L4)	13	17	$1201
Chevy Van G1500/G250 (5.7L/8/L4)	13	17	$1201
Chevy Van G1500/G250 (5.7L/8/L4)	13	18	$1201
Chrysler T&C (3.3L/6/L4)	17	24	$ 900
Chrysler T&C (3.8L/6/L4)	16	22	$1001
Chrysler T&C (3.8L/6/L4)	17	24	$ 900
Dodge Caravan 2wd (2.4L/4/L3)	20	26	$ 819
Dodge Caravan 2wd (3.0L/6/L3)	19	25	$ 857
Dodge Caravan 2wd (3.3L/6/L4)	18	24	$ 900
Dodge Caravan 2wd (3.8L/6/L4)	17	24	$ 900
Dodge Caravan 4wd (3.8L/6/L4)	16	22	$1001
Dodge Dakota 2wd (2.5L/4/M5)	21	25	$ 783
Dodge Dakota 2wd (3.9L/6/L4)	16	20	$1058
Dodge Dakota 2wd (3.9L/6/M5)	16	22	$1001
Dodge Dakota 2wd (5.2L/8/L4)	14	18	$1125
Dodge Dakota 2wd (5.2L/8/M5)	14	20	$1058
Dodge Dakota 4wd (3.9L/6/L4)	14	18	$1125
Dodge Dakota 4wd (3.9L/6/M5)	15	18	$1125
Dodge Dakota 4wd (5.2L/8/L4)	13	17	$1285
Dodge Dakota 4wd (5.2L/8/M5)	13	18	$1201
Dodge Ram PU 1500 2wd (3.9L/6/L4)	14	18	$1125
Dodge Ram PU 1500 2wd (3.9L/6/M5)	16	20	$1001
Dodge Ram PU 1500 2wd (5.2L/8/L4)	13	17	$1201
Dodge Ram PU 1500 2wd (5.2L/8/M5)	14	19	$1125
Dodge Ram PU 1500 2wd (5.9L/8/L4)	12	17	$1285
Dodge Ram PU 1500 4wd (5.2L/8/L4)	12	16	$1384
Dodge Ram PU 1500 4wd (5.2L/8/M5)	13	17	$1201
Dodge Ram PU 1500 4wd (5.9L/8/L4)	11	15	$1384
Dodge Ram PU 2500 2wd (5.2L/8/L4)	13	17	$1201
Dodge Ram PU 2500 2wd (5.2L/8/M5C)	13	16	$1285
Dodge Ram PU 2500 2wd (5.9L/8/L4)	12	17	$1285
Dodge Ram PU 2500 2wd (5.9L/8/M5C)	12	16	$1285
Dodge Ram PU 2500 4wd (5.2L/8/L4)	12	16	$1384
Dodge Ram PU 2500 4wd (5.2L/8/M5C)	12	15	$1384
Dodge Ram PU 2500 4wd (5.9L/8/L4)	11	15	$1384

Vehicle (eng./trans.)	City	Hwy	Cost
Dodge Ram PU 2500 4wd (5.9L/8/M5C)	12	15	$1384
Dodge Ram Van B1500/B250 (3.9L/6/L3)	15	17	$1125
Dodge Ram Van B1500/B250 (3.9L/6/L3)	15	17	$1125
Dodge Ram Van B1500/B250 (5.2L/8/A3)	13	14	$1384
Dodge Ram Van B1500/B250 (5.2L/8/A3)	12	14	$1384
Dodge Ram Van B1500/B250 (5.2L/8/L4)	13	17	$1201
Dodge Ram Van B1500/B250 (5.2L/8/L4)	13	17	$1201
Dodge Ram Van B1500/B250 (5.9L/8/L4)	12	17	$1285
Dodge Ram Van B1500/B250 (5.9L/8/L4)	12	17	$1285
Dodge Ram Van B3500 Van (5.2L/8/L4)	13	17	$1201
Dodge Ram Van B3500 Van (5.9L/8/L4)	12	17	$1285
Dodge Ram Van B3500 Wgn (5.2L/8/L4)	13	17	$1201
Dodge Ram Van B3500 Wgn (5.9L/8/L4)	11	14	$1499
Ford Aerostar (3.0L/6/L4)	18	24	$ 900
Ford Aerostar (4.0L/6/L4)	17	23	$ 947
Ford Aerostar (4.0L/6/L4)	15	20	$1058
Ford Bronco 4wd (5.0L/8/L4)	13	17	$1201
Ford Bronco 4wd (5.0L/8/M5)	14	17	$1201
Ford Bronco 4wd (5.8L/8/L4)	12	16	$1384
Ford E150 Club Wgn (4.9L/6/L4)	12	16	$1285
Ford E150 Club Wgn (5.0L/8/L4)	13	18	$1201
Ford E150 Club Wgn (5.8L/8/L4)	12	17	$1285
Ford E150 Econoline (4.9L/6/A3)	14	15	$1285
Ford E150 Econoline (4.9L/6/L4)	13	17	$1201
Ford E150 Econoline (5.0L/8/L4)	14	18	$1201
Ford E150 Econoline (5.8L/8/L4)	13	17	$1285
Ford E250 Econoline (4.9L/6/A3)	12	14	$1384
Ford E250 Econoline (4.9L/6/L4)	12	16	$1285
Ford E250 Econoline (5.8L/8/L4)	13	17	$1285
Ford Explorer 2wd (4.0L/6/L4)	16	21	$1001
Ford Explorer 2wd (4.0L/6/M5)	18	23	$ 900
Ford Explorer 2wd (5.0L/8/L4)	14	18	$1125
Ford Explorer 4wd (4.0L/6/L4)	15	20	$1058
Ford Explorer 4wd (4.0L/6/M5)	16	20	$1001
Ford F150 PU (4.9L/6/L4)	13	17	$1201
Ford F150 PU (4.9L/6/L4)	14	18	$1201
Ford F150 PU (4.9L/6/M5)	15	19	$1058
Ford F150 PU (4.9L/6/M5)	14	17	$1125
Ford F150 PU (5.0L/8/L4)	13	17	$1201
Ford F150 PU (5.0L/8/L4)	14	18	$1125
Ford F150 PU (5.0L/8/M5)	14	17	$1201
Ford F150 PU (5.0L/8/M5)	15	19	$1125
Ford F150 PU (5.8L/8/L4)	13	17	$1285
Ford F150 PU (5.8L/8/L4)	12	16	$1285
Ford F250 PU (4.9L/6/L4)	13	17	$1201
Ford F250 PU (4.9L/6/M5)	14	18	$1125
Ford F250 PU (5.0L/8/L4)	14	18	$1201
Ford F250 PU (5.0L/8/M5)	14	18	$1125
Ford F250 PU (5.8L/8/L4)	13	17	$1285
Ford Ranger 2wd (2.3L/4/L4)	20	25	$ 819
Ford Ranger 2wd (2.3L/4/M5)	22	27	$ 751

Vehicle (eng./trans.)	City	Hwy	Cost
Ford Ranger 2wd (3.0L/6/L4)	18	24	$ 900
Ford Ranger 2wd (3.0L/6/M5)	19	25	$ 857
Ford Ranger 2wd (4.0L/6/L4)	17	23	$ 947
Ford Ranger 2wd (4.0L/6/M5)	18	23	$ 900
Ford Ranger 4wd (2.3L/4/M5)	20	25	$ 819
Ford Ranger 4wd (3.0L/6/L4)	17	23	$ 947
Ford Ranger 4wd (3.0L/6/M5)	18	24	$ 900
Ford Ranger 4wd (4.0L/6/L4)	16	21	$1001
Ford Ranger 4wd (4.0L/6/M5)	17	21	$1001
Ford Windstar Fwd Van (3.0L/6/L4)	17	25	$ 900
Ford Windstar Fwd Van (3.8L/6/L4)	17	23	$ 900
Ford Windstar Fwd Wgn (3.0L/6/L4)	17	25	$ 900
Ford Windstar Fwd Wgn (3.8L/6/L4)	17	23	$ 900
GMC Jimmy 2wd (4.3L/6/L4)	17	22	$ 947
GMC Jimmy 2wd (4.3L/6/M5)	18	24	$ 900
GMC Jimmy 4wd (4.3L/6/L4)	16	21	$1001
GMC Jimmy 4wd (4.3L/6/M5)	17	22	$ 947
GMC Jimmy AWD (4.3L/6/L4)	16	21	$1001
GMC Safari 2wd Cargo (4.3L/6/L4)	17	22	$ 947
GMC Safari 2wd Passen (4.3L/6/L4)	16	20	$1001
GMC Safari AWD Cargo (4.3L/6/L4)	16	21	$1001
GMC Safari AWD Passen (4.3L/6/L4)	15	19	$1058
GMC Savana G1500/g250 (4.3L/6/L4)	15	19	$1125
GMC Savana G1500/g250 (4.3L/6/L4)	15	19	$1125
GMC Savana G1500/g250 (5.0L/8/L4)	14	18	$1201
GMC Savana G1500/g250 (5.0L/8/L4)	13	17	$1201
GMC Savana G1500/g250 (5.7L/8/L4)	13	18	$1201
GMC Savana G1500/g250 (5.7L/8/L4)	13	17	$1201
GMC Sierra C1500 (4.3L/6/L4)	17	22	$ 947
GMC Sierra C1500 (4.3L/6/M5)	17	22	$ 947
GMC Sierra C1500 (5.0L/8/L4)	15	19	$1125
GMC Sierra C1500 (5.0L/8/M5)	15	20	$1058
GMC Sierra C1500 (5.7L/8/L4)	15	19	$1125
GMC Sierra C1500 (5.7L/8/M5)	14	20	$1125
GMC Sierra C1500 (6.5L/8/L4)	16	21	$1001
GMC Sierra C2500 (5.0L/8/L4)	15	19	$1125
GMC Sierra C2500 (5.0L/8/M5)	15	20	$1058
GMC Sierra C2500 (5.7L/8/L4)	14	18	$1201
GMC Sierra C2500 (5.7L/8/M5)	13	17	$1285
GMC Sierra C2500 (6.5L/8/L4)	16	20	$1058
GMC Sierra K1500 (4.3L/6/L4)	16	20	$1001
GMC Sierra K1500 (4.3L/6/M5)	15	21	$1058
GMC Sierra K1500 (5.0L/8/L4)	14	18	$1125
GMC Sierra K1500 (5.0L/8/M5)	14	19	$1125
GMC Sierra K1500 (5.7L/8/L4)	13	17	$1201
GMC Sierra K1500 (5.7L/8/M5)	13	18	$1201
GMC Sierra K1500 (6.5L/8/L4)	15	19	$1125
GMC Sonoma Sonoma 2wd (2.2L/4/L4)	20	27	$ 783
GMC Sonoma Sonoma 2wd (2.2L/4/M5)	23	30	$ 693
GMC Sonoma Sonoma 2wd (4.3L/6/L4)	19	24	$ 857
GMC Sonoma Sonoma 2wd (4.3L/6/M5)	18	25	$ 857

Vehicle (eng./trans.)	City	Hwy	Cost
GMC Sonoma Sonoma 4wd (4.3L/6/L4)	16	21	$1001
GMC Sonoma Sonoma 4wd (4.3L/6/M5)	17	22	$ 947
GMC Suburban C1500 (5.7L/8/L4)	13	18	$1201
GMC Suburban K1500 (5.7L/8/L4)	13	17	$1285
GMC Yukon C1500 (5.7L/8/L4)	14	17	$1201
GMC Yukon K1500 (5.7L/8/L4)	13	17	$1201
GMC Yukon K1500 (6.5L/8/L4)	15	18	$1125
Geo Tracker 2wd (1.6L/4/L4)	22	25	$ 751
Geo Tracker 2wd (1.6L/4/M5)	24	26	$ 720
Geo Tracker Convertible (1.6L/4/L3)	23	24	$ 783
Geo Tracker Convertible (1.6L/4/L3)	23	24	$ 783
Geo Tracker Convertible (1.6L/4/M5)	24	26	$ 720
Geo Tracker Convertible (1.6L/4/M5)	24	26	$ 720
Geo Tracker Van 4x4 (1.6L/4/L4)	22	25	$ 751
Geo Tracker Van 4x4 (1.6L/4/M5)	24	26	$ 720
Honda Odyssey (2.2L/4/L4)	20	24	$ 819
Isuzu Hombre 2wd (2.2L/4/M5)	23	30	$ 693
Isuzu Oasis (2.2L/4/L4)	20	24	$ 819
Isuzu Trooper (3.2L/6/L4)	14	18	$1125
Isuzu Trooper (3.2L/6/M5)	16	18	$1058
Jeep Cherokee 2wd (2.5L/4/M5)	19	23	$ 857
Jeep Cherokee 2wd (4.0L/6/L4)	15	21	$1001
Jeep Cherokee 2wd (4.0L/6/M5)	18	23	$ 900
Jeep Cherokee 4wd (2.5L/4/M5)	19	22	$ 900
Jeep Cherokee 4wd (4.0L/6/L4)	15	19	$1058
Jeep Cherokee 4wd (4.0L/6/M5)	17	22	$ 947
Jeep Grand Cherokee 2wd (4.0L/6/L4)	15	21	$1058
Jeep Grand Cherokee 4wd (4.0L/6/L4)	15	20	$1058
Jeep Grand Cherokee 4wd (5.2L/8/L4)	14	18	$1201
Kia Sportage 2wd (2.0L/4/M5)	19	23	$ 857
Kia Sportage 4wd (2.0L/4/L4)	18	21	$ 900
Kia Sportage 4wd (2.0L/4/M5)	18	22	$ 900
Mazda B2300/B300 PU (2.3L/4/L4)	20	25	$ 819
Mazda B2300/B300 PU (2.3L/4/M5)	22	27	$ 751
Mazda B2300/B300 PU (2.3L/4/M5)	20	25	$ 819
Mazda B2300/B300 PU (3.0L/6/L4)	18	24	$ 900
Mazda B2300/B300 PU (3.0L/6/L4)	17	23	$ 947
Mazda B2300/B300 PU (3.0L/6/M5)	18	24	$ 900
Mazda B2300/B300 PU (3.0L/6/M5)	19	25	$ 857
Mazda B2300/B300 PU (4.0L/6/L4)	17	23	$ 947
Mazda B2300/B300 PU (4.0L/6/L4)	16	21	$1001
Mazda B2300/B300 PU (4.0L/6/M5)	18	23	$ 900
Mazda B2300/B300 PU (4.0L/6/M5)	17	21	$1001
Mazda MPV (3.0L/6/L4)	16	22	$1001
Mazda MPV (3.0L/6/L4)	15	19	$1125
Mercury Villager Fwd Van (3.0L/6/L4)	17	23	$ 900
Mercury Villager Fwd Wgn (3.0L/6/L4)	17	23	$ 900
Mitsubishi Mighty Max 2wd (2.4L/4/L4)	19	22	$ 900
Mitsubishi Mighty Max 2wd (2.4L/4/M5)	21	25	$ 819
Mitsubishi Montero (3.0L/6/L4)	15	18	$1125
Mitsubishi Montero (3.0L/6/L4)	16	19	$1058
Mitsubishi Montero (3.0L/6/M5)	15	18	$1058
Mitsubishi Montero (3.0L/6/M5)	16	18	$1058
Mitsubishi Montero (3.5L/6/L4)	14	18	$1266
Nissan Pathfinder 2wd (3.3L/6/L4)	16	20	$1001
Nissan Pathfinder 2wd (3.3L/6/M5)	17	20	$1001
Nissan Pathfinder 4wd (3.3L/6/L4)	15	19	$1058
Nissan Pathfinder 4wd (3.3L/6/M5)	16	18	$1058
Nissan Quest (3.0L/6/L4)	17	23	$ 900
Oldsmobile Silhouette 2wd (3.4L/5/L4)	19	26	$ 857
Plymouth Voyager 2wd (2.4L/4/L3)	20	26	$ 819
Plymouth Voyager 2wd (3.0L/6/L3)	19	25	$ 857
Plymouth Voyager 2wd (3.3L/6/L4)	18	24	$ 900
Plymouth Voyager 4wd (3.8L/6/L4)	16	22	$1001
Pontiac Trans Sport 2wd (3.4L/5/L4)	19	26	$ 857
Suzuki Sidekick 2 Door 2wd (1.6L/4/L3)	23	24	$ 783
Suzuki Sidekick 2 Door 2wd (1.6L/4/M5)	23	26	$ 751
Suzuki Sidekick 2 Door 4wd (1.6L/4/L3)	23	24	$ 783
Suzuki Sidekick 2 Door 4wd (1.6L/4/M5)	23	26	$ 751
Suzuki Sidekick 4 Door 2wd (1.6L/4/L4)	22	25	$ 751
Suzuki Sidekick 4 Door 2wd (1.6L/4/M5)	23	26	$ 751
Suzuki Sidekick 4 Door 4wd (1.6L/4/L4)	22	25	$ 751
Suzuki Sidekick 4 Door 4wd (1.6L/4/M5)	23	26	$ 751
Suzuki Sidekick Sport 4wd (1.8L/4/L4)	21	24	$ 783
Suzuki Sidekick Sport 4wd (1.8L/4/M5)	23	25	$ 783
Suzuki X-90 2wd (1.6L/4/M5)	25	28	$ 693
Suzuki X-90 4wd (1.6L/4/L4)	23	27	$ 720
Suzuki X-90 4wd (1.6L/4/M5)	25	28	$ 693
Toy. Land Cruiser Wgn 4wd (4.5L/6/L4)	13	15	$1285
Toyota Previa (2.4L/4/L4)	18	22	$ 947
Toyota Previa All-Trac (2.4L/4/L4)	17	20	$1001
Toyota RAV4 (2.0L/4/L4)	22	27	$ 751
Toyota RAV4 (2.0L/4/M5)	22	27	$ 751
Toyota RAV4 2wd (2.0L/4/L4)	24	29	$ 693
Toyota RAV4 2wd (2.0L/4/M5)	24	30	$ 666
Toyota T100 2wd (2.7L/4/L4)	19	22	$ 900
Toyota T100 2wd (2.7L/4/M5)	20	24	$ 857
Toyota T100 2wd (3.4L/6/L4)	17	20	$1001
Toyota T100 2wd (3.4L/6/M5)	17	21	$ 947
Toyota T100 4wd (3.4L/6/L4)	16	18	$1058
Toyota T100 4wd (3.4L/6/M5)	17	19	$1001
Toyota Tacoma 2wd (2.4L/4/A4)	22	25	$ 783
Toyota Tacoma 2wd (2.4L/4/M5)	23	28	$ 720
Toyota Tacoma 2wd (3.4L/6/L4)	19	22	$ 900
Toyota Tacoma 2wd (3.4L/6/M5)	19	23	$ 900
Toyota Tacoma 4wd (2.7L/4/L4)	18	21	$ 947
Toyota Tacoma 4wd (2.7L/4/M5)	19	23	$ 900
Toyota Tacoma 4wd (3.4L/6/L4)	17	19	$1001
Toyota Tacoma 4wd (3.4L/6/M5)	17	19	$1001

MAINTENANCE

After you buy a vehicle, maintenance costs will be a significant portion of your operating expenses. This chapter allows you to consider and compare some of these costs *before* deciding which vehicle to purchase. These costs include preventive maintenance servicing—such as changing the oil and filters—as well as the cost of repairs after your warranty expires. On the following pages, we compared the costs of preventive maintenance and of nine likely repairs for the 1996 models. Since the cost of a repair also depends on the shop and the mechanic, this chapter includes tips for finding a good shop and for communicating effectively with a mechanic.

Preventive maintenance is the periodic servicing, specified by the manufacturer, that keeps your vehicle running properly. For example, regularly changing the oil and oil filter. Every owner's manual specifies a schedule of recommended servicing for at least the first 50,000 miles, and the tables on the following pages estimate the cost of following this preventive maintenance schedule.

If for some reason you do not have an owner's manual with the preventive maintenance schedule, contact the manufacturer to obtain one.

Note: Some dealers and repair shops create their own maintenance schedules which call for more frequent (and thus more expensive) servicing than the manufacturer's recommendations. If the servicing recommended by your dealer or repair shop doesn't match what the maker recommends, make sure you understand and agree to the extra items.

The tables also list the costs for nine repairs that typically occur during the first 100,000 miles. There is no precise way to predict exactly when a repair will be needed. But if you keep a vehicle for 75,000 to 100,000 miles, it is likely that you will experience most of these repairs at least once. The last column provides a relative indication of how expensive these nine repairs are for many vehicles. Repair cost is rated as *Very Good* if the total for nine repairs is in the bottom fifth of all the vehicles rated, and *Very Poor* if the total is in the top fifth.

Most repair shops use "flat-rate manuals" to estimate repair costs. These manuals list the approximate time required for repairing many items. Each automobile manufacturer publishes its own manual and there are several independent manuals as well. For many repairs, the time varies from one manual to another. Some repair shops even use different manuals for different repairs. To determine a repair bill, a shop multiplies the time listed in its manual by its hourly labor rate and then adds the cost of parts.

Our cost estimates are based on flat-rate manual repair times multiplied by a nationwide average labor rate of $45 per hour. All estimates also include the cost of replaced parts and related adjustments.

Prices in the following tables may not predict the exact costs of these repairs. For example, the labor rate for your area may be more or less than the national average. However, the prices will provide you with a relative comparison of maintenance costs for various automobiles.

In This Chapter . . .

	PM Costs to 50,000Miles	Water Pump	Alternator	Front Brake Pads	Starter	Fuel Injection	Fuel Pump	Struts	Lower Ball Joints	CVJ or Univ. Joint	Relative Maint. Cost
Minivans											
Chevrolet Astro	660	192	210	80	256	567	219	150	190	87	Good
Chevy Lumina Minivan	660	128	226	109	346	163	235	260	114	232	Vry. Gd.
Chrys. Town and Cntry.	608	150	315	125	188	238	313	195	128	293	Good
Dodge Caravan	608	150	315	125	255	118	249	260	255	313	Good
Ford Aerostar	587	226	388	127	309	171	241	124	180	186	Good
Ford Windstar	587	283	414	145	274	197	253	314	192	362	Ave.
Honda Odyssey	880	237	375	112	432	113	445	127	270	335	Ave.
Isuzu Oasis	880	237	375	112	432	113	445	127	270	335	Ave.
Mazda MPV	826	190	248	92	355	304	174	339	610	427	Poor
Mercury Villager	613	187	401	150	280	254	323	241	149	190	Good
Nissan Quest	613	187	401	150	280	254	323	241	149	190	Good
Oldsmobile Silhouette	660	128	226	109	346	163	235	260	114	232	Vry. Gd.
Plymouth Voyager	608	150	315	125	255	118	249	260	255	313	Good
Pontiac Trans Sport	660	128	226	109	346	163	235	260	114	232	Vry. Gd.
Toyota Previa	788	133	370	108	313	226	356	421	178	399	Poor
Full Size Van											
Chevy Van/Chevy Expr.	747	202	239	80	437	280	136	122	310	87	Vry. Gd.
Dodge Ram Van/Wagon	834	195	307	111	313	160	375	87	280	64	Vry. Gd.
Ford Econoline/Club Wgn.	649	228	474	139	312	211	348	132	193	67	Good
GMC Savana	747	202	239	80	437	280	136	122	310	87	Vry. Gd.
Small Sport Utility											
Geo Tracker	639	208	558	151	464	219	536	455	165	86	Vry. Pr.
Jeep Wrangler	706	187	309	117	233	99	246	81	366	88	Vry. Gd.
Kia Sportage	700	135	239	131	255	218	315	341	155	408	Good
Suzuki Sidekick	639	208	558	151	464	219	536	455	165	86	Vry. Pr.
Average	724	206	380	122	335	197	296	294	292	259	

	PM Costs to 50,000Miles	Water Pump	Alternator	Front Brake Pads	Starter	Fuel Injection	Fuel Pump	Struts	Lower Ball Joints	CVJ or Univ. Joint	Relative Maint. Cost
Small Sport Utility (cont.)											
Suzuki X-90	639	143	423	134	496	245	497	273	173	437	Poor
Toyota RAV4	803	167	554	144	371	174	361	89	206	415	Ave.
Mid-Size Sport Utility											
Chevrolet Blazer	757	165	210	115	235	320	229	139	260	287	Good
Ford Explorer	649	245	418	107	313	137	208	119	261	43	Vry. Gd.
GMC Jimmy	757	165	210	115	235	320	229	139	260	287	Good
Honda Passport	747	231	292	111	296	181	380	100	205	75	Vry. Gd.
Isuzu Rodeo	747	231	292	111	296	181	380	100	205	75	Vry. Gd.
Isuzu Trooper	747	293	362	157	335	202	439	114	223	123	Good
Jeep Cherokee	706	184	304	112	230	96	255	78	141	109	Vry. Gd.
Jeep Grand Cherokee	706	194	309	112	180	99	328	128	169	79	Vry. Gd.
Land Rover Discovery	1237	285	533	100	627	258	305	249	311	597	Vry. Pr.
Mitsubishi Montero	932	265	362	118	631	275	391	167	260	91	Poor
Nissan Pathfinder	803	262	290	103	325	196	341	127	207	71	Vry. Gd.
Oldsmobile Bravada	757	165	210	115	235	320	229	139	260	287	Good
Toyota 4Runner	803	336	470	108	370	256	350	89	321	122	Ave.
Large Sport Utility											
Chevrolet Suburban	757	165	188	115	145	294	166	132	176	92	Vry. Gd.
Chevrolet Tahoe	757	154	234	110	308	284	166	133	266	83	Vry. Gd.
Ford Bronco	649	181	388	148	320	181	348	88	1178	42	Vry. Pr.
GMC Suburban	757	165	188	115	145	294	166	132	176	92	Vry. Gd.
GMC Yukon	757	154	234	110	308	284	166	133	266	83	Vry. Gd.
Land Rover Range Rover	1237	285	825	113	627	258	391	288	367	152	Vry. Pr.
Toyota Land Cruiser	803	204	386	98	302	286	350	89	321	123	Good
Average	724	206	380	122	335	197	296	294	292	259	

	PM Costs to 50,000Miles	Water Pump	Alternator	Front Brake Pads	Starter	Fuel Injection	Fuel Pump	Struts	Lower Ball Joints	CVJ or Univ. Joint	Relative Maint. Cost
Compact Pickup											
Chevrolet S-Series	767	163	214	114	295	181	206	143	161	88	Vry.Gd.
Dodge Dakota	720	148	298	148	220	113	322	77	251	66	Vry.Gd.
Ford Ranger	650	188	338	107	308	147	203	125	692	49	Good
GMC Sonoma	767	163	214	114	295	181	206	143	161	88	Vry.Gd.
Isuzu Hombre	767	163	214	114	295	181	206	143	161	88	Vry.Gd.
Mazda B-Series Pickup	650	188	338	107	308	147	203	125	692	49	Good
Mitsubishi Mighty Max	932	253	562	73	591	240	340	119	175	339	Poor
Nissan Pickup	803	263	290	93	324	173	294	101	183	88	Vry.Gd.
Toyota Tacoma	793	318	475	106	370	261	350	87	217	450	Poor
Standard Pickup											
Chevrolet C/K Series	757	164	234	109	222	287	171	104	134	87	Vry.Gd.
Dodge Ram Pickup	834	165	304	114	302	133	333	88	252	69	Vry.Gd.
Ford F-Series Pickup	650	210	427	150	320	188	348	116	269	83	Good
GMC Sierra	757	164	234	109	222	287	171	104	134	87	Vry.Gd.
Toyota T100	793	249	515	113	366	169	350	131	117	450	Ave.
Average	724	206	380	122	335	197	296	294	292	259	

Service Contracts

Each year nearly 50 percent of new vehicle buyers buy "service contracts." Ranging from $400 to $1500 in price, a service contract is one of the most expensive options you can buy. In fact, service contracts are a major source of profit for many dealers.

A service contract is not a warranty. It is more like an insurance plan that, in theory, covers repairs that are not covered by your warranty or that occur after the warranty runs out.

Service contracts are generally a very poor value. The companies who sell contracts are very sure that, on average, your repairs will cost considerably less than what you pay for the contract—if not, they wouldn't be in business.

One alternative to buying a service contract is to deposit the cost of the contract into a savings account. If the vehicle needs a major repair, not covered by your warranty, chances are good that the money in your account will cover the cost. Most likely, you'll be building up your down payment for your next vehicle!

If you believe that you really need a service contract, contact an insurance company, such as GEICO. You can save up to 50-percent by buying from an insurance company.

Here are some important questions to ask before buying a service contract:

How reputable is the company responsible for the contract? If the company offering the contract goes out of business, you will be out of luck. Recently, a number of independent service contract companies have gone under, so be very careful about who you buy from. Check with your Better Business Bureau or office of consumer affairs if you are not sure of a company's reputation. Service contracts from car and insurance companies are more likely to remain in effect than those from independent companies.

Exactly what does the contract cover and for how long? Service contracts vary considerably—different items are covered and different time limits are offered. This is true even among service contracts offered by the same company. For example, Ford's plans range from 3 years/ 50,000 miles maximum coverage to 6 years/100,000 miles maximum coverage, with other options for only powertrain coverage.

If you plan to resell your vehicle in a few years, you won't want to purchase a long-running service contract. Some service contracts automatically cancel when you resell the vehicle, while others require a hefty transfer fee before extending privileges to the new owner.

Some automakers offer a "menu" format which lets you pick the items you want covered in your service contract. Find out if the contract pays for preventive maintenance, towing, and rental car expenses. If not written into the contract, assume they are not covered.

Finally, think twice before purchasing travel services offered in the contract. Such amenities are offered by auto clubs, and you should compare prices before adding them into your contract cost.

How will the repair bills be paid? It is best to have the service contractor pay bills directly. Some contracts require you to pay the repair bill, and reimburse you later.

Where can the vehicle be serviced? Can you take the vehicle to any mechanic if you have trouble on the road? What if you move?

What other costs can be expected? Most service contracts will have a deductible expense. Compare deductibles on various plans. Also, some companies charge the deductible for each individual repair while other companies charge per visit, regardless of the number of repairs made.

Turbocharging

A turbocharger is an air pump that forces more air into the engine for combustion. Most turbo chargers consist of an air compressor driven by a small turbine wheel that is powered by the engine's exhaust. The turbine takes advantage of energy otherwise lost and forces increased efficiency from the engine. Turbochargers are often used to increase the power and sometimes the fuel efficiency of small engines. Engines equipped with turbochargers are more expensive than standard engines. The extra power may not be necessary when you consider the added expense and the fact that turbocharging adds to the complexity of the engine.

Tips for Dealing with a Mechanic

Call around. Don't choose a shop simply because it's nearby. Calling a few shops may turn up estimates cheaper by half.

Don't necessarily go for the lowest price. A good rule is to eliminate the highest and lowest estimates; the mechanic with the highest estimate is probably charging too much and the lowest may be cutting too many corners.

Check the shop's reputation. Call your local consumer affairs agency and the Better Business Bureau. They don't have records on every shop, but if their reports on a shop aren't favorable, you can disqualify it.

Look for Certification: Mechanics can be certified by the National Institute for Automotive Service Excellence, an industry-wide yardstick for competence. Certification is offered in eight areas of repair and shops with certified mechanics are allowed to advertise this fact. However, make sure the mechanic working on your car is certified for the repair.

Take a look around. A well-kept shop reflects pride in workmanship. A skilled and efficient mechanic would probably not work in a messy shop.

Don't sign a blank check. Your service order should have specific instructions or describe your vehicle's symptoms. Signing a vague work order could make you liable to pay for work you didn't want. Be sure you are called for approval before the shop does extra work.

Show interest. Ask about the repair. A mechanic may become more helpful just knowing that you're interested. But don't act like an expert if you really don't understand what's wrong. Demonstrating your ignorance, on the other hand, may set you up to be taken by a dishonest mechanic, so strike a balance.

Express your satisfaction. If you're happy with the work, compliment the mechanic and ask for him or her the next time you come in. You'll get to know each other, and the mechanic will get to know your vehicle.

Develop a "sider." If you know a mechanic, ask about work on the side—evenings or weekends. The labor will be cheaper.

Test drive, then pay! Before you pay for a major repair, you should take the vehicle for a test drive. The extra few minutes that you spend checking out the repair could save you a trip back to the mechanic. If you find that the problem still exists, there will be no question that the repair wasn't properly completed. It is much more difficult to prove the repair wasn't properly made after you've left the shop.

Repair Protection By Credit Card

TIP

Paying your auto repair bills by credit card can provide a much-needed recourse if you are having problems with an auto mechanic. According to federal law, you have the right to withhold payment for sloppy or incorrect repairs. Of course, you may withhold no more than the amount of the repair in dispute.

In order to use this right, you must first try to work out the problem with the mechanic. Also, unless the credit card company owns the repair shop (this might be the case with gasoline credit cards used at gas stations), two other conditions must be met. First, the repair shop must be in your home state (or within 100 miles of your current address), and second, the cost of repairs must be over $50. Until the problem is settled or resolved in court, the credit card company cannot charge you interest or penalties on the amount in dispute.

If you decide to take action, send a letter to the credit card company and a copy to the repair shop, explaining the details of the problem and what you want as settlement. Send the letter by certified mail with a return receipt requested.

Sometimes the credit card company or repair shop will attempt to put a "bad mark" on your credit record if you use this tactic. Legally, you can't be reported as delinquent if you've given the credit card company notice of your dispute. But, a creditor can report that you are disputing your bill, which goes in your record. However, you have the right to challenge any incorrect information and add your side of the story to your file.

For more information, write to the Federal Trade Commission, Credit Practices Division, 601 Pennsylvania Avenue, NW, Washington, DC 20580.

With the popularity of self-service gasoline stations, many of us overlook the simplest and most vital maintenance task of all: checking various items to prevent serious problems down the road. In about fifteen minutes a month, you can make the following checks yourself. *Warning:* Many new vehicles have electric cooling fans that operate when the engine is off. Be sure to keep your hands away from the fan if the engine is warm.

Coolant: We'll start with the easiest fluid to check. Most vehicles have a plastic reservoir next to the radiator. This bottle will have "full hot" and "full cold" marks on it. If coolant is below "full cold" mark, add water to bring it up to that mark. (Antifreeze should be used if you want extra protection in cold weather.) *Caution:* If vehicle is hot, do not open the radiator cap. Pressure and heat that can cause a severe burn may be released.

Brakes: The most important safety item on the vehicle is the most ignored. A simple test will signal problems. (With power brakes, turn on engine to test.) Push the brake pedal down and hold it down. It should stop firmly and stay about halfway to the floor. If the stop is mushy or the pedal keeps moving to the floor, you should have your brakes checked. Checking the brake fluid on most vehicles is also very easy. Your owner's manual tells you where to find the fluid reservoir, which indicates minimum and maximum fluid levels. If you add your own brake fluid, buy it in small cans and keep them tightly sealed. Brake fluid absorbs moisture, and excess moisture can damage your brake system. Have the brakes checked if you need to replace brake fluid regularly.

Oil: A few years ago, the phrase "fill it up and check the oil" was so common that it seemed like one word. Today, checking the oil often is the responsibility of the driver. To check your oil, first turn off the engine. Find the dipstick (look for a loop made of flat wire located on the side of the engine). If the engine has been running, be careful, because the dipstick and surrounding engine parts will be hot. Grab the loop, pull out the dipstick, clean it off, and reinsert it into the engine. Pull it out again and observe the oil level. "Full" and "add" are marked at the end of the stick. If the level is between "add" and "full," you are OK. If it is below "add," you should add enough oil until it reaches the "full" line. To add oil, remove the cap at the top of the engine. You may have to add more than one quart. Changing your oil regularly (every 3000 miles) is the single most important way to protect your engine. Many owner's manuals also contain directions for doing so. Change the oil filter whenever you change the oil.

Transmission Fluid: An automatic transmission is a very complicated and expensive item. Checking your transmission fluid level is easy and can prevent a costly repair job. As in the oil check, you must first find the transmission fluid dipstick. Usually it is at the rear of the engine and looks like a smaller version of the oil dipstick. To get an accurate reading, the engine should be warmed up and running. If fluid is below the "add" line, pour in one pint at a time, but do not overfill the reservoir.

While you check the fluid, also note its color. It should be a bright, cherry red. If it is a darker, reddish brown, the fluid needs changing. If it is very dark, nearly black, and has a burnt smell (like varnish), your transmission may be damaged. You should take it to a specialist.

Automatic transmission fluid is available at most department stores; check your owner's manual for the correct type for your vehicle.

Power Steering: The power steering fluid reservoir is usually connected by a belt to the engine. To check it, simply unscrew the cap and look in the reservoir. There will be markings inside; some vehicles have a little dipstick built in to the cap.

Belts: You may have one or more belts connected to your engine. A loose belt in the engine can lead to electrical, cooling, or even air conditioning problems. To check, simply push down on the middle of each belt. It should feel tight. If you can push down more than half an inch, the belt needs tightening.

Battery: If your battery has caps on the top, lift off the caps and check that fluid comes up to the bottom of the filler neck. If it doesn't, add water (preferably distilled). If it is very cold outside, add water only if you are planning to drive the vehicle immediately. Otherwise the newly added water can freeze and damage your battery.

Also, look for corrosion around the battery connections. It can prevent electrical circuits from being completed, leading you to assume your perfectly good battery is "dead." If cables are corroded, remove and clean with fine sandpaper or steel wool. The inside of the connection and the battery posts should be shiny when you put the cables back on. *Caution:* Do not smoke or use any flame when checking the battery.

Tires: Improperly inflated tires are a major cause of premature tire failure. Check for proper inflation at least once a month. The most fuel-efficient inflation level is the maximum pressure listed on the side of the tire. Because many gas station pumps do not have gauges, and those that do are generally inaccurate, you should invest in your own tire gauge.

Air Filter: Probably the easiest item to maintain is your air filter. You can usually check the filter by just looking at it. If it appears dirty, change it—it's a simple task. If you are not sure how clean your filter is, try the following: Once the engine warms up, put the vehicle in park or neutral and, with the emergency brake on, let the vehicle idle. Open the filter lid and remove the filter. If the engine begins to run faster, change the filter.

Battery Safety

Almost all motorists have had to jump start a vehicle because of a dead battery. But that innocent-looking battery can cause some serious injuries.

Batteries produce hydrogen gas when they discharge or undergo heavy use (such as cranking the engine for a long period of time). A lit cigarette or a spark can cause this gas to explode. Whenever you work with the battery, always remove the negative (or ground) cable first and reconnect it last; it is usually marked with a minus sign. This precaution will greatly reduce the chance of causing a spark that could ignite any hydrogen gas present.

For a safe jump start:

1 Connect each end of the red cable to the positive (+) terminal on each battery.

2 Connect one end of the black cable to the negative (-) terminal of the *good* battery.

3 Connect the other end of the black cable to exposed metal away from the battery of the vehicle being started.

4 To avoid damaging electrical parts, make sure the engine is idling before disconnecting the cables.

Saving Gasoline

TIP

A cold-running engine dramatically reduces fuel economy. Most engines operate efficiently at 180 degrees, and an engine running at 125 degrees can waste one out of every ten gallons of gas. Your engine temperature is controlled by a thermostat valve. A faulty thermostat can be a major cause of poor fuel economy. If you feel that your vehicle should be getting better mileage, have your thermostat checked. They are inexpensive and relatively easy to replace.

Warranties

Along with your new vehicle comes a warranty, which is a promise from the manufacturer that the vehicle will perform as it should. Most of us never read the warranty—until it is too late. In fact, because warranties are often difficult to read and understand, most of us don't really know what our warranties offer. This chapter will help you understand what to look for in a new vehicle warranty, tip you off to secret warranties, and provide you with the best and worst among the 1996 warranties.

There are two types of warranties: one provided by the manufacturer and one implied by law.

Manufacturers' warranties are either "full" or "limited." The best warranty you can get is a full warranty because, by law, it must cover all aspects of the product's performance. Any other guarantee is called a limited warranty, which is what most manufacturers offer. Limited warranties must be clearly marked as such, and you must be told exactly what is covered.

Warranties implied by law are warranties of merchantability and fitness. The "warranty of merchantability" ensures that your new vehicle will be fit for the purpose for which it is used—that means safe, efficient, and trouble-free transportation. The "warranty of fitness" guarantees that if the dealer says a vehicle can be used for a specific purpose, it will perform that purpose.

Any claims made by the salesperson are also considered warranties. They are called expressed warranties and you should have them put in writing if you consider them to be important. If the vehicle does not live up to promises made to you in the showroom, you may have a case against the seller.

The manufacturer can restrict the amount of time the limited warranty is in effect. And in most states, the manufacturer can also limit the time that the warranty implied by law is in effect.

Through the warranty, the manufacturer is promising that the way the vehicle was made and the materials used are free from defects, provided that the vehicle is used in a normal fashion for a certain period after you buy it. This period of time is usually measured in both months and miles—whichever comes first is the limit.

While the warranty is in effect, the manufacturer will perform, at no charge to the owner, repairs that are necessary because of defects in materials or in the way the vehicle was manufactured.

The warranty does not cover parts that have to be replaced because of normal wear, such as filters, fuses, light bulbs, wiper blades, clutch linings, brake pads, or the addition of oil, fluids, coolants, and lubricants. Tires, batteries, and the emission control system are covered by separate warranties. Options, such as a stereo system, should have their own warranties as well. Service should be provided through the dealer. A separate rust (corrosion) warranty is also included.

The costs for the required maintenance listed in the owner's manual are not covered by the warranty. Problems resulting from misuse, negligence, changes you make in the vehicle, accidents, or lack of required maintenance are also not covered.

Any implied warranties, including the warranties of merchantability and fitness, are limited to 12 months or 12,000 miles. Also, the manufacturer is not responsible for other problems caused by repairs,

In This Chapter...

such as the loss of time or use of your vehicle, or any expenses they might cause.

In addition to the rights granted to you in the warranty, you may have other rights under your state laws.

To keep your warranty in effect, you must operate and maintain your vehicle according to the instructions in your owner's manual. Remember, it is important to keep a record of all maintenance performed on your vehicle.

To have your vehicle repaired under the warranty, take it to an authorized dealer or service center. The work should be done in a reasonable amount of time during normal business hours.

Be careful not to confuse your warranty with a service contract. The *service contract* must be purchased separately; and, the warranty is yours at no extra cost when you buy the vehicle. (See page 51 for more on service contracts.)

Corrosion Warranty: All manufacturers warrant against corrosion. The typical corrosion warranty lasts for six years or 100,000 miles, whichever comes first.

Some dealers offer extra rust protection at an additional cost. Before you purchase this option, compare the extra protection offered to the corrosion warranty already included in the price of the vehicle—it probably already provides sufficient protection against rust. (See page 93 for more important information on rust-proofing.)

Emission System Warranty: The emission system is warranted by federal law. Any repairs required during the first two years or 24,000 miles will be paid for by the manufacturer if an original engine part fails because of a defect in materials or workmanship, and the failure causes your vehicle to exceed federal emissions standards. Major components, such as an onboard computer emissions control unit, are covered for eight years or 80,000 miles.

Using leaded fuel in a vehicle designed for unleaded fuel will void your emission system warranty and may prevent the car from passing your state's inspection. Because an increasing number of states are requiring an emissions test before a vehicle can pass inspection, you may have to pay to fix the system if you used the wrong type of fuel. Repairs to emission systems are usually very expensive.

Dealer Options & Your Warranty

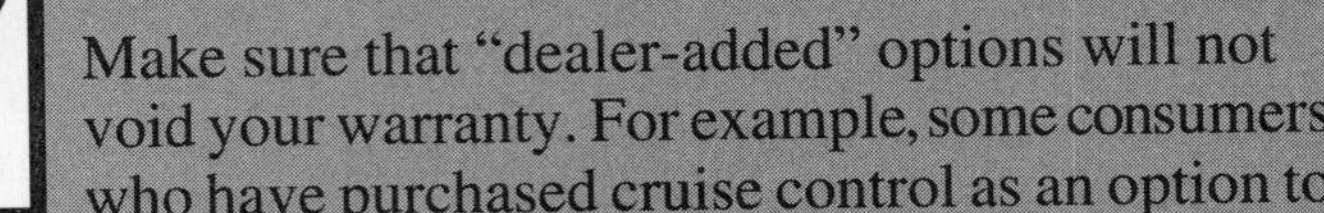

Make sure that "dealer-added" options will not void your warranty. For example, some consumers who have purchased cruise control as an option to be installed by the dealer have found that their warranty is void when they take the vehicle in for engine repairs. Also, some manufacturers warn that dealer-supplied rustproofing will void your corrosion warranty. If you are in doubt, contact the manufacturer before you authorize the installation of dealer-supplied options. If the manufacturer says that adding the option will not void your warranty, get it in writing.

Getting Warranty Service

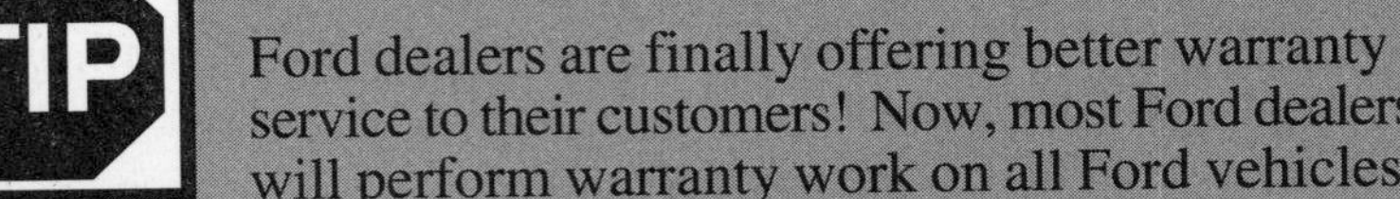

Ford dealers are finally offering better warranty service to their customers! Now, most Ford dealers will perform warranty work on all Ford vehicles, regardless of where the vehicle was purchased. Previously, only the selling dealer was required to perform repairs under warranty. Individual Ford dealers can still set their own policy, however, so it is best to call and ask before taking your vehicle in for warranty service. GM, Japanese and European dealers also provide this service to their customers, and Chrysler "recommends" that dealers follow this policy.

Secret Warranties

If dealers report a number of complaints about a certain part and the manufacturer determines that the problem is due to faulty design or assembly, the manufacturer may permit dealers to repair the problem at no charge to the customer even though the warranty is expired. In the past, this practice was often reserved for customers who made a big fuss. The availability of the free repair was never publicized, which is why we call these *secret* warranties.

Manufacturers deny the existence of secret warranties. They call these free repairs "policy adjustments" or "goodwill service." Whatever they are called, most consumers never hear about them.

Many secret warranties are disclosed in service bulletins that the manufacturers send to dealers. These bulletins outline free repair or reimbursement programs, as well as other problems and their possible causes and solutions.

Because of problems with secret warranties in the past, three companies are now required to make many of their bulletins available to the public. *Ford* was required to disclose both bulletins and goodwill adjustments under an FTC Consent Order through 1988. Now Ford's toll-free "defect line," 800-241-3673, provides information only on goodwill adjustments. *General Motors* bulletins from the past three years (which may cover models made earlier) and indexes to the bulletins are available at GM dealers. You may also call 800-551-4123 to obtain a form to order them directly from GM. The indexes are free, but there is a charge for the bulletins. *Volkswagen* is also required to make this information available to consumers. You can order an index of all service bulletins, which includes information on obtaining the actual bulletins, by calling 800-544-8021.

Service bulletins from other manufacturers may be on file at the National Highway Traffic Safety Administration. For copies of the bulletins on file, send a letter with the make, model and year of the car and the year you believe the service bulletin was issued, to the NHTSA's Technical Reference Library, Room 5108, NHTSA, Washington, DC 20590. If you write to the government, ask for "service bulletins" rather than "secret warranties."

If you find that a secret warranty is in effect and repairs are being made at no charge after the warranty has expired, contact the Center for Auto Safety, 2001 S Street NW, Washington, DC 20009. They will publish the information so others can benefit.

Disclosure Laws: Spurred by the proliferation of secret warranties and the failure of the FTC to take action, California, Connecticut, Virginia, and Wisconsin have passed legislation that requires consumers to be notified of secret warranties on their cars. Several other states have introduced similar warranty bills.

Typically, the laws require the following: Direct notice to consumers within a specified time after the adoption of a warranty adjustment policy; notice of the disclosure law to new car buyers; reimbursement, within a number of years after payment, to owners who paid for covered repairs before they learned of the extended warranty service; and dealers must inform consumers who complain about a covered defect that it is eligible for repair under warranty.

New York's bill has another requirement—the establishment of a toll-free number for consumer questions. Consumer groups, such as CAS, support this requirement, but it has met opposition from Ford, GM, Toyota, and other auto manufacturers.

If you live in a state with a secret warranty law already in effect, write your state attorney general's office (in care of your state capitol) for information. To encourage passage of such a bill, contact your state representative (in care of your state capitol).

A Secret Warranty: Here is an example of a secret warranty uncovered by the Center for Auto Safety. Ford is liable for up to $1 billion for bad paint—mainly on blue, silver and grey 1985-92 F-Series trucks. Ford set up an "Owners Dialogue Program" in 1993 to report peeling F-Series pickups, Broncos and Mustangs for free but abandoned the program when it became too costly. CAS is also aware of paint problems on the Aerostar, Bronco, Bronco II, Econoline, Escort, EXP, LTD, Mustang, Probe, Ranger, Sable, Taurus, Tempo, Thunderbird and Tracer. If your Ford has had problems with the paint peeling, voice your complaint to CAS, the Federal Trade Commission, or your local attorney general's office or state representative.

If you believe you may be covered, first contact a dealer. If they are not willing to help, write to the manufacturer of your vehicle.

Uncovered Secret Warranties

Secret warranties are, by nature, difficult to find out about. However, following are a few examples recently uncovered by the Center for Auto Safety. If you think you may be covered, first contact your dealer. If they are unwilling to help, write to vehicle's manufacturer.

Ford is liable for up to $1 billion for bad paint—mainly on blue, silver, and grey 1985-92 F-Series trucks. The Center is also aware of paint problems on the Aerostar, Bronco, Bronco II, Econoline, Escort, EXP, LTD, Mustang, Probe, Ranger, Sable, Taurus, Tempo, Thunderbird and Tracer. If your Ford has had problems with peeling paint, voice your complaint to the Center for Auto Safety, the Federal Trade Commission or your local attorney general's office or state representative.

At the Center for Auto Safety's urging, General Motors has adopted the most comprehensive paint policy in the industry. GM will repaint vehicles with defective paint at no cost within the first six years of the vehicle's life, regardless of mileage or whether you bought the vehicle new or used. GM will pay repair costs except for normal wear including bumps, scrapes and dents. If the paint on your vehicle is peeling or blistering, contact the service manager at yourlocal dealership, who has the authorization to make the repair free of charge. For further information or for a refund of a previous paint job, contact the GM official responsible for the program: Elizabeth A. Marsh, Associate Coordinator, Legal Staff, General Motors Corp., New Center One Building, 3031 West Grand Boulevard, P.O.Box 33130, Detroit, MI, 48232. Or call your respective GM customer assistance division.

Honda has recently attempted to evade Connecticut's secret warranty law by conducting a free repair program through its regional offices and declaring it a "goodwill adjustment." The defect involves the misalignment, and subsequent premature tire wear, on 1989-90 Honda Civics. As the Center for Auto Safety learned, the defect involved was serious enough to cause at least one accident. That particular instance fell under the secret warranty category, as only the VIN number was verified, without the usual review of repair records, purchase history or vehicle inspection, before the work was performed. Again, if you think your vehicle may be involved, contact a local dealership's service manager or the regional office of Honda.

To find out more about secret warranties and other items the manufacturers don't want you to know about, the Center for Auto Safety's recently released book "Little Secrets of the Auto Industry" is available by sending a check for $11.95 to the Center for Auto Safety, 2001 S Street, NW, Washington, D.C. 20009-1160.

Comparing Warranties

Warranties are difficult to compare because they contain lots of fine print and confusing language. The following table will help you understand this year's new car warranties. Because the table does not contain all the details about each warranty, you should review the actual warranty to make sure you understand its fine points. Remember, you have the right to inspect a warranty before you buy—it's the law.

The table provides information on five areas covered by a typical warranty:

The **Basic Warranty** covers most parts of the vehicle against manufacturer's defects. The tires, batteries, and items you may add to the vehicle are covered under separate warranties. The table describes coverage in terms of months andmiles; for example, 36/36,000 means the warranty is good for 36 months or 36,000 miles, whichever comes first. This is the most important part of your warranty.

The **Powertrain Warranty** usually lasts longer than the basic warranty. Because each manufacturer's definition of the powertrain is different, it is important to find out exactly what your warranty will cover. Powertrain coverage should include parts of the engine, transmission, and drivetrain. The warranty on some luxury vehicles will often cover some additional systems such as steering, suspension, and electrical systems.

The **Corrosion Warranty** usually applies only to actual holes due to rust. Read this section carefully, because many corrosion warranties *do not* apply to what the manufacturer may describe as cosmetic rust or bad paint.

The **Roadside Assistance** column indicates whether or not the warranty includes a program for helping with problems on the road. Typically, these programs cover such things as lock outs, jump starts, flat tires, running out of gas and towing. Most of these are offered for the length of the basic warranty. Some have special limitations or added features, which we have pointed out. Because each one is different, check your's out carefully.

The last column contains the **Warranty Rating Index,** which provides an overall assessment of this year's warranties. The higher the Index number, the better the warranty. The Index number incorporates the important features of each warranty. In developing the Index, we gave the most weight to the basic and powertrain components of the warranties. The corrosion warranty was weighted somewhat less, and the roadside assistance feature received the least weight. We also considered special features such as whether you had to bring the vehicle in for corrosion inspections, or if rental vehicles were offered when warranty repairs were being done.

After evaluating all the features of the new warranties, here are this year's best and worst ratings.

1996 Warranties: The Best and The Worst

The Best		The Worst	
Isuzu	1228	Suzuki	670
Kia	1126	Honda	834
Mitsubishi	1124	Ford	942
		Mercury	942

The higher the index number, the better the warranty. See the following table for complete details.

Manufacturer	Basic Warranty	Powertrain Warranty	Corrosion Warranty	Roadside Assistance	Index	Warranty Rating
Chevrolet	36/36,000	36/36,000	72/100,000	36/36,000	956	Very Poor
Chrysler	36/36,000	36,36,000	84/100,000	36/36,000	980	Very Poor
Dodge	36/36,000	36,36,000	84/100,000	36/36,000	980	Very Poor
Ford	36/36,000	36/36,000	60/unlimited	36/36,000	942	Very Poor
GMC	36/36,000	36/36,000	72/100,000	36/36,000	956	Very Poor
Geo	36/36,000	36/36,000	72/100,000	36/36,000	956	Very Poor
Honda	36/36,000	36/36,000	60/unlimited	None	834	Very Poor
Isuzu	36/50,000	60/60,000	72/100,000	60/60,000	1228	Good
Jeep	36/36,000	36,36,000	84/100,000	36/36,000	980	Very Poor
Kia	36/36,000	60/60,000	60/100,000	36/36,000[1]	1126	Average
Land Rover	36/42,000	36/42,000	72/unlimited	36/42,000	1059	Poor
Mazda	36/50,000	36/50,000	60/unlimited	36/50,000	1061	Poor
Mercury	36/36,000	36/36,000	60/unlimited	36/36,000	942	Very Poor
Mitsubishi	36/36,000	60/60,000	60/unlimited	36/36,000	1124	Average
Nissan	36/36,000	60/60,000	60/unlimited	36/36,000[2]	1032	Poor
Oldsmobile	36/36,000	36/36,000	72/100,000	36/36,000[1]	1006	Poor
Plymouth	36/36,000	36,36,000	84/100,000	36/36,000	980	Very Poor
Pontiac	36/36,000	36/36,000	72/100,000	36/36,000	956	Very Poor
Suzuki[3]	36/36,000	36/36,000	36/unlimited	None	670	Very Poor
Toyota	36/36,000	60/60,000	60/unlimited	Optional	978	Very Poor

[1] Covers trip interruption expenses.
[2] Limited roadside services.
[3] Suzuki Soft Tops have a 24/24,000 Basic Warranty on the soft top itself.

INSURANCE

Insurance is a big part of ownership expenses, yet often it's forgotten in the showroom. As you shop, remember that the vehicle's design and accident history may affect your insurance rates. Some vehicles cost less to insure because experience has shown that they are damaged less, less expensive to fix after a collision, or stolen less.

This chapter provides you with the information you need to make a wise insurance purchase. We discuss the different types of insurance, offer special tips on reducing this cost and include information on occupant injury and theft—factors that can affect your insurance.

More and more consumers are saving hundreds of dollars by shopping around for insurance. In order to be a good comparison shopper, you need to know a few things about automobile insurance. First, there are six basic types of coverage:

Collision Insurance: This pays for the damage to your vehicle after an accident.

Comprehensive Physical Damage Insurance: This pays for damages when your vehicle is stolen or damaged by fire, floods, or other perils.

Property Damage Liability: This pays claims and defense costs if your vehicle damages someone else's property.

Medical Payments Insurance: This pays for your vehicle's occupants' medical expenses resulting from an accident.

Bodily Injury Liability: This provides money to pay claims against you and to pay for the cost of your legal defense if your vehicle injures or kills someone.

Uninsured Motorists Protection: This pays for injuries caused by an uninsured or a hit-and-run driver.

A number of factors determine what these coverages will cost you. A vehicle's design can affect both the chances and severity of an accident. A vehicle with a well-designed bumper may escape damage altogether in a low-speed crash. Some vehicles are easier to repair than others or may have less expensive parts. Vehicles with four doors tend to be damaged less than vehicles with two doors.

The reason one vehicle may get a discount on insurance while another receives a surcharge also depends upon the way it is traditionally driven. Sports cars, for example, are usually surcharged due, in part, to the typical driving habits of their owners. Four-door sedans and station wagons generally merit discounts.

Insurance companies use this and other information to determine whether to offer a *discount* on insurance premiums for a particular vehicle, or whether to levy a *surcharge*.

Not all companies offer discounts or surcharges, and many vehicles receive neither. Some companies offer a discount or impose a surcharge on collision premiums only. Others apply discounts and surcharges on both collision and comprehensive coverage. Discounts and surcharges usually range from 10 to 30 percent. Allstate offers discounts of up to 35 percent on certain vehicles. Remember that one company may offer a discount on a particular vehicle while another may not.

Check with your insurance agent to find out whether your company has a rating program. The Truck Rating pages at the end of the book indicate the expected insurance rates for each of the 1996 models.

In This Chapter ...

No-Fault Insurance

One of the major expenses of vehicular accidents has been the cost of determining who is "at fault." Often, both parties hire lawyers and wait for court decisions, which can take a long time. Another problem with this system is that some victims receive considerably less than others for equivalent losses.

To resolve this, many states have instituted "no-fault" vehicle insurance. The concept is that each person's losses are covered by his or her personal insurance protection, regardless of who is at fault. Lawsuits are permitted only under certain conditions.

While the idea is the same from state to state, the details of the no-fault laws vary. These variations include the amounts paid in similar situations, conditions of the right to sue, and the inclusion or exclusion of property damage.

The concept of no-fault means that your insurance company pays for your losses regardless of who is responsible and that lawsuits are restricted by the severity of the injuries. Ironically, some no-fault states still permit lawsuits to determine who is at fault.

Although the laws in each state may vary, here is a list of states with and without no-fault laws.

No-Fault States

Colorado	Massachusetts	New York
Florida	Michigan	North Dakota
Hawaii	Minnesota	Pennsylvania*
Kansas	New Jersey*	Utah
Kentucky*		

States Without No-Fault

Alabama	Louisiana	Oregon
Alaska	Maine	Rhode Island
Arizona	Maryland	South Carolina
Arkansas	Mississippi	South Dakota
California	Missouri	Tennessee
Connecticut	Montana	Texas
Delaware	Nebraska	Vermont
District of Columbia	Nevada	Virginia
Georgia	New Hampshire	Washington
Idaho	New Mexico	West Virginia
Illinois	North Carolina	Wisconsin
Indiana	Ohio	Wyoming
Iowa	Oklahoma	

*NJ, KY, PA have a policy option for choosing no-fault.

Insurance Industry Statistics

TIP

The insurance industry regularly publishes information about the accident history of cars currently on the road. The most reliable source of this rating information is the Highway Loss Data Institute (HLDI). These ratings, which range from very good to very poor, are based on the frequency of medical claims under personal injury protection coverages. A few companies will charge you more to insure a car rated poor than for one rated good.

A car's accident history may not match its crash test performance. Such discrepancies arise because the accident history includes driver performance. A sports car, for example, may have good crash test results but a poor accident history because its owners tend to drive relatively recklessly.

If you want more information about the injury history, bumper performance, and theft rating of today's cars, write to HLDI, 1005 North Glebe Road, Arlington, VA 22201.

Reducing Insurance Costs

After you have shopped around and found the best deal by comparing the costs of different coverages, consider these other factors that will affect your final insurance bill.

Your Annual Mileage: The more you drive, the more your vehicle will be "exposed" to a potential accident. The insurance cost for a vehicle rarely used will be less than the cost for a frequently used one.

Where You Drive: If you regularly drive and park in the city, you will most likely pay more than if you drive in rural areas.

Youthful Drivers: Usually the highest premiums are paid by male drivers under the age of 25. Whether or not the under-25-year-old male is married also affects insurance rates. (Married males pay less.) As the driver gets older, rates are lowered.

In addition to shopping around, take advantage of certain discounts to reduce your insurance costs. Most insurance companies offer discounts of 5 to 30 percent on various parts of your insurance bill. The availability of discounts varies among companies and often depends on where you live. Many consumers do not benefit from these discounts simply because they don't ask about them.

To determine whether you are getting all the discounts that you're entitled to, ask your insurance company for a complete list of the discounts that it offers.

Here are some of the most common insurance discounts:

Driver Education/Defensive Driving Courses: Many insurance companies offer (and in some cases mandate) discounts to young people who have successfully completed a state-approved driver education course. Typically, this can mean a $40 reduction in the cost of coverage. Also, a discount of 5-15 percent is available in some states to those who complete a defensive driving course.

Good Student Discounts: Many insurance companies offer discounts of up to 25 percent on insurance to full-time high school or college students who are in the upper 20 percent of their class, on the dean's list, or have a B or better average.

Good Driver Discounts: Many companies offer discounts to drivers with an accident and violation-free record.

Mature Driver Credit: Drivers ages 50 and older may qualify for up to a 10 percent discount, or a lower price bracket.

Sole Female Driver: Some companies offer discounts of 10 percent for females, ages 30 to 64, who are the only driver in a household, citing favorable claims experience.

Non-Drinkers and Non-Smokers: A limited number of companies offer incentives ranging from 10-25% to those who abstain.

Farmer Discounts: Many companies offer farmers either a discount of 10-30% or a lower price bracket.

Car Pooling: Commuters sharing driving may qualify for discounts of 5-25% or a lower price bracket.

Insuring Driving Children: Children away at school don't drive the family car very often, so it's usually less expensive to insure them on the parents' policy rather than separately. If you do insure them separately, discounts of 10-40% or a lower price bracket are available.

Desirable Vehicles: Premiums are usually much higher for vehicles with high collision rates or that are the favorite target of thieves.

Passive Restraints/Anti-Lock Brake Credit: Many companies offer discounts (from 10 to 30 percent) for automatic belts and air bags. Some large companies are now offering a 5 percent discount to owners of vehicles with anti-lock brakes.

Anti-Theft Device Credits: Discounts of 5 to 15 percent are offered in some states for vehicles equipped with a hood lock and an alarm or a disabling device (active or passive) that prevents the vehicle from being started.

Multi-Car Discount: Consumers insuring more than one vehicle in the household with the same insurer can save up to 20 percent.

Account Credit: Some companies offer discounts of up to 10 percent for insuring your home and auto with the same company.

Long-Term Policy Renewal: Although not available in all states, some companies offer price breaks of 5-20 percent to customers who renew a long-term policy.

First Accident Allowance: Some insurers offer a "first accident allowance," which guarantees that if a customer achieves five accident-free years, his or her rates won't go up after the first at-fault accident.

Deductibles: Opting for the largest reasonable deductible is the obvious first step in reducing premiums. Increasing your deductible to $500 from $200 could cut your collision premium about 20 percent. Raising the deductible to $1,000 from $200 could lower your premium about 45 percent. Discounts may vary by company.

Collision Coverage: The older the vehicle, the less the need for collision insurance. Consider dropping collision insurance entirely on an older vehicle. Regardless of how much coverage you carry, the insurance company will only pay up to the vehicle's "book value." For example, if your vehicle requires $1,000 in repairs but its "book value" is only $500, the insurance company is required to pay only $500.

Uninsured Motorist Coverage/Optional Coverage: The necessity of both of these policies depends upon the extent of your health insurance coverage. In states where they are not required, consumers with applicable health insurance may not want uninsured motorist coverage. Also, those with substantial health insurance coverage may not want an optional medical payment policy.

Rental Cars: If you regularly rent cars, special coverage on your personal auto insurance can cover you while renting for far less than rental agencies offer.

Tip: Expensive fender bender repairs can add up for both you andyour insurance company. To reduce repairs, look for a vehicle with bumpers that can withstand a 5-mph impact without damage.

Vehicle Theft

The risk of your vehicle being stolen is an important factor in the cost of your insurance. In fact, each year over 1.5 million vehicles are stolen. As a result, the market is flooded with expensive devices designed to prevent theft. Before you spend a lot of money on anti-theft devices, consider this: Of the vehicles stolen, nearly 80 percent were unlocked and 40 percent actually had the keys in the ignition. Most of these thefts are by amateurs. While the most important way to protect your vehicle is to keep it locked and remove the keys, this precaution will not protect you from the pros. If you live or travel in an area susceptible to auto thefts or have a high-priced vehicle, here are some steps you can take to prevent theft.

Inexpensive Theft Prevention:

☑ Replace door lock buttons with tapered tips. They make it difficult to hook the lock with a wire hanger. (But it will also keep you from breaking into your own vehicle!)

☑ Buy an alarm sticker (even if you don't have an alarm) for one of your windows.

☑ Buy an electric etching tool (about $15) and write your driver's license number in the lower corners of the windows and on unpainted metal items where it can be seen. Many police departments offer this service at no charge. They provide a sticker and enter the number into their records. The purpose of these identifying marks is to deter the professional thief who is planning to take the vehicle apart and sell the components. Since the parts can be traced, your vehicle becomes much less attractive.

☑ Remove the distributor wire. This is a rather inconvenient but effective means of rendering your vehicle inoperable. If you are parking in a particularly suspect place or leaving your vehicle for a long time you may want to try this. On the top of the distributor, there is a short wire running to the coil. Removing the wire makes it impossible to start the vehicle.

A recently popular anti-theft device is a long rod that locks the steering wheel into place, sold under a variety of names. It costs $50 and requires a separate key without which the car can only be driven straight, if the ignition will engage at all. Beware, however, that thieves now use a spray can of freon to freeze the lock, making it brittle enough to be smashed open with a hammer.

More Serious Measures:

☑ Cutting off the fuel to the engine will keep someone from driving very far with your vehicle. For around $125, you can have a fuel cutoff device installed that enables you to open or close the gasoline line to the engine. One drawback is that the thief will be able to drive a few blocks before running out of gas. If your vehicle is missing, you'll have to check your neighborhood first!

☑ Another way to deter a pro is to install a second ignition switch for about $150. To start your vehicle, you activate a hidden switch. The device is wired in such a complicated manner that a thief could spend hours trying to figure it out. Time is the thief's worst enemy, and the longer it takes to start your vehicle, the more likely the thief is to give up.

☑ The most common anti-theft devices on the market are alarms. These cost from $100 to $500 installed. Their complexity ranges from simply sounding your horn when someone opens your door to setting off elaborate sirens when someone merely approaches the vehicle. Alarms require an exterior key-operated switch to turn them off and on. Some people buy the switch, mount it on their vehicle, and hope that its presence will intimidate the thief.

The Highway Loss Data Institute regularly compiles statistics on motor vehicle thefts. In rating vehicles, they consider the frequency of theft and the loss resulting from the theft. The result is an index based on "relative average loss payments per insured vehicle year." The next page indicates the current theft ratings of some popular vehicles.

Theft Ratings

Vehicle	Theft Rate Index
Ford E-150 Club Wagon	17
Nissan Quest	25
Ford Aerostar 4wd	27
Mercury Villager	32
Mazda B-Series	35
Dodge Dakota 4wd	38
Ford Aerostar 2wd	42
Dodge Dakota 2wd	43
Ford Ranger 2wd	43
GMC Sonoma	43
Ford Ranger 4wd	51
Chevrolet S-Series 2wd	57
Chevrolet Astro 4wd	57
Dodge Ram 4wd	58
Dodge Ram 2wd	59
Toyota Previa 4wd	60
GMC Safari 2wd	63
Ford E-250 Econoline	64
Ford F-150 4wd	64
Mazda MPV 2wd	64
GMC Sierra 2500 4wd	72
Ford F-150 2wd	74
Oldsmobile Silhouette	75
Toyota Previa 2wd	80
Ford E-150 Econoline	81
Ford F-250 2wd	82

Vehicle	Theft Rate Index
Suzuki Sidekick 4dr, 4wd	83
Ford F-350 4wd	85
Toyota Tacoma 2wd	88
GMC Safari 4wd	89
Chevrolet CK-2500 4wd	91
Isuzu Trooper 4dr, 4wd	92
Pontiac Trans Sport	97
Ford F-250 4wd	99
Toyota T100	100
Mitsubishi Mighty Max	100
Chevrolet Lumina Minivan	100
Chevrolet S-Series 4wd	101
Chevrolet Astro 2wd	102
Nissan Pickup 2wd	106
Dodge B250 Cargo Van	119
Isuzu Rodeo 4wd	120
Isuzu Rodeo 2wd	124
Mazda MPV 4wd	132
Nissan Pickup 4wd	135
Ford F-350 2wd	143
Toyota Tacoma 4wd	146
GMC Safari Cargo Van	150
Chevrolet Astro Cargo Van	162
Jeep Cherokee 2dr,2wd	168
Chevrolet CK-2500 2wd	169
Geo Tracker 4wd	173

Vehicle	Theft Rate Index
Ford Bronco	176
Chevrolet CK-3500 4wd	178
GMC Sierra 1500 4wd	183
Jeep Cherokee 2dr, 4wd	188
Chevrolet CK-1500 4wd	191
GMC Suburban 1500 4wd	196
Jeep Cherokee 4dr,2wd	203
GMC Sierra 1500 2wd	211
GMC Sierra 2500 2wd	220
Geo Tracker 2wd	221
Toyota 4Runner 2wd	229
Suzuki Sidekick 2dr	239
Chevrolet CK-1500 2wd	248
Jeep Cherokee 4dr,4wd	254
GMC Yukon 4wd	268
Jeep Wrangler	284
Chevy Suburban 1500 4wd	295
Chevrolet CK-3500 2wd	315
GMC Suburban 1500 2wd	330
Chevy Suburban 1500 2wd	342
Jeep Grand Cherokee 2wd	385
Jeep Grand Cherokee 4wd	395
Toyota 4Runner 4wd	498
Chevrolet Blazer 2dr, 4wd	583
Toyota Land Cruiser	1729
Mitsubishi Montero 4wd	1815

Note: Lower numbers indicate a lower likelihood of being stolen.

Tires

For most of us, buying tires has become an infrequent task. The reason—most vehicles now come with radial tires, which last much longer than the bias and bias-belted tires of the past. However, when we do get around to buying tires, making an informed purchase is not easy. The tire has to perform more functions simultaneously than any other part of the vehicle (steering, bearing the load, cushioning the ride, and stopping). And not only is the tire the hardest-working item on the vehicle, but there are nearly 1,800 tire lines to choose from. With only a few major tire manufacturers selling all those tires, the difference in many tires may only be the brand name.

This chapter contains all the information you need to select the best tires for your vehicle.

Because it is so difficult to compare tires, it is easy to understand why many consumers mistakenly use price and brand name to determine quality. The difficulty in comparing one tire to another is compounded by the advertising terminology that is used to describe tires. One company's definition of "first line" or "premium" may be entirely different from another's. But there is help. The U.S. government now requires tires to be rated according to their safety and expected mileage.

A little-known system grades tires on their *treadwear*, *traction*, and *heat resistance*. The grades are printed on the sidewall and are also attached to the tire on a paper label. In addition, every dealer can provide you with the grades of the tires he or she sells.

Treadwear: The treadwear grade gives you an idea of the mileage you can expect from a tire. It is shown in numbers—300, 310, 320, 330 and so forth. A tire graded 400 should give you 33 percent more mileage than one graded 300. In order to *estimate* the expected actual mileage, multiply the treadwear grade by 200. Under average conditions a tire graded 300 should last 60,000 miles. Because individual driving habits vary considerably, it is best to use the treadwear as a *relative* basis of comparison rather than an absolute predictor of mileage. Also remember that tire wear is affected by regional differences in the level of abrasive material used in road surfaces.

Traction: Traction grades of A, B, and C describe the tire's ability to stop on wet surfaces. Tires graded A will stop on a wet road in a shorter distance than tires graded B or C. Tires rated C have poor traction. If you drive frequently on wet roads, buy a tire with a higher traction grade.

Heat Resistance: Heat resistance is also graded A, B, and C. This grading is important because hot-running tires can result in blowouts or tread separation. An A rating means the tire will run cooler than one rated B or C, and it is less likely to fail if driven over long distances at highway speeds. In addition, tires that run cooler tend to be more fuel efficient. If you do a lot of high speed driving, a high heat resistance grade is best.

The tables at the end of this section give you a list of the highest rated tires on the market. For a complete listing of all the tires on the market, you can call the Auto Safety Hotline, toll free, at 800-424-9393 or 800-424-9153 (TTY). (In Washington, DC, the number is 202-366-7800.)

In This Chapter...

Tire Pricing: Getting the Best Value

There are few consumer products on the market today as price competitive as tires. While this situation provides a buyer's market, it does require some price shopping.

The price of a tire is based on its size, and tires come in as many as nine sizes. For example, the list price of the same Goodyear Arriva tire can range from $74.20 to $134.35, depending on its size. Some manufacturers do not provide list prices, leaving the appropriate markup to the individual retailer. Even when list prices are provided, dealers rarely use them. Instead, they offer tires at what is called an "everyday low price," which can range from 10 to 25 percent below list.

The following tips can help you get the best buy.

1 Check to see which manufacturer makes the least expensive "offbrand." Only twelve major manufacturers produce the over 1,800 types of tires sold in the U.S., so you can save money and still get high quality.

2 Remember, generally the wider the tire, the higher the price.

3 Don't forget to inquire about balancing and mounting costs when comparing tire prices. In some stores, the extra charges for balancing, mounting, and valve stems can add up to more than $25. Other stores may offer them as a customer service at little or no cost. That good buy in the newspaper may turn into a poor value when coupled with these extra costs. Also, compare warranties; they do vary from company to company.

4 Never pay list price for a tire. A good rule of thumb is to pay at least 30 to 40 percent off the suggested list price.

5 Use the treadwear grade the same way you would the "unit price" in a supermarket. It is the best way to ensure that you are getting the best tire value. The tire with the lowest cost per grade point is the best value. For example, if tire A costs $100 and has a treadwear grade of 300, and tire B costs $80 and has a treadwear grade of 200:

Tire A:
$100÷300 = $.33 per point

Tire B:
$80÷200 = $.40 per point

Since 33 cents is less than 40 cents, tire A is the better buy even though its initial cost is more.

New Tire Registration

You may be missing out on free or low-cost replacement tires or, worse, driving on potentially hazardous ones, if you don't fill out the tire registration form when you buy tires. The law once required all tire sellers to submit buyers' names automatically to the manufacturer, so the company could contact them if the tires were ever recalled. While this is still mandatory for tire dealers and distributors owned by tire manufacturers, it is not required of independent tire dealers. A recent government study found that 70 percent of independent tire dealers had not registered a single tire purchase. Ask for the tire registration card when you buy tires, and remember to fill it out and send it in. This information will allow the company to notify you if the tire is ever recalled.

Brand Name	Model	Description	Grades			Expected Mileage		
			Trac.	Heat	Tred.	High	Medium	Low
Dunlop	Elite 65	15 & 16	A	B	540	162,000	108,000	81,000
Falken	FK315	All	A	B	540	162,000	108,000	81,000
Kelly	Aqua Tour	All	A	B	540	162,000	108,000	81,000
Ohtsu	HS311	All	A	B	540	162,000	108,000	81,000
Toyo	800+ 75	All	A	B	540	162,000	108,000	81,000
Toyo	800+ 70	15	A	B	540	162,000	108,000	81,000
Vogue	CBR VII 65/70/75 S	14 & 15	A	B	540	162,000	108,000	81,000
Centennial	Interceptor	15 & 16	A	B	520	156,000	104,000	78,000
Co-Op	Golden Mark 65/70	All	A	B	520	156,000	104,000	78,000
Cooper	Grand Classic STE SR	All	A	B	520	156,000	104,000	78,000
Cordovan	Grand Prix ST	All	A	B	520	156,000	104,000	78,000
Dean	Touring Edition	All	A	B	520	156,000	104,000	78,000
Dunlop	Elite 65	14'	A	B	520	156,000	104,000	78,000
Falls	Mark VII	All	A	B	520	156,000	104,000	78,000
Hallmark	Ultimate Touring	All	A	B	520	156,000	104,000	78,000
Lee	STL Trak	All	A	B	520	156,000	104,000	78,000
Michelin	XH4	14 & 15	A	B	520	156,000	104,000	78,000
Monarch	Ultra Touring GT	All	A	B	520	156,000	104,000	78,000
Multi-Mile	Grand Am ST	All	A	B	520	156,000	104,000	78,000
Remington	Touring	15 & 16	A	B	520	156,000	104,000	78,000
Sigma	Supreme ST	All	A	B	520	156,000	104,000	78,000
Star	Centurion Touring	All	A	B	520	156,000	104,000	78,000
Toyo	800+ 75	14	A	B	520	156,000	104,000	78,000
Toyo	800+ 70	175/70R14	B	B	520	156,000	104,000	78,000
Toyo	800+ 70	All	B	B	520	156,000	104,000	78,000
Pirelli	P300 60/65/80	All	A	A	500	150,000	100,000	75,000
Atlas	Pinnacle TE 70	13	A	B	500	150,000	100,000	75,000
Atlas	Pinnacle TE 70/75	14 & 15	A	B	500	150,000	100,000	75,000
Centennial	Interceptor	14	A	B	500	150,000	100,000	75,000
Dayton	Touring 70	All	A	B	500	150,000	100,000	75,000
Dayton	Touring 70/75S	All	A	B	500	150,000	100,000	75,000
Duralon	IV Plus	All	A	B	500	150,000	100,000	75,000
Duralon	Touring Plus IV	All	A	B	500	150,000	100,000	75,000
Gillette	Kodiak LE	All	A	B	500	150,000	100,000	75,000
Peerless	Permasteel LE	All	A	B	500	150,000	100,000	75,000
Remington	Touring	14	A	B	500	150,000	100,000	75,000
Sumitomo	SC890 75	15	A	B	500	150,000	100,000	75,000
Toyo	800+ 75	235/75RL15	A	B	500	150,000	100,000	75,000
Co-Op	Golden Mark 75	All	A	B	480	144,000	96,000	72,000
Cordovan	Grand Prix STE	All	A	B	480	144,000	96,000	72,000
Douglas	Premium WTE	All	A	B	480	144,000	96,000	72,000
Douglas	Premium Touring	All	A	B	480	144,000	96,000	72,000
Dunlop	Elite 65	13	A	B	480	144,000	96,000	72,000
Hallmark	Prestige PWR4	All	A	B	480	144,000	96,000	72,000
Kelly	Navigator 800S	All	A	B	480	144,000	96,000	72,000
Lee	GT VI Trak	All	A	B	480	144,000	96,000	72,000
Michelin	XH4	13	A	B	480	144,000	96,000	72,000
Monarch	Ultra Trak	All	A	B	480	144,000	96,000	72,000
Multi-Mile	Grand Am STE	All	A	B	480	144,000	96,000	72,000
Republic	Weather King	All	A	B	480	144,000	96,000	72,000
Sigma	Supreme STE	All	A	B	480	144,000	96,000	72,000
Star	Imperial	All	A	B	480	144,000	96,000	72,000
Vanderbilt	Turbo Tech Tour G/T	All	A	B	480	144,000	96,000	72,000

Brand Name	Model	Description	Grades			Expected Mileage		
			Trac.	Heat	Tred.	High	Medium	Low
Vogue	Premium	All	A	B	480	144,000	96,000	72,000
Winston	Signature Premium	All	A	B	480	144,000	96,000	72,000
Cordovan	Grand Prix STE	XL	A	C	480	144,000	96,000	72,000
Hallmark	Prestige PWR4	235/75R15	A	C	480	144,000	96,000	72,000
Kelly	Navigator 800S	235/75R15	A	C	480	144,000	96,000	72,000
Lee	GT VI Trak	235/75R15	A	C	480	144,000	96,000	72,000
Monarch	Ultra Trak	235/75R15	A	C	480	144,000	96,000	72,000
Multi-Mile	Grand Am STE	XL	A	C	480	144,000	96,000	72,000
Republic	Weather King XL	P235/75R15	A	C	480	144,000	96,000	72,000
Sigma	Supreme STE	XL	A	C	480	144,000	96,000	72,000
Star	Imperial	235/75R15	A	C	480	144,000	96,000	72,000
Big-O	Legacy 65	P205/65R15	A	B	460	138,000	92,000	69,000
Big-O	Legacy 70/75	15	A	B	460	138,000	92,000	69,000
Brigadier	Touring 65	P205/65R15	A	B	460	138,000	92,000	69,000
Brigadier	Touring 70/75	15	A	B	460	138,000	92,000	69,000
Centennial	Interceptor	13	A	B	460	138,000	92,000	69,000
Continental	CT24	15	A	B	460	138,000	92,000	69,000
General	Ameri Tech 4 75	15	A	B	460	138,000	92,000	69,000
General	Ameri Tech ST	P215,P225/75R15	A	B	460	138,000	92,000	69,000
General	Ameri Tech ST 70	15	A	B	460	138,000	92,000	69,000
General	GS	All	A	B	460	138,000	92,000	69,000
Kumho	782	All	A	B	460	138,000	92,000	69,000
Pirelli	P300 70/75	70/75	A	B	460	138,000	92,000	69,000
Remington	Touring	13	A	B	460	138,000	92,000	69,000
Reynolds	Touring 70/75	15	A	B	460	138,000	92,000	69,000
Reynolds	Touring 65	P205/65R15	A	B	460	138,000	92,000	69,000
Sonic	Sentinel 65	P205/65R15	A	B	460	138,000	92,000	69,000
Sonic	Sentinel 70/75	15	A	B	460	138,000	92,000	69,000
Touring	65	P205/65R15	A	B	460	138,000	92,000	69,000
Touring	70/75	15	A	B	460	138,000	92,000	69,000
Toyo	800+ 70	13	A	B	460	138,000	92,000	69,000
Toyo	800+ 80	All	A	B	460	138,000	92,000	69,000
Vogue	CBR VII 60 V	16	A	A	440	132,000	88,000	66,000
Atlas	Pinnacle TE 80	13	A	B	440	132,000	88,000	66,000
Big-O	Legacy 70/75	14	A	B	440	132,000	88,000	66,000
Brigadier	Touring 70/75	14	A	B	440	132,000	88,000	66,000
Continental	CS24	14	A	B	440	132,000	88,000	66,000
Delta	Supreme 70/75	15	A	B	440	132,000	88,000	66,000
General	Ameri Tech ST 70	14	A	B	440	132,000	88,000	66,000
General	Ameri Tech 4 75	14	A	B	440	132,000	88,000	66,000
General	Ameri Tech 4 70	P205/70R14	A	B	440	132,000	88,000	66,000
Hercules	Mega TR	15	A	B	440	132,000	88,000	66,000
Medalist	Precept 70/75	15	A	B	440	132,000	88,000	66,000
Montgomery Ward	Yokohama	14 & 15	A	B	440	132,000	88,000	66,000
National	XT6000 70/75	15	A	B	440	132,000	88,000	66,000
Republic	Land Rover	All	A	B	440	132,000	88,000	66,000
Reynolds	Touring 70/75	14	A	B	440	132,000	88,000	66,000
Sears	RD Handler + 60-70	All	A	B	440	132,000	88,000	66,000
Sonic	Sentinel 70/75	14	A	B	440	132,000	88,000	66,000
Sumitomo	SC890 75	14	A	B	440	132,000	88,000	66,000
Touring	70/75	14	A	B	440	132,000	88,000	66,000
Cooper	Discover STE	All	B	B	440	132,000	88,000	66,000
Falls	Courser STD	All	B	B	440	132,000	88,000	66,000
Starfire	Bronco CTD	All	B	B	440	132,000	88,000	66,000

COMPLAINTS

Americans spend billions of dollars on motor vehicle repairs every year. While many of those repairs are satisfactory, there are times when getting your vehicle fixed can be a very difficult process. In fact, vehicle defects and repairs are the number one cause of consumer complaints in the U.S., according to the Federal Trade Commission.

This chapter is designed to help you resolve your complaint, whether it's for a new vehicle still under warranty or for one you've had for years. In addition, we offer a guide to arbitration, the names and addresses of consumer groups, federal agencies, and the manufacturers themselves. Finally, we tell you how to take the important step of registering your complaint with the U.S. Department of Transportation.

No matter what your complaint, keep accurate records. Copies of the following items are indispensable in helping to resolve your problems:

- your service invoices
- bills you have paid
- letters you have written to the manufacturer or the repair facility owner
- written repair estimates from your independent mechanic.

Resolving Complaints: If you are having trouble, here are some basic steps to help you resolve your problem.

First, return your vehicle to the repair facility that did the work. Bring a written list of the problems, and make sure that you keep a copy of the list. Give the repair facility a reasonable opportunity to examine your vehicle and attempt to fix it. Speak directly to the service manager (not to the service writer who wrote up your repair order), and ask him or her to test drive the vehicle with you so that you can point out the problem.

If that doesn't resolve the problem, take the vehicle to a diagnostic center for an independent examination. This may cost $45 to $60. Get a written statement defining the problem and outlining how it may be fixed. Give your repair shop a copy. If your vehicle is under warranty, do not allow any warranty repair by an independent mechanic; you may not be reimbursed by the manufacturer.

If your repair shop does not respond to the independent assessment, present your problem to a mediation panel. These panels hear both sides of the story and try to come to a resolution.

If the problem is with a new vehicle dealer, or if you feel that the manufacturer is responsible, you may be able to use one of the manufacturer's mediation programs discussed on page 74.

If the problem is solely with an independent dealer, a local Better Business Bureau (BBB) may be able to mediate your complaint. It may also offer an arbitration hearing. In any case, the BBB should enter your complaint into its files on that establishment.

When contacting any mediation program, determine how long the process takes, who makes the final decision, whether you are bound by that decision, and whether the program handles all problems or only warranty complaints.

If there are no mediation programs in your area, contact private consumer groups, local government agencies, or your local "action line" newspaper columnist, newspaper editor, or radio or TV broadcaster. A phone call or letter from them may persuade a repair facility to take action. Send a copy of your letter to the repair shop.

In This Chapter...

One of your last resorts is to bring a law suit against the dealer, manufacturer, or repair facility in small claims court. The fee for filing such an action is usually small, and you generally act as your own attorney, saving attorney's fees. There is a monetary limit on the amount you can claim, which varies from state to state. Your local consumer affairs office, state attorney general's office, or the clerk of the court can tell you how to file such a suit.

Finally, talk with an attorney. It's best to select an attorney who is familiar with handling automotive problems. If you don't know of one, call the lawyer referral service listed in the telephone directory (or see box) and ask for the names of attorneys who deal with automobile problems. If you can't afford an attorney, contact the Legal Aid Society.

Warranty Complaints: If your vehicle is under warranty or you are having problems with a factory-authorized dealership, here are some special guidelines:

Have the warranty available to show the dealer. Make sure you call the problem to the dealer's attention before the end of the warranty period.

If you are still unsatisfied after giving the dealer a reasonable opportunity to fix your vehicle, contact the manufacturer's representative (also called the zone representative) in your area. This person can authorize the dealer to make repairs or take other steps to resolve the dispute. Your dealer will have your zone representative's name and telephone number. Explain the problem and ask for a meeting and a personal inspection of your vehicle.

If you can't get satisfaction from the zone representative, call or write the manufacturer's owner relations department. Your owner's manual contains this phone number and address. In each case, as you move up the chain, indicate the steps you have already taken.

Your next option is to present your problem to a complaint-handling panel or to the arbitration program in which the manufacturer of your vehicle participates. See page 74 for additional information.

If you complain of a problem during the warranty period, you have a right to have the problem fixed even after the warranty runs out. If your warranty has not been honored, you may be able to "revoke acceptance," which means that you return the vehicle to the dealer. If you are successful, you may be entitled to a replacement vehicle, or to a full refund of the purchase price and reimbursement of legal fees under the Magnuson-Moss Warranty Act. Or, if you are covered by one of the state Lemon Laws (see page 82), you may be able to return the vehicle and receive a refund or replacement from the manufacturer.

Legal Aid

If you need legal assistance with your repair problem, the Center for Auto Safety has a list of lawyers who specialize in helping consumers with auto repair problems. For the names of some attorneys in your area, send a stamped, self-addressed envelope to: Center for Auto Safety, 2001 S Street, NW, Washington, DC 20009-1160

In addition, the Center has published *The Lemon Book,* a detailed, 368-page guide to resolving automobile complaints. The book is available for $15.95 from the Center.

Attorneys Take Note: For information on litigation assistance provided by the Center for Auto Safety, including The Lemon Law Litigation Manual, please contact the Center for Auto Safety at the above address.

Auto Safety Hotline

One of the most valuable but often unused services of the government is the Auto Safety Hotline. By calling the Hotline to report safety problems, your particular concern or problem will become part of the National Highway Traffic Safety Administration's (NHTSA) complaint database. This complaint program is extraordinarily important to government decision makers who often take action based on this information. In addition, it provides consumer groups, like the Center for Auto Safety, with the evidence they need to force the government to act. Unless government engineers or safety advocates have evidence of a wide-scale problem, little can be done to get the manufacturers to correct the defect.

Few government services have the potential to do as much for the consumer as this complaint database, so we encourage you to voice your concerns to the government.

Your letter can be used as the basis of safety defect investigations and recall campaigns. When you file a complaint, be sure to indicate that your name and address can be made public. Without names and addresses, it is more difficult for consumer groups to uncover safety defects.

Hotline Complaints: When you call the Hotline to report a safety problem, you will be mailed a questionnaire asking for information that the agency's technical staff will need to evaluate the problem. This information also gives the government an indication of which vehicles are causing consumers the most problems.

You can also use this questionnaire to report defects in tires and child safety seats. In fact, we strongly encourage you to report problems with child safety seats. Now that they are required by law in all fifty states, we have noticed that numerous design and safety problems have surfaced. If the government knows about these problems, they will be more likely to take action so that modifications are made to these life-saving devices.

After you complete and return the questionnaire, the following things will happen:

1. A copy will go to NHTSA's safety defect investigators.

2. A copy will be sent to the manufacturer of the vehicle or equipment, with a request for help in resolving the problem.

3. You will be notified that your questionnaire has been received.

4. Your problem will be recorded in the complaint database which we use to provide you with complaint ratings.

Hotline Services: Hotline operators can also provide information on recalls. If you want recall information on a particular automobile, simply tell the Hotline operator the make, model, and year of the vehicle, or the type of equipment involved. You will receive any recall information that NHTSA has about that vehicle or item. This information can be very important if you are not sure whether your vehicle has ever been recalled. If you want a printed copy of the recall information, it will be mailed within twenty-four hours at no charge.

If you have other vehicle-related problems, the Hotline operators can refer you to the appropriate federal, state, and local government agencies. If you need information about federal safety standards and regulations, you'll be referred to the appropriate experts.

You may call the Hotline day or night, seven days a week. If you call when no operators are available, a recorded message will ask you to leave your name and address and a description of the information you want. The appropriate materials will be mailed to you.

Complaints and Safety Information

Auto Safety Hotline
800-424-9393
(in Washington, DC: 202-366-0123)
TTY for hearing impaired:
800-424-9153
(in Washington, DC: 202-366-7800)

The toll-free Auto Safety Hotline can provide information on recalls, record information about safety problems, and refer you to the appropriate government experts on other vehicle related problems. You can even have recall information mailed to you within 24 hours of your call at no charge.

Arbitration

An increasingly popular method of resolving automobile repair problems is through arbitration. This procedure requires that both parties present their cases to a mediator or panel that makes a decision based on the merits of the complaint. You can seek repairs, reimbursement of expenses, or a refund or replacement for your vehicle through arbitration.

In theory, arbitration can be an effective means of resolving disputes. It is somewhat informal, relatively speedy, and you do not need a lawyer to present your case. If you resolve your problem through arbitration, you avoid the time and expense of going to court.

Almost all manufacturers now offer some form of arbitration, usually for problems that arise during the warranty period. Some companies run their own and others subscribe to programs run by groups like the Better Business Bureau or the American Automobile Association. Your owner's manual will identify which programs you can use. Also, contact your state attorney general to find out what programs your state offers.

How it works: Upon receiving your complaint, the arbitration program will attempt to mediate a resolution between you and the manufacturer or dealer. If you are not satisfied with the proposed solution, you have the right to have your case heard at an arbitration hearing.

These hearings vary among the programs. In the BBB program, each party presents its case in person to a volunteer arbitrator. The other programs will decide your case based on written submissions from both you and the manufacturer.

If an arbitration program is incorporated into your warranty, you may have to use that program before filing a legal claim. However, you may always go to small claims court instead of using arbitration. Federal law requires that arbitration programs incorporated into a warranty be nonbinding on the consumer. That is, if you do not like the result, you can seek other remedies.

Arbitration programs have different eligibility requirements, so be sure you are eligible for the program you are considering.

Let the Federal Trade Commission, the Center for Auto Safety (their addresses are on pages 80 and 79, respectively), and your state attorney general (c/o your state capitol) know of your experience with arbitration. It is particularly important to contact these offices if you have a complaint about how your case was handled.

Ford Dispute Settlement Board: This was one of the first panels established by a manufacturer. Each case is considered by a four-person panel that includes one dealer, who has no vote. In most cases, no oral presentations are given. Only cases under warranty are reviewed. For information, call 800-392-3673.

Chrysler Customer Arbitration Board: No oral presentations are allowed under this program—decisions are based on written submissions by each party. A Chrysler zone representative and dealer are on the panel but cannot vote. The panel will only hear cases under warranty. (In Maryland, Chrysler will sometimes hear cases beyond the warranty.) For information, call 800-992-1997.

Better Business Bureau Arbitration Programs (Auto Line): The BBB always tries to mediate a dispute before recommending arbitration. Fewer than 10 percent of the disputes it handles actually go to arbitration. Theoretically, each party receives a list of potential arbitrators with a background description of each person and then ranks them according to preference. The arbitrator with the most votes handles the case. But in actual fact, the consumer rarely has a voice in the selection of an arbitrator.

The arbitrators are volunteers from the local community and sometimes are not automobile experts. This can both help and harm your case. As a result, it is important to be well prepared when participating in the BBB program. If you're not, the potential exists for the dealer or manufacturer to appear as the "expert" on automobiles. For more information, contact your local BBB or 800-955-5100.

Automobile Consumer Action Program: AUTOCAP was established by the National Automobile Dealers Association to assist consumers in resolving auto sales or service disputes with dealers and manufacturers. The program is sponsored on a voluntary basis by state and local dealer associations. Currently, most AUTOCAPs do not operate under the FTC guidelines required for warranty cases. Sixty-five percent of the cases that

AUTOCAP considers are resolved in preliminary mediation. Of those cases that go to arbitration, 45 percent are resolved in favor of the consumer, 22 percent are a compromise, and 33 percent are in favor of the company. For more information and the name of your local panel, contact: AUTOCAP, 8400 Westpark Drive, McLean, Virginia 22102; 703-821-7144.

State-Run Arbitration

State-run arbitration programs are often more fair to consumers than national programs. The following states have set up state programs (or guidelines) which are far better than their national counterparts. If you live in one of these areas, contact your attorney general's office for information. Even if your state is not listed below, you can contact your state attorney general's office (in care of your state capitol) for advice on arbitration.

Connecticut	Hawaii	New Hampshire	South Carolina
D. C.	Maine	New Jersey	Texas
Florida	Massachusetts	New York	Vermont
Georgia	Montana	Rhode Island	Washington

Ten Tips for Arbitration

Arbitration is designed to be easier and less intimidating than going to court. However, the process can still be nerve-racking, especially if you've never been through it before. Here are some tips to help make the process as simple and straightforward as possible.

1 Before deciding to go to arbitration, get a written description of how the program works, and make sure you understand the details. If you have any questions, contact the local representatives of the program. Remember, the manufacturer or dealer probably has more experience with this process than you do.

2 Make sure the final decision is nonbinding on you. If the decision is binding, you give up your right to appeal.

3 Determine whether the program allows you to appear at the hearing. If not, make sure your written statement is complete and contains all the appropriate receipts and documentation. If you think of something that you want considered after you have sent in your material, send it and specifically request that the additional information be included.

4 Make sure the program follows the required procedures. If the arbitration program is incorporated into the vehicle's warranty, for example, the panel must make a decision on your case within 40 days of receiving your complaint.

5 Contact the manufacturer's zone manager and re quest copies of any technical service bulletins that apply to your vehicle. (See "Secret Warranties" on page 57 for a description of technical service bulletins and how to get them.) Service bulletins may help you prove that your vehicle is defective.

6 Well before the hearing, ask the program representative to send you copies of all material submitted by the other party. You may want to respond to this information.

7 Make sure all your documents are in chronological order, and include a brief outline of the events. Submit copies of all material associated with your problem and a copy of your warranty.

8 Even though you may be very angry about the situation, try to present your case in a calm, logical manner.

9 If you are asking for a refund or a replacement for your vehicle in accordance with your state's Lemon Law, do not assume that the arbitrator is completely familiar with the law. Be prepared to explain how it entitles you to your request.

10 In most programs, you have to reject the decision in order to go to court to pursue other action. If you accept the decision, you may limit your rights to pursue further action. You will, however, have additional claims if the manufacturer or dealer does not properly follow through on the decision or if your vehicle breaks down again.

Complaint Index

Thanks to the efforts of the Center for Auto Safety, we are able to provide you with the vehicle complaints on file with the National Highway Traffic Safety Administration (NHTSA). Each year, thousands of Americans call the government to register complaints about their vehicles. The government collects this information but has never released it to the public.

The complaint index is the result of our analysis of these complaints. It is based on a ratio of the number of complaints for each vehicle to the sales of that vehicle. In order to predict the expected complaint performance of the 1996 models, we have examined the complaint history of that car's *series*. The term *series* refers to the fact that when a manufacturer introduces a new model, that vehicle remains essentially unchanged for 4-6 years. For example, the Chevrolet Lumina Minivan was introduced in 1990 and remains essentially the same vehicle for 1996. As such, we have compiled the complaint experience for that series in order to give you some additional information to use in deciding which car to buy. For those vehicles just introduced in 1995 or 1996, we do not yet have enough data to develop a complaint index.

The following table presents the complaint indexes for the best and worst 1996 models. Higher index numbers mean the vehicle generated a greater number of complaints. Lower numbers indicate fewer complaints. After calculating the indexes, we compared the results among all 1996 vehicles.

1996 Complaint Ratings

The Best

Vehicle	Index
Chevy S-Series Pickup	0
Nissan Pickup	602
Dodge Ram Van/Wagon	1059
Toyota T100	1238
GMC Savana	1322
Mitsubishi Mighty Max	1429
GMC Sierra	1432
Chevy C/K Series Pickup	1757
Ford F-Series Pickup	1796
Geo Tracker	1959
Suzuki Sidekick	2119
Ford Econoline/Clb Wgn.	2296
Toyota 4Runner	2644
Dodge Ram	2899
Chevy Astro	2987
Mitsubishi Montero	3010
Isuzu Trooper	3112
Ford Ranger	3183
Toyota Previa	3254
Olds Silhouette	3344

The Worst

Vehicle	Index
GMC Suburban	12067
Chevy Surburban	11724
GMC Sonoma	10066
Jeep Grand Cherokee	9328
GMC Yukon	8613
Nissan Quest	6749
Honda Passport	6403
Mazda B-Series Pickup	6383
Chevy Lumina	6295
Land Rover Range Rover	6032
Mazda MPV	5662
Mercury Villager	5538
Toyota Land Cruiser	5014
Jeep Wrangler	4923
Jeep Cherokee	4833
Isuzu Rodeo	4487
Pontiac Trans Sport	4282
Ford Aerostar	3828
GMC Safari	3625
Ford Bronco	3541

Center for Auto Safety

Every year automobile manufacturers spend millions of dollars making their voices heard in government decision making. For example, General Motors and Ford have large staffs in Detroit and Washington that work solely to influence government activity. But who looks out for the consumer?

For over twenty years, the nonprofit Center for Auto Safety (CAS) has told the consumer's story to government agencies, to Congress and to the courts. Its efforts focus on all consumers rather than only those with individual complaints.

The Center for Auto Safety was established in 1970 by Ralph Nader and Consumers Union. As consumer concerns about auto safety issues expanded, so did the work of CAS. It became an independent group in 1972, and the original staff of two has grown to fourteen attorneys and researchers. CAS' activities include:

Initiating Safety Recalls: CAS analyzes over 50,000 consumer complaints each year. By following problems as they develop, CAS requests government investigations and recalls of defective vehicles. CAS was responsible for the Ford Pinto faulty gas tank recall, the Firestone 500 steel-belted radial tire recall, and the record recall of over 3 million Evenflo One Step child seats.

Representing the Consumer in Washington: CAS follows the activities of federal agencies and Congress to ensure that they carry out their responsibilities to the American taxpayer. CAS brings a consumer's point of view to vehicle safety policies and rule-making. Since 1970, CAS has submitted more than 500 petitions and comments on federal safety standards.

One major effort in this area has been the successful fight for adoption of automatic crash protection in passenger cars. These systems are a more effective and less intrusive alternative to crash protection than mandatory safety belt laws or belts that must be buckled in order to start the car.

Three years ago, the Center for Auto Safety uncovered a fire defect that dwarfed the highly publicized flammability of the Ford Pinto. It had to do with the side-saddle gas tanks on full size 1973-87 GM pickups and 1988-90 crew cabs that tend to explode on impact. Over 1,300 people have been killed in fire crashes involving these trucks. After mounting a national campaign to warn consumers to steer clear of these GM fire hazards, the U.S. Department of Transportation granted CAS' petition and conducted one of its biggest defect investigations in history. The result—GM was asked to recall its pickups. GM, sadly, denied this request.

Thanks to a petition originally filed by CAS, NHTSA adopted a new registration system to better enable manufacturer notification to parents with defective child seats. This will enable more parents to find out about potentially hazardous safety seats.

Exposing Secret Warranties: CAS played a prominent role in the disclosure of secret warranties, "policy adjustments," as they are called by manufacturers. These occur when an auto maker agrees to pay for repair of certain defects beyond the warranty period but refuses to notify consumers. (See "Secret Warranties" in the Warranty Chapter.)

Improving Rust Warranties: Rust and corrosion cost American car owners up to $14 billion annually. CAS has been successful in its efforts to get domestic and foreign auto companies to lengthen their all-important corrosion warranties.

Lemon Laws: CAS' work on Lemon Laws aided in the enactment of state laws which make it easier to return a defective new automobile and get money back.

Tire Ratings: After a suspension between 1982-84, consumers have reliable treadwear ratings to help them get the most miles for their dollar. CAS' lawsuit overturned DOT's revocation of this valuable new tire information program.

Initiating Legal Action: When CAS has exhausted other means of obtaining relief for consumer problems, it will initiate legal action. For example, in 1978 when the Department of Energy attempted to raise the price of gasoline 4 cents per gallon without notice or comment, CAS succeeded in stopping this illegal move through a lawsuit, thus saving consumers $2 billion for the six month period that the action was delayed.

A Center for Auto Safety lawsuit against the Environmental Protection Agency, in 1985, forced the EPA to recall polluting cars, rather than let companies promise to make cleaner cars in the future. As part of the settlement, GM (which was responsible for the polluting cars) funded a $7 million methanol bus demonstration program in New York City.

Publications: CAS has many publications on automobiles, motor homes, recreational vehicles, and fuel economy, including a number of free information packets. For each of the packets listed below, or for a complete description of all of the CAS' publications, send a separate stamped, self-addressed, business-sized envelope with 52 cents postage to the address below. Unless otherwise noted, the packets listed cover all known major problems for the models indicated and explain what to do about them. Requests for information should include make, model, and year of vehicle (with VIN number), as well as the type of problem you are experiencing. (Allow 2 to 3 weeks for delivery.)

Audi Defects (1978-92)
Cad. Seville/Eldorado/DeVille/ Fleetwood/Brougham/Allante HT-4100 Defects (1982-87)
Chrys. Paint/Water Leaks (1983-1995)
Chrys. Ultradrive Trans. (1989-95)
Chrys. FWD Cars (1981-95)
Chrys. Trucks/Vans (1981-95)
Chrys. Cirrus/Stratus/Neon (1994-95)
Chrys. LHS/Intrepid/Concorde (1993-95)
Chrys. Minivan (1984-95)
Ford Aerostar (1986-95)
Ford Cr. Vic./Gr. Marquis/ Lincoln Cont./Town Car/ Mark Series (1983-95)
Ford Escort/Lynx/Tracer (1981-95)
Ford F-Series Pickup Truck/Van Defects (1981-95)
Ford Taurus/Sable (1986-95)
Ford Tempo/Topaz (1984-95)
Ford Mustang/Capri/Probe (1979-95)
Ford Paint (1985-95)
GM Compact Cars-Prizm/Metro/ Storm/LeMans/Sprint/Nova (1985-95)
GM Saturn Defects (1991-1995)
GM Auto. Trans.: FWD (1981-93)
GM Auto. Trans.: RWD (1981-92)
GM Beretta/Corsica (1987-95)
GM Cut. Supr./Gr. Prix/Lumina/ Regal (1988-95)
GM Celebrity/6000/Century/Cut. Ciera & Cruiser (1982-95)
GM Camaro/Firebird (1982-95)
GM Citation/Omega/Phoenix/ Skylark (1981-85)
GM Achieva/Calais/Gr. Am/ Skylark/Somerset Regal (1985-95)
GM Buick Roadmaster/Chevrolet Caprice (1981-95)
GM Cavalier/Cimarron/Firenza/ Skyhawk/Sunbird/J2000 (1982-95)
GM LeSabre/Delta 88 & 98/ Bonneville/Electra & Park Ave. (1986-95)
GM Power Steering Failure (1980-88)
GM Large Pickup/Suburban & Blazer/Jimmy Utility Vehicle (1984-95)
GM S-series Truck/Blazer/Jimmy (1982-95)
GM Big Vans/Astro/Safari/APVs (1980-95)
GM Pontiac Fiero (1984-88)
GM Paint (1985-95)
Honda/Acura Defects (1988-95)
Hyundai Defects (1986-95)
Jeep–all models(1984-95)
Lemon Law Fact Sheet and Chart (1995)
Lemon Lawyer Recommendations (1995)
Mazda Car/Truck Defects (1988-95)
Mercedes Defects (1980-95)
Minivan Safety (1995)
Mitsubishi Defects (1983-95)
Nissan Car and Truck Defects (1988-95)
Renault/Eagle/Dodge Defects (1981-95)
Toyota Defects (1988-95)
Volkswagen Defects (1980-95)
Volvo Defects (1980-95)

CAS depends on the public for its support. Annual consumer membership is $15 ($20 for overseas). All contributions to this nonprofit organization are tax-deductible. Annual membership includes a quarterly newsletter called "LEMON TIMES." To join, send a check to:

Center for Auto Safety
2001 S St. NW, Suite 410
Washington, DC 20009-1160

Lemon Aid

The Center for Auto Safety has published *The Lemon Book,* a detailed, 368 page guide to resolving automobile complaints. Co-authored by Ralph Nader and the CAS Executive Director, Clarence Ditlow, this handbook is designed to help car buyers avoid lemons and tells you what to do if you wind up with one. To obtain this valuable book, send $15.95 to the Center for Auto Safety, 2001 S St., NW, Suite 410, Washington, DC 20009-1160. CAS is a non-profit consumer group supported, in part, by the sales of its publications.

Consumer Groups and Government

Here are the names of additional consumer groups which you may find helpful:

Consumer Action San Francisco
116 New Montgomery St., #233
San Francisco, CA 94105
(415) 777-9635
Focus: General problems of California residents.

Consumers for Auto Reliability and Safety Foundation
1500 W. El Camino Ave, #419
Sacramento, CA 95833-1945
(916) 759-9440
Focus: Auto safety, air bags, and lemon laws.

Consumers Education and Protective Association
6048 Ogontz Avenue
Philadelphia, PA 19141
(215) 424-1441
Focus: Pickets on behalf of members to resolve auto purchase and repair problems.

SafetyBelt Safe, U.S.A.
P.O. Box 553
Altadena, CA 91003
(800) 745-SAFE or
(310) 673-2666
Focus: Provides excellent information and training on child safety seats and safety belt usage.

VIGOR (Victims Group Opposed to Unsafe Restraint Systems)
3286 Avenida Anacapa Street
Carlsbad, CA 92009
(619) 943-0670
Focus: Promotes the replacement of lap-only seat belts in existing vehicles.

Several federal agencies conduct automobile-related programs. Listed below is each agency with a description of the type of work it performs as well as the address and phone number for its headquarters in Washington, D.C.

National Highway Traffic Safety Administration
400 7th Street, SW, NOA-40
Washington, D.C. 20590
202-366-9550

NHTSA issues safety and fuel economy standards for new motor vehicles; investigates safety defects and enforces recall of defective vehicles and equipment; conducts research and demonstration programs on vehicle safety, fuel economy, driver safety, and automobile inspection and repair; provides grants for state highway safety programs in areas such as police traffic services, driver education and licensing, emergency medical services, pedestrian safety, and alcohol abuse.

Environmental Protection Agency
401 M Street, SW
Washington, D.C. 20460
202-260-2090

EPA is responsible for the control and abatement of air, noise, and toxic substance pollution. This includes setting and enforcing air and noise emission standards for motor vehicles and measuring fuel economy in new vehicles (EPA Fuel Economy Guide).

Federal Trade Commission
PA Avenue & 6th Street, NW
Washington, D.C. 20580
202-326-2000

FTC regulates advertising and credit practices, marketing abuses, and professional services and ensures that products are properly labeled (as in fuel economy ratings). The commission covers unfair or deceptive trade practices in motor vehicle sales and repairs, as well as in non-safety defects.

Federal Highway Administration
400 7th Street, SW,
Room 3401, HHS1
Washington, D.C. 20590
202-366-1153

FHA develops standards to ensure highways are constructed to reduce occurrence and severity of accidents.

Department of Justice
Consumer Litigation
Civil Division
1331 Pennsylvania Avenue
National Place Bldg., Suite 950N
Washington, DC 20004
202-514-6786

The Department of Justice enforces the federal law that requires manufacturers to label new automobiles and forbids removal or alteration of labels before delivery to consumers. Labels must contain the make, model, vehicle identification number, dealer's name, suggested base price, manufacturer option costs, and manufacturer's suggested retail price.

Chrysler Corporation
Mr. Robert Eaton
Chairman and CEO
12000 Chrysler Drive
Highland Park, MI 48288-0001
(313) 956-5741

Ford Motor Company
Mr. Alex Trotman
Chairman, President and CEO
The American Road
Dearborn, MI 48103
(313) 322-3000
(313) 446-9475 (fax)

General Motors Corporation
Mr. John F. Smith, Jr.
CEO and President
3044 W. Grand Blvd.
Detroit, MI 48202
(313) 556-5000
(313) 556-5108 (fax)

American Honda Motor Co.
Mr. K. Amemiya
President
1919 Torrance Blvd.
Torrance, CA 90501-2746
(310) 783-2000
(310) 783-3900 (fax)

American Isuzu Motors Inc.
Mr. Yoshito Mochizuki
President
P.O. Box 2480
City of Industry, CA 91746
(310) 699-0500
(310) 692-7135 (fax)

Kia Motors America Inc.
Mr. H.R. Park
President and CEO
2 Cromwell
Irvine, CA 92718
(714) 470-7000
(714) 470-2801 (fax)

Land Rover of America
Mr. Charles R. Hughes
President
4390 Parliament Place
Lanham, MD 20706
(301) 731-9040
(301) 731-9054 (fax)

Mazda Motor of America, Inc.
Mr. George Toyama
President
7755 Irvine Center Dr.
Irvine, CA 92718
(714) 727-1990
(714) 727-6529 (fax)

Mitsubishi Motor Sales
Mr. Tohei Takeuchi
President and CEO
6400 Katella Ave.
Cypress, CA 90630-0064
(714) 372-6000
(714) 373-1019 (fax)

Nissan Motor Corp. U.S.A.
Mr. Robert Thomas
President and CEO
P.O. Box 191
Gardena, CA 90248-0191
(310) 532-3111
(310) 719-3343 (fax)

American Suzuki Motor Corp.
Mr. Masao Nagura
President
3251 E. Imperial Hwy.
Brea, CA 92621-6722
(714) 996-7040
(714) 524-2512 (fax)

Toyota Motors Sales, U.S.A., Inc.
Mr. Shinji Sakai
President and CEO
19001 S. Western Avenue
Torrance, CA 90509
(310) 618-4000
(310) 618-7800 (fax)

Volkswagen of America, Inc.
Mr. Clive Warrilow
President
3800 Hamlin Road
Auburn Hills, MI 48326
(810) 340-5000
(810) 340-4643 (fax)

Lemon Laws

Sometimes, despite our best efforts, we buy a vehicle that just doesn't work right. There may be little problem after little problem, or perhaps one big problem that never seems to be fixed. Because of the bad taste that such vehicles leave in the mouths of consumers who buy them, these vehicles are known as "lemons."

In the past, it's been difficult to obtain a refund or replacement if a vehicle was a lemon. The burden of proof was left to the consumer. Because it is hard to define exactly what constitutes a lemon, many lemon owners were unable to win a case against a manufacturer. But things are changing. As of 1993, all states have passed "Lemon Laws." Although there are some important state-to-state variations, all of the laws have similarities: They establish a period of coverage, usually one year from delivery or the written warranty period, whichever is shorter; they may require some form of noncourt arbitration; and most importantly they define a lemon. In most states a lemon is a new car, truck, or van that has been taken back to the shop at least four times for the same repair or is out of service for a total of 30 days during the covered period.

This time does not mean consecutive days. In some states the total time must be for the same repair; in others, it can be based on different repair problems.

Be sure to keep careful records of your repairs since some states now require only one of the three or four repairs to be within the specified time period.

Specific information about laws in your state can be obtained from your state attorney general's office (c/o your state capitol) or your local consumer protection office. The following table offers a general description of the Lemon Law in your state and what you need to do to set it in motion (*Notification/Trigger*). An **L** indicates that the law covers leased vehicles and we indicate where state-run arbitration programs are available. State-run programs are the best type of arbitration.

Alabama	**Qualification:** 3 unsuccessful repairs or 30 calendar days out of service within shorter of 24 months or 24,000 miles, provided 1 repair attempt or 1 day out of service is within shorter of 1 year or 12,000 miles. **Notification/Trigger:** Certified mail notice to manufacturer, who has 14 calendar days to make final repair.
Alaska	**Qualification:** 3 unsuccessful repairs or 30 business days out of service within shorter of 1 year or warranty. **Notification/Trigger**: Certified mail notice to manufacturer and dealer, or agent within 60 days after expiration of warranty or 1 year. Consumer must demand refund or replacement to be delivered within 60 days after mailing the notice. Final repair attemptwithin 30 days of receipt of notice.
Arizona	**Qualification:** 4 unsuccessful repairs or 30 calendar days out of service within shorter of 1 year or warranty. **Notification/Trigger:** Written notice to manufacturer and opportunity to repair.
Arkansas	**Qualification:** 3 unsuccessful repairs, or 1 unsuccessful repair of a problem likely to cause death or serious bodily injury within longer of 24 months or 24,000 miles. **Notification/Trigger:** Certified or registered mail notice to manufacturer. Manufacturer has 10 days to notify consumer of repair facility. Facility has 10 days to repair.
California	**Qualification:** 4 unsuccessful repairs or 30 calendar days out of service within shorter of 1 year or 12,000 miles. **Notification/Trigger:** Written notice to manufacturer and delivery of car to repair facility for repair attempt within 30 days. *State has certified guidelines for arbitration.* **L**
Colorado	**Qualification:** 4 unsuccessful repairs or 30 business days out of service within shorter of 1 year or warranty. **Notification/Trigger:** Prior certified mail notice for each defect occurance and opportunity to repair.
Conn.	**Qualification:** 4 unsuccessful repairs or 30 calendar days out of service within shorter of 2 years or 18,000 miles, or 2 repairs of problem likely to cause death or serious bodily injury within shorter of 1 year or warranty. **Notification/Trigger:** Report to manufacturer, agent or dealer. Written notice to manufacturer only if required in owner's manual or warranty. *State-run arbitration program is available.* **L**

Delaware	**Qualification:** 4 unsuccessful repairs or 30 calendar days out of service within shorter of 1 year or warranty. **Notification/Trigger:** Written notice to manufacturer and opportunity to repair. **L**
D. C.	**Qualification:** 4 unsuccessful repairs or 30 calendar days out of service or 1 unsuccesful repair of a safety-related defect, within shorter of 2 years or 18,000 miles. **Notification/Trigger:** Report of each defect occurance to manufacturer, agent or dealer. *State-run arbitration program is available.* **L**
Florida	**Qualification:** 3 unsuccessful repairs or 20 calendar days out of service within shorter of 12 months or 12,000 miles. **Notification/Trigger:** Written notice by certified or express mail to manufacturer who has 14 calendar days (10 if vehicle has been out of service 20 cumulative calendar days) for final repair attempt after delivery to designated dealer. *State-run arbitration program is available.* **L**
Georgia*	**Qualification:** 3 unsuccessful repair attempts or 30 calendar days out of service within shorter of 24,000 miles or 24 months, with 1 repair or 15 days out of service within shorter or 1 year or 12,000 miles; or one unsuccessful repair of a serious safety defect in the braking or steering system within shorter of 1 year or 12,000 miles. **Notification/Trigger:** Certified mail notice return receipt requested. Manufacturer has 7 days to notify consumer of repair facility. Facility has 14 days to repair. *State-run arbitration program is available.* **L**
Hawaii	**Qualification:** 3 unsuccessful repairs, or 1 unsuccessful repair of a nonconformity likely to cause death or serious bodily injury, or out of service within shorter of 2 years or 24,000 miles. **Notification/Trigger:** Written notice to manufacturer and opportunity to repair. *State-run arbitration program is available.* **L**
Idaho	**Qualification:** 4 repair attempts or 30 business days out of service within shorter of 12 months or 12,000 miles. **Notification/Trigger:** Written notice to manufacturer or dealer.
Illinois*	**Qualification:** 4 unsuccessful repairs or 30 business days out of service within shorter of 1 year or 12,000 miles. **Notification/Trigger:** Written notice to manufacturer and opportunity to repair.
Indiana	**Qualification:** 4 unsuccessful repairs or 30 business days out of service within the shorter of 18 months or 18,000 miles. **Notification/Trigger:** Written notice to manufacturer only if required in warranty. **L**
Iowa	**Qualification:** 3 unsuccessful repairs, or 1 unsuccessful repair of a nonconformity likely to cause death or serious bodily injury, or 20 calendar days out of service within shorter of 2 years or 24,000 miles. **Notification/Trigger:** Written notice to manufacturer and final opportunity to repair within 10 calendar days of receipt of notice. *State has certified guidelines for arbitration.* **L**
Kansas	**Qualification:** 4 unsuccessful repairs of the same problem or 30 calendar days out of service or 10 total repairs of any problem within shorter of 1 year or warranty. **Notification/Trigger:** Actual notice to manufacturer.
Kentucky	**Qualification:** 4 unsuccessful repairs or 30 calendar days out of service within shorter of 1 year or 12,000 miles. **Notification/Trigger:** Written notice to manufacturer.
Louisiana	**Qualification:** 4 unsuccessful repairs or 30 calendar days out of service within shorter of 1 year or warranty. **Notification/Trigger:** Report to manufacturer or dealer. **L**
Maine	**Qualification:** 3 unsuccessful repairs (when at least 2 times the same agent attempted the repair) or 15 business days out of service within shorter of 2 years or 18,000 miles. **Notification/Trigger:** Written notice to manufacturer or dealer only if required in warranty or owner's manual. Manufacturer has 7 business days after receipt for final repair attempt. *State-run arbitration program available.* **L**

Maryland	**Qualification:** 4 unsuccessful repairs, 30 calendar days out of service or 1 unsuccessful repair of braking or steering system within shorter of 15 months or 15,000 miles. **Notification/Trigger:** Certified mail notice, return receipt requested to manu. or factory branch and opportunity to repair within 30 calendar days of receipt of notice. **L**
Mass.	**Qualification:** 3 unsuccessful repairs or 15 business days out of service within shorter of 1 year or 15,000 miles. **Notification/Trigger:** Notice to manufacturer or dealer who has 7 business days to attempt a final repair. *State-run arbitration program is available*
Michigan	**Qualification:** 4 unsuccessful repairs or 30 calendar days out of service within shorter of 1 year or warranty. **Notification/Trigger:** Certified mail notice, return receipt requested, to manufacturer who has 5 business days to repair after delivery.
Minn.	**Qualification:** 4 unsuccessful repairs or 30 business days out of service or 1 unsuccessful repair of total braking or steering loss likely to cause death or serious bodily injury within shorter of 2 years or warranty. **Notification/Trigger:** At least one written notice to manufacturer, agent or dealer and opportunity to repair. **L**
Miss.	**Qualification:** 3 unsuccessful repairs or 15 business days out of service within shorter of 1 year or warranty. **Notification/Trigger:** Written notice to manufacturer who has 10 business days to repair after delivery to designated dealer.
Missouri	**Qualification:** 4 unsuccessful repairs or 30 business days out of service within shorter of 1 year or warranty. **Notification/Trigger:** Written notice to manufacturer who has 10 calendar days to repair after delivery to designated dealer.
Montana	**Qualification:** 4 unsuccessful repairs or 30 business days out of service after notice within shorter of 2 years or 18,000 miles. **Notification/Trigger:** Written noticeto manufacturer and opportunity to repair. *State-run arbitration program is available.*
Nebraska	**Qualification:** 4 unsuccessful repairs or 40 calendar days out of service within shorter of 1 year or warranty. **Notification/Trigger:** Certified mail notice to manufacturer and opportunity to repair.
Nevada	**Qualification:** 4 unsuccessful repairs or 30 calendar days out of service within shorter of 1 year or warranty. **Notification/Trigger:** Written notice to manufacturer.
N. H.	**Qualification:** 3 unsuccessful repairs by same dealer or 30 business days out of service within warranty. **Notification/Trigger:** Report to manufacturer, distributor, agent or dealer (on forms provided by manufacturer) and final opportunity to repair before arbitration. *State-run arbitration program is available.* **L**
N. J.	**Qualification:** 3 unsuccessful repairs or 20 calendar days out of service within shorter of 2 years or 18,000 miles. **Notification/Trigger:** Certified mail notice, written notice to manufacturer who has 15 days to repair. *State-run arbitration program available.* **L**
N. M.	**Qualification:** 4 unsuccessful repairs or 30 business days within shorter of 1 year or warranty. **Notification/Trigger:** Written notice to manufacturer, agent or dealer and opportunity to repair.
N. Y.	**Qualification:** 4 unsuccessful repairs or 30 calendar days out of service within shorter of 2 years or 18,000 miles. **Notification/Trigger:** Certified notice to manufacturer, agent or dealer. *State-run arbitration program is available.* **L**

N. C.	**Qualification:** 4 unsuccessful repairs within the shorter of 24 months, 24,000 miles or warranty or 20 business days out of service during any 12 month period of the warranty. **Notification/Trigger:** Written notice to manufacturer and opportunity to repair within 15 calendar days of receipt only if required in warranty or owner's manual. **L**
N. D.	**Qualification:** 4 unsuccessful repairs or 30 business days out of service within shorter of 1 year or warranty. **Notification/Trigger:** Direct written notice and opportunity to repair to manufacturer. **L**
Ohio	**Qualification:** 3 unsuccessful repairs of same nonconformity, 30 calendar days out of service, 8 total repairs of any problem, or 1 unsuccessful repair of problem likely to cause death or serious bodily injury within shorter of 1 year or 18,000 miles. **Notification/Trigger:** Report to manufacturer, its agent or dealer.
Okla.	**Qualification:** 4 unsuccessful repairs or 45 calendar days out of service within shorter of 1 year or warranty. **Notification/Trigger:** Written notice to manufacturer and opportunity to repair.
Oregon	**Qualification:** 4 unsuccessful repairs or 30 business days out of service within shorter of 1 year or 12,000 miles. **Notification/Trigger:** Direct written notice to manufacturer and opportunity to repair. **L**
Penn.	**Qualification:** 3 unsuccessful repairs or 30 calendar days out of service within shorter of 1 year, 12,000 miles, or warranty. **Notification/Trigger:** Delivery to authorized service and repair facility. If delivery impossible, written notice to manufacturer or its repair facility obligates them to pay for delivery.
R. I.	**Qualification:** 4 unsuccessful repairs or 30 calendar days out of service within shorter of 1 year or 15,000 miles. **Notification/Trigger:** Report to dealer or manufacturer who has 7 days for final repair opportunity. **L**
S. C.	**Qualification:** 3 unsuccessful repairs or 30 calendar days out of service within shorter of 1 year or 12,000 miles. **Notification/Trigger:** Written notice to manufacturer by certified mail and oppportunity to repair only if manufacturer informed consumer of such at time of sale. Manufacturer has 10 days to notify consumer of repair facility. Facility has 10 days to repair. *State-run arbitration program is available*. **L**
S. D.	**Qualification:** 4 unsuccessful repairs, at least 1 of which occurred during the shorter of 1 year or 12,000 miles, or 30 calendar days out of service during the shorter of 24 months or 24,000 miles. **Notification/ Trigger:** Certified mail notice to manufacturer and final opportunity to repair. Manufacturer has 7 calendar days to notify consumer of repair facility. Facility has 14 days to repair. If manufacturer has established a state recognized informal dispute settlement procedure, consumer must use program before instituting a cause of action.
Tenn.	**Qualification:** 4 unsuccessful repairs or 30 calendar days out of service within shorter of 1 year or warranty. **Notification/Trigger:** Certified mail notice to manufacturer and final opportunity to repair within 10 calendar days. **L**
Texas	**Qualification:** 4 unsuccessful repairs when 2 occured within shorter of 1 year or 12,000 miles, and other 2 occur within shorter of 1 year or 12,000 miles from date of 2nd repair attempt; or 2 unsuccessful repairs of a serious safety defect when 1 occured within shorter of 1 year or 12,000 miles and other occured within shorter of 1 year or 12,000 miles from date of 1st repair; or 30 calendar days out of service within shorter of 2 years or 24,000 miles and at least 2 attempts were made within shorter of 1 year or 12,000 miles. **Notification/Trigger:** Written notice to manufacturer. *State-run arbitration program is available*. **L**
Utah	**Qualification:** 4 unsuccessful repairs or 30 business days out of service within shorter of 1 year or warranty. **Notification/Trigger:** Report to manufacturer, agent or dealer. **L**

Vermont	**Qualification:** 3 unsuccessful repairs when at least 1st repair was within warranty, or 30 calendar days within warranty **Notification/Trigger:** Written notice to manufacturer (on provided forms) after 3rd repair attempt, or 30 days. Arbitration must be held within 45 days after notice, during which time manufacturer has 1 final repair. *State-run arbitration program is available.* **L**
Virginia	**Qualification:** 3 unsuccessful repairs, or 1 repair attempt of a serious safety defect, or 30 calendar days out of service within 18 months. **Notification/Trigger:** Written notice to manufacturer. If 3 unsuccessful repairs or 30 days already exhausted before notice, manufacturer has 1 more repair attempt not to exceed 15 days.
Wash.	**Qualification:** 4 unsuccessful repairs, 30 calendar days out of service (15 during warranty period), or 2 repairs of serious safety defects, first reported within shorter of the warranty or 24 months or 24,000 miles. One repair attempt and 15 of the 30 days must fall within manufacturer's express warranty of at least 1 year or 12,000 miles. **Notification/Trigger:** Written notice to manufacturer. *State-run arbitration program is available.* **L** *Note: Consumer should receive replacement or refund within 40 calendar days of request.*
W. V.	**Qualification:** 3 unsuccessful repairs or 30 calendar days out of service or 1 unsuccessful repair of problem likely to cause death or serious bodily injury within shorter of 1 year or warranty. **Notification/Trigger:** Prior written notice to manufacturer and at least one opportunity to repair.
Wisc.	**Qualification:** 4 unsuccessful repairs or 30 calendar days out of service within shorter of 1 year or warranty. **Notification/Trigger:** Report to manufacturer or dealer. **L***Note: Consumer should receive replacement or refund within 30 calendar days after offer to return title.*
Wyoming	**Qualification:** 3 unsuccessful repairs or 30 business days out of service within 1 year. **Notification/Trigger:** Direct written notice to manufacturer and opportunity to repair.

SHOWROOM STRATEGIES

Buying a vehicle means matching wits with a seasoned professional. But if you know what to expect, you'll have a much better chance of getting a really good deal! This chapter offers practical advice on buying a vehicle, tips on getting the best price, information on buying vs. leasing, and tips on avoiding lemons. We'll also take a peek at some future options that will increase driving safety.

For most of us, the auto showroom can be an intimidating environment, and for good reason. We're matching wits with seasoned, professional negotiators over a very complex product. Being prepared is the best way to turn a potentially intimidating showroom experience into a profitable one. Here's some advice on handling what you'll find in the showroom.

Beware of silence. Silence is often used to intimidate, so be prepared for long periods of time when the salesperson is "talking with the manager." This tactic is designed to make you want to "just get the negotiation over with." Instead of becoming a victim, do something that indicates you are serious about looking elsewhere. Bring the classified section of the newspaper with you and begin circling other vehicles or review brochures from other manufacturers. By sending the message that you have other options, you increase your bargaining power and speed the process.

Don't fall in love with a vehicle. Never look too interested in any particular vehicle. Advise family members who go with you against being too enthusiastic about any one vehicle. *Tip:* Beat the dealers at their own game—bring along a friend who tells you that the price is "too much compared to the *other* deal."

Keep your wallet in your pocket. Don't leave a deposit, even if it's refundable. You'll feel pressure to rush your shopping, and you'll have to return and face the salesperson again, perhaps before you are ready.

Shop at the end of the month. Salespeople anxious to meet sales goals are more willing to negotiate a lower price at this time.

Buy last year's model. The majority of new vehicles are the same as the previous year, with minor cosmetic changes. You can save considerably by buying in early fall when dealers are clearing space for "new" models. The important trade-off you make using this technique is that the car maker may have added air bags or anti-lock brakes to an otherwise unchanged vehicle.

Buying from stock. You can often get a better deal on a vehicle that the dealer has on the lot. However, these vehicles usually have expensive options you may not want or need. Do not hesitate to ask the dealer to remove an option (and its accompanying charge) or sell you the vehicle without charging for the option. Another advantage of buying from stock is that the longer the vehicle sits there, the more interest the dealer pays on the vehicle, which increases the dealer's incentive to sell.

Ordering a vehicle. Domestic vehicles can be ordered from the manufacturer. Simply offering a fixed amount over invoice may be attractive because it's a sure sale and the dealership has not invested in the vehicle. All the salesperson has to do is take your order.

In This Chapter...

If you do order a vehicle, make sure when it arrives it includes only the options you requested. Don't fall for the trick where the dealer offers you unordered options at a "special price," because it was their mistake. If you didn't order the option, don't pay for it.

Don't trade in. Although it is more work, you can almost always do better by selling your old vehicle yourself than by trading it in. To determine what you'll gain by selling the vehicle yourself, check the NADA "Blue Book" at your credit union or library. The difference between the trade-in price (what the dealer will give you) and the retail price (what you can typically sell it for) is your extra payment for selling the vehicle yourself.

If you do decide to trade your car in at the dealership, *keep the buying and selling separate.* First, negotiate the best price for your new vehicle, then find out how much the dealer will give you for your old vehicle. Keeping the two deals separate ensures that you know what you're paying for your new vehicle and simplifies the entire transaction.

Avoiding Lemons

One way to avoid the sour taste of a lemon after you've bought your car is to protect yourself *before* you sign on the dotted line. These tips will help you avoid problems down the road.

1 **Avoid new models.** Any new car in its very first year of production often turns out to have a lot of defects. Sometimes, the manufacturer isn't able to remedy the defects until the second, third, or even fourth year of production. If the manufacturer has not worked out problems by the third model year, the car will likely be a lemon forever.

2 **Avoid the first cars off the line.** Most companies close down their assembly lines every year to make annual style changes. In addition to adding hundreds of dollars to the price of a new car, these changes can introduce new defects. It can take a few months to iron out these bugs. Ask the dealer when the vehicle you are interested in was manufactured, or look on the metal tag found on the inside of the driver-side door frame to find the date of manufacture.

3 **Avoid delicate options.** Delicate options have the highest frequency-of-repair records. Power seats, power windows, power antennas, and special roofs are nice conveniences—until they break down. Of all the items on the vehicles, they tend to be the most expensive to repair.

4 **Inspect the dealer's checklist.** Request a copy of the dealer's pre-delivery service and adjustment checklist (also called a "make-ready list") at the time your new vehicle is delivered. Write the request directly on the new vehicle order. This request informs the dealer that you are aware of the dealer's responsibility to check your new car for defects.

5 **Examine the car on delivery.** Most of us are very excited when it comes time to take the vehicle home. This is the time where a few minutes of careful inspection can save hours of aggravation later. Carefully look over the body for any damage, check for the spare tire and jack equipment, make sure all electrical items work, and make sure all the hubcaps and body molding are on. You may want to take a short test drive. Finally, make sure you have the owner's manual, warranty forms, and all the legal documents.

Getting the Best Price

One of the most difficult aspects of buying a new vehicle is getting the best price. Most of us are at a disadvantage negotiating because we don't know how much the car actually cost the dealer. The difference between what the dealer paid and the sticker price represents the negotiable amount.

Until recently, the key to getting the best price was finding out the dealer cost. Many shoppers now ask to see the factory invoice, so some dealers promote their vehicles by offering to sell at only $49 or $99 over invoice. This sounds like a good deal, but these vehicles often have options you may not want, and most invoice prices do not reveal the extra, hidden profit to the dealer.

Now that most savvy consumers know to check the so-called "dealer invoice," the industry has camouflaged this number. Special incentives, rebates, and kickbacks can account for $500 to $2,000 worth of extra profit to a dealer selling a vehicle at "dealer invoice." The non-profit Center for the Study of Services recently discovered that in 37% of cases when dealers are forced to bid against each other for the sale, they offered the buyer a price below the "dealer invoice"—an unlikely event if the dealer was actually losing money. The bottom line is that "dealer invoice" doesn't mean anything anymore.

Because the rules have changed, we believe that most consumers are ill-advised to try and negotiate with a dealer. Introducing competition is the best way to get the lowest price on a new vehicle. What this means is that you have to convince 3-4 dealers that you are, in fact, prepared to buy a vehicle; that you have decided on the make, model, and features; and that your decision now rests solely on which dealer will give you the best price. You can try to do this by phone, but often dealers will not give you the best price, or will quote you a price over the phone that they will not honor later. Instead, you should try to do this in person. As anyone who has ventured into an auto showroom simply to get the best price knows, the process can be lengthy and arduous. Nevertheless, if you can convice the dealer that you are serious and are willing to take the time to go to a number of dealers, it will pay off. Otherwise, we suggest you use the CarBargains service listed on the next page.

If you find a big savings at a dealer far from your home, call a local dealer with the price. They may very well match it. If not, pick up the vehicle from the distant dealer, knowing your trip has saved you hundreds. You can still bring it to your local dealer for warranty work and repairs. Here are some other showroom strategies:

Beware of misleading advertising. New vehicle ads are meant to get you into the showroom. They usually promise low prices, big rebates, high trade-in, and spotless integrity—don't be deceived. Advertised prices are rarely the true selling price. They usually exclude transportation charges, service fees, or document fees. And always look out for the asterisk, both in advertisements and on invoices. It can be a signal that the advertiser has something to hide.

Don't talk price until you're ready to buy. On your first trips to the showroom, simply look over the vehicles, decide what options you want, and do your test driving.

Shop the corporate twins. Page 16 contains a list of corporate twins—nearly identical vehicles that carry different name plates. Check the price and options of the twins of the vehicle you like. A higher priced twin may have more options, so it may be a better deal than the lower priced vehicle without the options you want.

Watch out for dealer preparation overcharges. Before paying the dealer to clean your vehicle, make sure that preparation is not included in the basic price. The price sticker will state: "Manufacturer's suggested retail price of this model includes dealer preparation."

If you must negotiate . . . Negotiate from the "invoice" price. Rather than see how much you can get off the sticker price, simply make an offer close to or at the "invoice" price. If the sales person says that your offer is too low to make a profit, ask to see the factory invoice.

TIP

The 180 Degree Turn

If you try to negotiate a car purchase, remember that you have the most important weapon in the bargaining process: *the 180-degree turn.* Be prepared to walk away from a deal, even at the risk of losing the "very best deal" your salesperson has ever offered, and you will be in the best position to get a genuine "best deal." Remember: dealerships need you, the buyer, to survive.

Price Shopping Service

Even with the information that we provide you in this chapter of *The Truck, Van & 4x4 Book*, most of us will *not* be well prepared to negotiate a good price for the vehicles we are considering. In fact, as we indicated on the previous page, we don't believe that you can negotiate the best price with *a* dealer. The key to getting the best price is to get the dealers to compete with each other. This page describes a new and easy way to find the best price by actually getting the dealers to compete.

CarBargains is a service of the non-profit Center for the Study of Services, a Washington, D.C., consumer group, set up to provide comparative price information for many products and services.

CarBargains will "shop" the dealerships in your area and obtain at least five price quotes for the make and model of the vehicle that you want to buy. The dealers who submit quotes know that they are competing with other area dealerships and have agreed to honor the prices that they submit. It is important to note that CarBargains is not an auto broker or "car buying" service; they have no affiliation with dealers.

Here's how the service works:

1. You provide CarBargains with the make, model, and style of vehicle you wish to buy (Ford Bronco XL, for example) by phone or mail.

2. Within two weeks, CarBargains will send you dealer quote sheets from at least 5 local dealers who have bid against one another to sell you that vehicle. The offer is actually a commitment to a dollar amount above (or below) "factory invoice cost" for that model.

You will also receive a printout with the exact dealer cost for the vehicle and each available option. Included in the information will be the name of the sales manager responsible for honoring the quote.

3. Use the factory invoice cost printout to add up the invoice cost for the base vehicle and the options you want and then determine which dealer offers the best price using the dealer quote sheets. Contact the sales manager of that dealership and arrange to purchase the vehicle.

If a vehicle with the options you want is not available on the dealer's lot, you can have the dealer order the vehicle from the factory or, in some cases, from another dealer at the agreed price.

When you receive your quotes, you will also get some suggestions on low-cost sources of financing and a valuation of your used car (trade-in).

The price for this service may seem expensive, but when you consider the savings that will result by having dealers bid against each other as well as the time and effort of trying to get these bids yourself, we believe it's a great value. First of all, the dealers know they have a bona fide buyer (you've paid $150 for the service) and they know they are bidding against 5-7 of their competitors.

To obtain CarBargains' competitive price quotes, send a check for $150 to CarBargains, 733 15th St., NW, Suite 820CB, Washington, DC 20005. Include your complete mailing address, phone number (in case of questions), and the exact make, model, and year of the vehicle you want to buy. You should receive your bids within 2-3 weeks. For faster service, call them at 800-475-7283. They will accept Visa or Mastercard on phone orders.

Auto Brokers

While CarBargains is a non-profit organization created to help you find the best price for the vehicle you want to purchase, auto brokers are typically in the business to make money. As such, what ever price you end up paying for the vehicle will include additional profit for the broker. While many brokers are legitimately trying to get their customers the best price, others have developed special relationships with certain dealers and may not do much shopping for you. As a consumer, it is difficult to tell which are which. If you use a broker, make sure the contract to purchase the vehicle is with the dealer, not the broker. In addition, it is best to pay the broker *after* the services is rendered, not before. There have been cases where the auto broker makes certain promises, takes your money, and you never hear from him or her again. If CarBargains is not for you, then we suggest you consider using a buying service associated with your credit union or auto club, which can arrange for the purchase of a vehicle at some fixed price over "dealer invoice."

Depreciation

Over the past 20 years, new vehicle depreciation costs have steadily increased. A recent study conducted by the Runzheimer International management consulting firm shows that depreciation and interest now account for slightly over 50 percent of the costs of owning and operating a vehicle. This number is up from 41 percent in 1976. On the other hand, the relative cost of gasoline has dropped by half, from 35 cents to 17 cents of every dollar spent on the average vehicle. Other costs, including insurance, maintenance, and tires, have remained at relatively steady shares of the automotive dollar.

The high cost of depreciation is largely due to skyrocketing new vehicle prices. While there is no reliable method of predicting retained value, your best bet is to purchase a popular new vehicle. Chances are that it will also be popular as a usedvehicle. Vehicles are generally poor investments in terms of retaining their value. There are some exceptions, however, and the following table indicates the current resale values for some 1991 vehicles. The highest-priced vehicles are not necessarily the best quality. Supply and demand, as well as appearance, are extremely important factors in determining used vehicle prices.

Vehicle	1991 Price	1995 Price	% of Cost
Chevrolet Astro	13,460	9,775	73%
Chevrolet Blazer	17,590	14,425	82%
Chevy C/K Series Pickup*	10,625	10,050	95%
Chevrolet Lumina APV ▪	13,592	8,450	62%
Chevrolet S10	8,382	6,725	81%
Chevrolet S10 Blazer	13,845	11,775	85%
Chevrolet Suburban*	16,720	15,925	95%
Daihatsu Rocky	11,297	8,250	73%
Dodge Caravan ▪	12,266	8,225	67%
Dodge Dakota	10,172	9,575	94%
Dodge Ram 50	7,787	6,725	86%
Dodge Ram Pickup	7,787	6,725	86%
Dodge Ramcharger ▪	15,003	9,975	67%
Ford Aerostar	12,520	8,225	66%
Ford Bronco	17,620	15,225	86%
Ford Econoline/Club Wgn	17,512	12,425	71%
Ford Explorer	13,938	13,050	94%
Ford F Series Pickup	10,971	9,425	86%
Ford Ranger	8,279	6,850	83%
Geo Tracker	8,999	7,425	82%
GMC CK Series Pickup	10,645	10,050	94%
GMC Jimmy	17,694	14,425	82%
GMC Jimmy S15	17,674	14,425	82%
GMC S15	14,060	11,800	84%
GMC Safari	13,544	9,775	72%
GMC Sonoma	8,466	6,775	80%
GMC Suburban*	16,775	15,950	95%
GMC Vandura/Rally	13,964	10,375	76%
Isuzu Amigo	9,979	8,850	90%
Isuzu Pickup	7,979	6,475	81%
Isuzu Rodeo*	12,499	12,100	97%
Isuzu Trooper/Trooper II	13,699	12,600	92%
Jeep Cherokee/Wagoneer	13,822	11,375	82%
Jeep Comanche	8,537	7,650	90%
Jeep Grand Wagoneer ▪	29,065	14,865	51%
Jeep Wrangler	12,800	11,700	91%
Mazda B Series Pickup	7,989	7,125	89%
Mazda MPV	12,415	10,975	88%
Mazda Navajo	17,560	14,000	80%
Mitsubishi Mighty Max	7,689	6,350	83%
Mitsubishi Montero	15,489	12,325	80%
Nissan Pathfinder*	16,120	15,825	98%
Nissan Pickup	8,279	7,650	92%
Oldsmobile Bravada	23,795	16,525	69%
Oldsmobile Silhouette ▪	18,195	12,150	67%
Plymouth Voyager	13,195	9,375	71%
Pontiac Trans Sport	15,619	11,725	75%
Suzuki Samurai	5,999	4,700	78%
Suzuki Sidekick	10,299	7,700	75%
Toyota Pickup	8,198	7,425	91%
Toyota Previa	18,698	16,675	89%
Volkswagen Vanagon	14,575	11,200	77%

* Top five in retained value.
▪ Bottom five in retained value.

Leasing vs. Buying

As vehicle prices continue to rise and dealer ads scream out the virtues of leasing, many buyers are wondering whether they should lease rather than buy. Here is some information to help you make the right decision.

With a lease, you pay a monthly fee for a predetermined length of time in exchange for the use of a vehicle. Usually, however, you pay for maintenance, insurance, and repairs as if the vehicle were your own. There are two types of leases—*closed-* and *open-ended.* Most consumer leases are closed-ended, and you simply return the vehicle at the lease's end. Your monthly payment depends on the original cost of the vehicle and what the company thinks the vehicle can sell for after the lease is up. An open-ended lease is riskier because you pay the difference between the vehicle's expected value and its actual resale value when the lease ends. If the lessor underestimated the resale value of your payments, you'll pay a lump sum at the end.

While these terms describe general types of leases, within these categories the details may vary considerably. Some companies combine these concepts with a vehicle purchase option. They guarantee to sell you the vehicle at the end of the lease for a predetermined amount, called the residual value. If, at the end, the vehicle is worth more than the pre-determined price, you may want to buy it. If it's worth less, simply turn it in.

Generally speaking, leasing costs more than buying outright or financing. In fact, when you lease a vehicle, you have all the headaches and responsibilities of ownership with none of the benefits. In addition, leased vehicles are often not covered by the Lemon Laws. However, if the benefit of the lower monthly payments outweighs the overall added costs, consider the following when shopping for a lease:

Know the make and model of the vehicle you want. Tell the agent exactly how you want the vehicle equipped. You don't have to pay for options you don't request. Decide in advance how long you will keep the vehicle.

Find out the price of the options on which the lease is based. Typically, it will be full retail price. The price can be negotiated (albeit with some difficultly)—before you settle on the monthly payment.

Find out how much you are required to pay at delivery. Most leases require at least the first month's payment. Others have a security deposit, registration fees, or other "hidden" costs. When shopping around, make sure price quotes include taxes—sales tax, monthly use tax, or gross receipt tax. Ask how the length of the lease affects your monthly cost.

Find out the annual mileage limit. Don't accept a contract with a lower limit than you need. Most standard contracts allow 15,000 to 18,000 miles per year. If you go under the allowance one year, you can go over it the next.

Avoid "capitalized cost reduction" or "equity leases." Here the lessor offers to lower the monthly payment by asking you for more money up front. This defeats the principal benefit of a lease. By paying more initially, you lose the opportunity to use or earn interest on this money. These opportunity costs are based on the interest rate that you would otherwise earn.

Ask about early termination. If you terminate the lease before it is up, what are the financial penalties? Ask the dealer *exactly* what you would owe at the end of each year if you wanted out of the lease. Remember, if your vehicle is stolen, the lease will typically be terminated. While your insurance should cover the value of the vehicle, you still may owe additional amounts per your lease contract.

Avoid maintenance contracts. Getting work done privately is cheaper in the long run—and don't forget, this is a new vehicle with a standard warranty.

Arrange for your own insurance. You can generally find less expensive insurance than the programs offered by the lessor.

Ask how quickly you can expect delivery. If your agent can't deliver in a reasonable time, maybe he or she can't meet the price quoted.

Find out the service charges at the end of the lease. Usually around $100, they can go up to $250.

Retain your option to buy the vehicle at the end of the lease at a predetermined price. The price should equal the residual value; if it is more, then the lessor is trying to make an additional profit. Regardless of how the end-of-lease value is determined, if you want the vehicle make an offer based on the current "Blue Book" value at the end of the lease.

Find out how the lease price was figured. Lease prices are generally based on the manu- facturer's suggested retail price, less the predetermined residual value. The best values are vehicles with a high expected residual value. To protect themselves, lessors tend to underestimate residual value, but you can do little about this estimate.

Here's what First National Lease Systems Automotive Lease Guide estimates the residual values for a few 1996 vehicles will be after four years:

Chevy Blazer 2WD	47%
Ford Explorer XL 4WD	50%
Ford Windstar LX	45%
Ford Ranger Splash	43%
GMC Sonoma SLS 4WD	39%
Honda Passport DX 2WD	49%
Isuzu Trooper	46%
Jeep Wrangler Sahara	47%
Land Rover Range Rover	47%
Nissan Pickup 2WD	41%
Plymouth Voyager SE	46%
Toyota 4-Runner 4WD	55%

The following table compares the typical costs of leasing vs. buying the same vehicle. Your actual costs will vary slightly, but you can use this format to compare the vehicles you are considering. Our example assumes that the residual value of a purchased vehicle is 60 percent after two years and 45 percent after four.

Finally, keep in mind that at the end of a lease period you have nothing—but at the end of your finance period you will own a vehicle.

Financing vs. Leasing

	2 Years		4 Years	
	Lease	Finance*	Lease	Finance*
Number of Months	24	24	48	48
Manu. Suggested Price	$15,000	$15,000	$15,000	$15,000
Cash Down Payment		$1,500		$1,500
Monthly Payment	$425	$678	$300	$366
Total Amt. of Payments**	$10,200	$16,272	$14,400	$17,568
Less Vehicle Value at End	$0	$9,000	$0	$6,750
Actual Cost	$10,200	$8,772	$14,400	$12,318

*Based on an annual percentage rate of 8%
**In a lease, this is the total amount paid for the use of the vehicle. When financing, this is the total amount paid to become the owner.

Don't Buy Rustproofing

For years, we've recommended *against* spending the hundreds of dollars dealers charge for rustproofing. Some manufacturers (GM, Nissan, Saturn, Subaru, Suzuki, Toyota, and Volkswagen) now also recommend against aftermarket rustproofing. General Motors' warranty presents one of the clearest arguments against buying this expensive item: *Some after-manufacture rustproofing may create a potential environment which reduces the corrosion resistance designed and built into your vehicle. Depending upon application technique, some after-manufacture rustproofing could result in damage or failure of some electrical or mechanical systems of your vehicle. Repairs to correct damage or malfunctions caused by after-manufacture rustproofing are not covered under any of your GM new vehicle warranties.* Other manufacturers who suggest that rustproofing may void your corrosion warranty include Nissan, Saturn, and Volkswagen.

Options

You may want to consider the following options for your new vehicle:

Childproof Locks: Many vehicles come with a simple lever that disconnects the inside rear door handles so the doors can only be opened from the outside. This device is especially important in family vans, yet only about half of the vans and sport utility vehicles on the market offer this valuable safety feature.

Cruise Control: A properly functioning cruise control system can be convenient and can even contribute to improved fuel efficiency on long trips. Unfortunately, in investigating the growing problem of sudden acceleration (when the vehicle suddenly lurches out of control), the Center for Auto Safety has related this problem to a failure in the cruise control system. If you do not regularly use cruise control, consider deleting it from the options on your new vehicle.

E-4WD: This electronically controlled system allows the 4WD clutch to engage and disengage whenever it is needed, without the driver having to switch it manually. E-4WD was introduced by Ford in 1991.

High-Tech Safety Belts: A few models have seat-belt tensioners on the front belts. In the event of a frontal crash, these devices take up any slack in the safety belt and reduce forward movement. Find out if the vehicles you are considering have these devices; they are an important advance in safety-belt technology.

Reinforced Door Beams: Injuries from side crashes or rollovers can be greatly reduced by building reinforcing beams into the vehicle's doors. This feature is especially important in sport utility vehicles because of their high tendency to roll over—yet few of the current models offer this added important protection.

Head Restraints: Head restraints help prevent whiplash injuries. They have only recently become uniformly available, since the safety requirement for head restraints went into effect in 1992 for trucks, vans, and 4x4s.

Anti-lock Braking System: Many manufacturers offer a safety feature called anti-lock braking or ABS. ABS shortens stopping distance on dry, wet, and even icy roads. By preventing brake lockup, ABS ensures steering control even in severe emergency braking. Beware—ABS that only operates on rear wheels is of marginal value. Look for all-wheel ABS. (See page 23 for a list of which vehicles have ABS.)

Future Options

Here are some options you can expect in the future:

Radar Brakes: Using radar to detect objects in front of you, radar provides a warning for the need to brake. It can also be used to apply the brakes to reduce the chances of crashing—for a driver who falls asleep, for example.

Side Airbags: Airbags that come out of the doors, and out of the back of the front seat would be triggered by "crash anticipation" sensors. Together with frontal airbags, the omnidirectional airbag system would protect in all directions and in rollover crashes. Volvo sent other manufacturers scrambling by offering this feature in the 850 Turbo in 1995.

Air Pads: Air pads are double layers of plastic with multiple compartments which look like ordinary trim in the uninflated condition. When the crash sensors for the airbags detect a crash, the air pads inflate out a few inches over all hard surfaces such as the window sills and the header over the windshield.

Night Vision Enhancement: Being developed by GM, this system uses cameras that detect infrared light and projects a visible image of what's ahead on a screen located on the vehicle's instrument panel. The system could also detect, through a heat-seeking infrared system, someone lurking in a darkened parking lot. This would be most useful at night or in heavy fog or rain. This device will see through fog, rain and darkness, and provide an image of any obstacles or problems in the road.

RATINGS

This chapter provides an overview of the most important features of the new 1996 cars. In this section of *The Truck, Van & 4x4 Book,* you can see on each "car page" all the ingredients you need to make a smart choice. In addition to some descriptive text and a photo, the page contains seven important information boxes:

THE DESCRIPTION

The vast majority of the information in *The Truck, Van & 4x4 Book* is purely objective—we research and present the facts so that you can make an informed choice among the models that fit your taste and pocketbook. For the second year we are adding, among other new features, some background details. Specifically, for every vehicle we include some general information to help you round out the hard facts. Much of the information in this section is subjective and you may not share our opinion. Nevertheless, like the photo, which will give you a general idea of what the vehicle looks like, the description will give you a snapshot of some of the features that we think are worth noting which may not show up in the statistics.

GENERAL INFORMATION

This is additional information you may want to consider when buying a new vehicle.

Fuel Economy: This is the EPA-rated fuel economy for city and highway driving measured in miles per gallon. Most models have a number of fuel economy ratings because of different engine and transmission options. We indicate the figure for what we expect to be the most popular model. For more individual ratings, see "The Fuel Economy Chapter."

Driving Range: Given the vehicle's expected fuel economy and gas tank size, this gives an idea of how far you can go on a full tank.

Parking Index: Using the vehicle's length, wheelbase and turning circle, we have calculated how easy it will be to maneuver this vehicle in tight spots. This rating of *very easy* to *very hard* is an indicator of how much difficulty you may have parking. If you regularly parallel park, or find yourself maneuvering in and out of tight spaces, this can be an important factor in your choice.

Theft Rating: This rating is given by the Insurance Institute for Highway Safety. It predicts the likelihood of the vehicle being stolen or broken into based on its past history. If no information appears, it means that the vehicle is too new to have a rating.

Corporate Twins: Often a company will make numerous models on the same platform. This is a list of this vehicle's twins.

Where made: Here we tell you where the vehicle was assembled.

Year of Production: We generally don't recommend buying a vehicle during it's first model year of production. In addition, we believe that the longer a company makes the same vehicle, the less likely the vehicle is to have manufacturing and design defects. Each year the model is made, the production process usually is improved and there are fewer minor design defects. Therefore, the longer a vehicle has

In This Chapter...

been made, the less likely you are to be plagued with defects. On the other hand, the newer a vehicle is, the more likely it is to have the latest in engineering.

PRICES

This box contains sample price information. When available, we list the base and the most luxurious version of the vehicle. The difference is often substantial. Usually the more expensive versions have fancy trim, larger engines and lots of automatic equipment. The least expensive versions usually have manual transmission and few extra features. In addition, some manufacturers try to sell popular options as part of a package. For example, to get air conditioning you may have to buy power steering and deluxe seats.

This information provides an idea of the price range and the expected dealer markup. Be prepared for higher retail prices when you get to the showroom. Manufacturers like to load their vehicles with factory options, and dealers like to add their own items such as fabric protection and paint sealant. Remember, prices and dealer costs can change during the year. Use these figures for general reference and comparisons, not as a precise indication of exactly how much the vehicle you are interested in will cost. See page 92 for a new buying service designed to ensure that you get the very best price.

THE RATINGS

These are ratings in nine important categories, as well as an overall rating. We have adopted the Olympic rating system with "10" being the best.

Overall Rating: This is the "bottom line." Using a combination of all of the ratings, this tells how this vehicle stacks up against the other '96s on a scale of 1 to 10. Due to the importance of crash tests, vehicles with no crash test results as of our publication date cannot be given an overall rating. More recent results may be available from the Auto Safety Hotline at 1-800-424-9393 (see page 73).

Crash Test Performance: This rating compares the 1996 models against all of the crash test results to date. We give the best performers a 10 and the worst a 1. Remember, it is important to compare crash test results relative to other vehicles in the same size class. For complete details, see "The Safety Chapter."

Safety Features: This is an evaluation of how much extra safety is built into the vehicle. We give credit for air bags, ABS, rollover propensity, built-in child restraints and belt height adjustors.

Fuel Economy: Here we compare the EPA mileage ratings of each vehicle. The gas misers get a 10 and the guzzlers get a 1. For more information, see "The Fuel Economy Chapter."

PM Cost: Each manufacturer suggests a preventive maintenance schedule designed to keep the vehicle in good shape and to protect your rights under the warranty. The cost of these schedules varies substantially from vehicle to vehicle—ranging from $0 to $1500 for the first 50,000 miles of driving. Those with the lowest PM costs get a 10 and the highest, a 1. See "The Maintenance Chapter" for the actual costs.

Repair Cost: It is virtually impossible to predict exactly what any new vehicle will cost you in repairs. As such, we take nine typical repairs that you are likely to experience *after* your warranty expires and compare those costs among this year's models. Those with the lowest cost get a 10 and the highest, a 1. For the details, see "The Maintenance Chapter."

Warranty: There are good warranties and not so good warranties. This is an overall assessment of the vehicle's warranty when compared to all 1996 warranties. The rating considers the important features of each warranty, with emphasis on the length of the basic and powertrain warranties. We give the highest rated warranties a 10 and the lowest a 1. See "The Warranty Chapter" for details.

Complaints: This is where you'll find how your vehicle stacks up against hundreds of others on the road, based on the U.S. government complaint data. We can only rate vehicles which have enough on-the-road complaint history, so if no information is listed, the vehicle has not been around long enough to have developed a complaint history—good or bad. The least complained about vehicles get a 10 and the most problematic, a 1.

Insurance Cost: Insurance companies have rated most of the vehicles on the road to determine how they plan to charge for insurance. Here, you'll find whether you can expect a *discount* or a *surcharge*. If the vehicle is likely to receive neither, we label it *regular*. Those receiving a discount get a 10, while those with a surcharge get a 1, any with neither get a 5.

SAFETY

For most of us, safety is a critical consideration in buying a new vehicle. This box will tell you, at a glance, whether or not the vehicle has the safety features you care about.

Crash Test: Here's where we tell you if its crash test was *very good, good, average, poor* or *very poor*, compared to all tests ever performed by the government.

Side Impact Protection: By 1999, light trucks, vans and sport utility vehicles must have increased side impact protection built in, and starting this year, some vehicles do. Find out which vehicles have this much needed protection. A *strong* rating means that the vehicle meets the 1999 requirement, a *weak* rating means it does not.

Air Bag: Here's where you'll find out which occupants benefit from this invaluable safety feature and who is left unprotected.

Anti-lock Brakes: This safety feature comes in two or four wheel versions. Two wheel ABS is of marginal value. An asterisk indicates if you have to pay extra to get ABS.

Belt Adjustors: This tells if the car maker offers a safety belt height/comfort adjustor. People often don't wear safety belts because they are uncomfortable. In fact, a belt's effectiveness is due, in part, to how well it fits your body. In order to make sure shoulder belts fit properly (squarely across the front of your chest) some manufacturers have installed devices that let you adjust the height of the belt. This allows for proper fit among drivers and passengers of various heights. In addition to allowing a safer fit, it helps prevent such problems as the belt scraping across the neck of a shorter driver. Availability is indicated for both front seat occupants, unless otherwise noted.

Child Safety Seats: Some manufacturers are offering "built-in" child safety seats which reduces the chances that your child rides unprotected.

Occupant Injury: This is the expected injury rating, as presented by the Insurance Institute for Highway Safety, based on actual experience. If the model or style is all new this year, it has no rating. A vehicle may have a good crash test rating, but a poor injury rating. This could be due to the way the vehicle is driven. For example, a sporty car may have a good crash test result, but a poor injury rating. This may be due to the fact that the car is typically driven by young males who are in accidents more frequently than others.

SPECIFICATIONS

Here are the "nuts and bolts." In this box, we have listed seven key specifications which enable you to evaluate how best that vehicle meets your particular needs.

Length: This is the overall length of the vehicle from bumper to bumper.

Head/Leg Room: This tells how roomy the front seat is.

Cargo Space: This gives you the cubic feet available for cargo. For vans, it is the back of the two front seats to the rear of the vehicle. It is difficult to give a specific volume for the cargo space of pickups since you can pile stuff to the sky. Check the length and width of the bed when selecting a pickup.

Payload: This is the amount of weight that is safe for the vehicle to carry, including passengers and cargo. Where variations are indicated, different models of the vehicle have different capacities. In such cases, we tried to choose a median value.

Tow Rating: Ratings of *very low, low, average, high* and *very high* indicate the vehicle's relative ability to tow trailers or other loads. The towing weight at which the vehicle is rated is also given.

Seating: This figure represents the maximum number of seating positions equipped with safety belts. When more than one number is listed (for example, 5/6/7) it means that different models have different seat configurations.

Wheel Size: See what your choices are for wheel diameters. Remember—larger wheels raise the center of gravity of the vehicle and increase your risk of rolling over.

COMPETITION

Here we tell you how the vehicle stacks up with what is expected to be its competition. Use this information to compare the overall rating of similar vehicles and as a stepping off point to broaden your choice of new vehicle possibilities. This may help you select a more economical or better performing vehicle than the one you were originally considering. We've added page references so you can easily check out the details on the competition. In cases where a competing vehicle was not crash tested, we could not give it an overall rating—but check it out on the referenced page for further details. This list is meant as a guideline, not as an all inclusive list of every possible competitive choice.

Using the Ratings Pages

When using the ratings pages remember:

1. Blanks mean data unavailable.
2. Crash tests are not available for all vehicles—when the crash rating is missing, we cannot give an overall rating.
3. Use the competition table as a guide to other possible choices.
4. For various specifications, we have chosen the numbers for the model expected to be the most popular. However, other models may be available.
5. The price information is meant as a guideline. See page 92 for a great way to get the very best price.

Chevrolet Astro

Minivan

A completely refurbished interior makes the Astro look and feel more like the more modern GM minivans: the Lumina, Oldsmobile Silhouette and Pontiac Trans Sport. It now has dual airbags, which should greatly help its past poor government crash test results, and integrated child safety seats are now optional. 4-wheel ABS also comes standard.

The Astro comes standard with a 4.3-liter V6 and automatic overdrive which provides ample power; but gas mileage is poor, even for a minivan. Handling is sloppy, although the optional touring suspension will help. Ride is unsettling once you get off the highway. Getting in and out of the front seats is tricky. The seats are reasonably comfortable, but make sure you have enough leg room in the front. Both the payload and towing capacities are suitable for most of your demands. This vehicle is greatly outclassed by its rivals.

The Ratings

	POOR — GOOD
COMPARATIVE RATING	
CRASH TEST	
SAFETY FEATURES	
FUEL ECONOMY	
PM COST	
REPAIR COST	
WARRANTY	
COMPLAINTS	
INSURANCE COST	

Safety

CRASH TEST	No government results
SIDE CRASH PROTECT.	Weak
AIRBAGS	Dual
ANTI-LOCK BRAKES	4-wheel
BELT ADJUSTORS	Standard
BUILT-IN CHILD SEAT	Optional
OCCUPANT INJURY	Average

General Information

FUEL ECONOMY	16/21	Poor
DRIVING RANGE	486	Very Long
PARKING INDEX	Hard	
THEFT RATING	Good	
CORPORATE TWINS	GMC Safari	
WHERE MADE	U.S.	
YEAR OF PRODUCTION	Twelfth	

Specifications

LENGTH (in.)	189.8	Average
HEAD/LEG ROOM (in.)	39.2/41.6	Average
CARGO SPACE (cu. ft.)	152	Very Large
PAYLOAD	1950	Average
TOW RATING (lbs.)	5500	High
SEATING	5/8	
WHEEL SIZE (in.)	15	

Specifications may vary.

Prices

Model	Retail	Mkup
Astro CS Passenger Base	19,176	10%
Astro Cargo Base	18,592	10%
Astro Upfit Base	18,335	10%

Competition

	POOR — GOOD	Pg.
Chevrolet Astro		99
Ford Aerostar		112
Ford Windstar		118
Honda Odyssey		127
Toyota Previa		155

Chevrolet Blazer

Mid-Size Sport Utility

Completely redesigned last year, the Blazer receives minor changes for '96. Standard safety features include driver's side air bag, 4-wheel ABS and daytime running lamps. Like other Chevy's, the Blazer also comes with 100,000 mile coolant and spark plugs. Unfortunately, the Blazer performed badly in government crash tests.

Chevrolet hopes the more contemporary styling will enable the Blazer to better compete with the Ford Explorer and Jeep Grand Cherokee. While there is plenty interior space, the cargo room is on the skimpy side. The 4.3-liter V6 provides plenty of power. With two body styles (2- or 4-door), three trim levels (base, LS or LST), two drive types (2- or 4-wheel) and five suspension packages (from smooth riding to off-roading), the Blazer offers many options. Shop carefully to avoid buying options you don't want in order to get the ones you do want.

General Information

FUEL ECONOMY	18/24	Poor
DRIVING RANGE	380	Short
PARKING INDEX	Average	
THEFT RATING		
CORPORATE TWINS	Jimmy, Bravada	
WHERE MADE	U.S.	
YEAR OF PRODUCTION	Second	

Prices

Model	Retail	Mkup
Blazer 2-door (4x2)	19,444	10%
Blazer 4-door (4x2)	21,150	10%
Blazer 2-door (4x4)	21,204	10%
Blazer 4-door (4x4)	23,252	10%

The Ratings

	POOR — GOOD
COMPARATIVE RATING	
CRASH TEST	
SAFETY FEATURES	
FUEL ECONOMY	
PM COST	
REPAIR COST	
WARRANTY	
COMPLAINTS	
INSURANCE COST	

Safety

CRASH TEST	Very Poor
SIDE CRASH PROTECT.	Weak
AIRBAGS	Driver
ANTI-LOCK BRAKES	4-wheel
BELT ADJUSTORS	None
BUILT-IN CHILD SEAT	None
OCCUPANT INJURY	Average

Specifications

LENGTH (in.)	181.2	Short
HEAD/LEG ROOM (in.)	39.7/42.4	Roomy
CARGO SPACE (cu. ft.)	67	Small
PAYLOAD	1300	Low
TOW RATING (lbs.)	5000	Average
SEATING	6	
WHEEL SIZE (in.)	15	

Specifications may vary.

Competition

	POOR — GOOD	Pg.
Chevrolet Blazer		100
Ford Explorer		115
GMC Jimmy		119
Mits. Montero		143
Olds Bravada		147

Chevrolet Chevy Van/Chevy Express

Full Size Van

Though the big Chevy van has received some facelifts over the years, it hasn't undergone a major overhaul since its introduction back in 1971. The Chevy Van is for cargo, while the Sport Van is for people. For 1996, the interiors were redesigned and the wheelbase extended, increasing head and leg room. Standard safety features include 4-wheel ABS and dual airbags.

Last year's engines were updated for '96, including the addition of a 5.0-liter V8, a 5.7-liter V8, and a 6.5-liter V8 turbo diesel engine. With the standard V8, performance is adequate, but don't expect good gas mileage on this heavy vehicle which is not aerodynamic in the least. You can tow more than three tons and haul up to 12 people. A vehicle this large is very hard to park. Rather sloppy handling gives away the Chevy van's age, as do the controls and dashboard layout.

The Ratings	POOR → GOOD
COMPARATIVE RATING*	□□□□□□□□□□
CRASH TEST	□□□□□□□□□□
SAFETY FEATURES	□□□□□□■□□□
FUEL ECONOMY	□□■□□□□□□□
PM COST	□□□□■□□□□□
REPAIR COST	□□□□□□□□■□
WARRANTY	□■□□□□□□□□
COMPLAINTS	□□□□□□□□□□
INSURANCE COST	□□□□■□□□□□

Safety	
CRASH TEST	No government results
SIDE CRASH PROTECT.	Weak
AIRBAGS	Dual
ANTI-LOCK BRAKES	4-wheel
BELT ADJUSTORS	Standard
BUILT-IN CHILD SEAT	None
OCCUPANT INJURY	

General Information		
FUEL ECONOMY	15/19	Poor
DRIVING RANGE	496	Very Long
PARKING INDEX	Very Hard	
THEFT RATING		
CORPORATE TWINS	GMC Savana	
WHERE MADE	U.S.	
YEAR OF PRODUCTION	First	

Specifications		
LENGTH (in.)	218.8	Very Long
HEAD/LEG ROOM (in.)	40.6/41.2	Roomy
CARGO SPACE (cu. ft.)	260	Very Large
PAYLOAD	2000	Average
TOW RATING (lbs.)	6500	High
SEATING	8/12	
WHEEL SIZE (in.)	15/16	

Specifications may vary.

Prices

Model	Retail	Mkup
Van Base	18,899	14%
Van Extended	19,902	14%
Sportvan Base	21,881	14%
Sportvan Extended	22,786	14%

Competition

	POOR → GOOD	Pg.
Chevy Van/Express	□□□□□□□□□□	101
Dodge Ram Van	□□□□□□□□□□	111
Ford Aerostar	□□□□□□□■□□	112
Ford Econoline	□□□□■□□□□□	114
GMC Savana	□□□□□□□□□□	121

* Due to the importance of crash tests, vehicles with no results as of publication date cannot be given an overall rating.

Chevrolet C/K Series Pickup

Standard Pickup

Although the styling changes little, the C/K pickups have several additions that will keep it popular in the standard-size pickup market in 1996. A driver's side airbag and 4-wheel ABS are standard, as well as daytime running lamps.

There are several engines to choose from: a V6, three gasoline V8s, and two diesel V8s which can be teamed with 5-speed manual or 4-speed automatic transmissions. The engines have been refined for '96, giving them even more power. The standard 4.3-liter V6 now has 40 more horse-power than last year's standard engine. There are three cab sizes: regular, extended or crew, and two box sizes, Fleetside or Sportside pickup box. Also available is a new easy-access system on the 1500 extended-cab models—a new panel which acts like a third door. A good choice, if you can wade through the options list.

The Ratings

	POOR □□□□□□□□ GOOD
COMPARATIVE RATING	□□□□□□□□□■
CRASH TEST	□□□□□□□□■□
SAFETY FEATURES	□□□□■□□□□□
FUEL ECONOMY	□□□■□□□□□□
PM COST	□□□□■□□□□□
REPAIR COST	□□□□□□□□□■
WARRANTY	□■□□□□□□□□
COMPLAINTS	□□□□□□□□□■
INSURANCE COST	□□□□■□□□□□

Safety

CRASH TEST	Very Good
SIDE CRASH PROTECT.	Weak
AIRBAGS	Driver
ANTI-LOCK BRAKES	4-wheel
BELT ADJUSTORS	Standard
BUILT-IN CHILD SEAT	None
OCCUPANT INJURY	Very Good

General Information

FUEL ECONOMY	17/22	Poor
DRIVING RANGE	646	Very Long
PARKING INDEX	Hard	
THEFT RATING	Very Poor (4WD=Poor)	
CORPORATE TWINS	GMC Sierra	
WHERE MADE	U.S.	
YEAR OF PRODUCTION	Ninth	

Specifications

LENGTH (in.)	194.5	Long
HEAD/LEG ROOM (in.)	39.9/41.7	Roomy
CARGO SPACE (cu. ft.)		
PAYLOAD	2400	High
TOW RATING (lbs.)	7500	Very High
SEATING	2/6	
WHEEL SIZE (in.)	15/16	

Specifications may vary.

Prices

Model	Retail	Mkup
C1500 Fleetside Base	14,016	10%
C1500 Sportside Base	16,239	14%
K1500 Fleetside Base	17,621	10%
K1500 Sportside Base	18,893	14%
C/K Crew Cab (4WD)	24,284	14%

Competition

	POOR □□□□□□□□ GOOD	Pg.
Chevy C/K Series	□□□□□□□□□■	102
Dodge Ram Pickup	□□□□□□□□□□	110
Ford F-Series	□□□□□□□□■□	116
GMC Sierra	□□□□□□□□□■	122
Toyota T100	□□□□■□□□□□	157

Chevrolet Lumina Minivan

Minivan

The Lumina Minivan, which is the twin of the Pontiac Trans Sport and Oldsmobile Silhouette, receives very few changes for 1996. A driver's side airbag and 4-wheel ABS are standard, and traction control is optional.

New for 1996 is a more powerful standard engine. The old 3.1-liter is replaced this year with a 3.4-liter V6 which delivers 60 more horsepower than the previous year's engine. This new engine even beats the 3.8-liter V8 that was optional last year. Rear child seats are an excellent option, and you have your choice of one seat or two, but be careful that you don't end up paying for other options that you don't need. Ride is smooth on good roads, but handling is a bit sluggish. Driving position and visibility take some getting used to and interior space is a bit cramped. Center and rear seats are easy to remove and install, but there isn't as much cargo room as in other minivans.

General Information		
FUEL ECONOMY	19/26	Poor
DRIVING RANGE	420	Average
PARKING INDEX	Hard	
THEFT RATING	Average	
CORPORATE TWINS	Silhouette, Trans Sport	
WHERE MADE	U.S.	
YEAR OF PRODUCTION	Seventh	

Prices		
Model	**Retail**	**Mkup**
Lumina Minivan	19,890	10%

The Ratings	POOR — GOOD
COMPARATIVE RATING	
CRASH TEST	
SAFETY FEATURES	
FUEL ECONOMY	
PM COST	
REPAIR COST	
WARRANTY	
COMPLAINTS	
INSURANCE COST	

Safety	
CRASH TEST	Good
SIDE CRASH PROTECT.	Weak
AIRBAGS	Driver
ANTI-LOCK BRAKES	4-wheel
BELT ADJUSTORS	Standard
BUILT-IN CHILD SEAT	Optional (two)
OCCUPANT INJURY	

Specifications		
LENGTH (in.)	191.5	Long
HEAD/LEG ROOM (in.)	39.2/40.0	Cramped
CARGO SPACE (cu. ft.)	113	Large
PAYLOAD	1250	Low
TOW RATING (lbs.)	3000	Low
SEATING	7	
WHEEL SIZE (in.)	15	

Specifications may vary.

Competition	POOR — GOOD	Pg.
Chevrolet Lumina		103
Ford Windstar		118
Honda Odyssey		127
Olds Silhouette		148
Toyota Previa		155

Chevrolet S-Series Pickup

Compact Pickup

The S-Series pickup adds some major new features for 1996. A driver's airbag and daytime running lights, which increase other drivers' visibility of your vehicle, are both standard. 4-wheel ABS is also now standard. With the addition of these features, the S-Series is safer and much more attractive.

The standard 2.2-liter 4-cylinder engine is adequate for most needs, but you may want to get the new optional 4.3-liter V6 which is much more powerful. Fuel economy on the standard engine is just average. You'll have the choice of 2- or 4-wheel drive, regular or extended cab, base or LS trim level, and seven suspension packages, so there is much to choose from—be sure to do your homework. You will have ample head and leg room and the tow rating is high among compact pickups. With these new additions, the S-Series pickup positions itself nicely against its compact pickup competition.

The Ratings	POOR ... GOOD
COMPARATIVE RATING	□□□□□□■□□□
CRASH TEST	□□■□□□□□□□
SAFETY FEATURES	□□□■□□□□□□
FUEL ECONOMY	□□□□□■□□□□
PM COST	□□□□■□□□□□
REPAIR COST	□□□□□□□□□■
WARRANTY	□■□□□□□□□□
COMPLAINTS	□□□□□□□□□■
INSURANCE COST	□□□□■□□□□□

Safety	
CRASH TEST	Poor
SIDE CRASH PROTECT.	Weak
AIRBAGS	Driver
ANTI-LOCK BRAKES	4-wheel
BELT ADJUSTORS	None
BUILT-IN CHILD SEAT	None
OCCUPANT INJURY	Good

General Information		
FUEL ECONOMY	23/30	Average
DRIVING RANGE	494	Very Long
PARKING INDEX	Average	
THEFT RATING	Good	
CORPORATE TWINS	GMC Sonoma	
WHERE MADE	U.S.	
YEAR OF PRODUCTION	Third	

Specifications		
LENGTH (in.)	188.6	Average
HEAD/LEG ROOM (in.)	39.5/42.4	Roomy
CARGO SPACE (cu. ft.)		
PAYLOAD	1650	Low
TOW RATING (lbs.)	5500	High
SEATING	3	
WHEEL SIZE (in.)	15	

Specifications may vary.

Prices		
Model	**Retail**	**Mkup**
S10 Fleetside Base	11,070	6%
S10 LS Fleetside Ext. Cab	13,585	10%
T10 Fleetside Base	15,710	6%
T10 LS Fleetside Base	16,715	10%
T10 LS Fleetside Ext. Cab	18,215	10%

Competition	POOR ... GOOD	Pg.
Chevy S-Series	□□□□□□■□□□	104
Dodge Dakota	□□□□□□□□■□	109
Ford Ranger	□□□□□□■□□□	117
GMC Sonoma	□■□□□□□□□□	123
Mazda B-Series	□□□■□□□□□□	139

Chevrolet Suburban

Large Sport Utility

The Suburban is a 4-door station wagon version of a Chevrolet C/K pickup, and no other manufacturer offers anything quite like it. Daytime running lamps have been added to the already standard ABS and drivers side airbag.

Since an unloaded Suburban weighs close to 5,000 pounds, the standard 5.7-liter V8 has a lot of work to do. Optional engines include a 7.4-liter V8 and a 6.5-liter turbo-diesel V8; all engines come with 4-speed automatic overdrive. Gas mileage is dreary with the 5.7-liter, abysmal with the 7.4-liter. 4-wheel drive is available. The interior is spacious and can be quite comfortable, if you choose one of the interior upgrades. The Suburban is becoming more popular with the car pool set and offers a variety of seating options. Handling is sluggish, but you don't buy a Suburban for its handling—you buy it for its sheer size.

General Information		
FUEL ECONOMY	13/18	Very Poor
DRIVING RANGE	630	Very Long
PARKING INDEX	Very Hard	
THEFT RATING	Very Poor	
CORPORATE TWINS	GMC Suburban	
WHERE MADE	U.S./Mexico	
YEAR OF PRODUCTION	Fifth	

Prices		
Model	**Retail**	**Mkup**
Suburban C1500 (2WD)	24,682	14%
Suburban K1500 (4WD)	26,988	14%
Suburban C2500 (2WD)	25,910	14%
Suburban K2500 (4WD)	28,129	14%

The Ratings	POOR — GOOD
COMPARATIVE RATING	
CRASH TEST	
SAFETY FEATURES	
FUEL ECONOMY	
PM COST	
REPAIR COST	
WARRANTY	
COMPLAINTS	
INSURANCE COST	

Safety	
CRASH TEST	Very Good
SIDE CRASH PROTECT.	Weak
AIRBAGS	Driver
ANTI-LOCK BRAKES	4-wheel
BELT ADJUSTORS	Standard
BUILT-IN CHILD SEAT	None
OCCUPANT INJURY	Very Good

Specifications		
LENGTH (in.)	220.0	Very Long
HEAD/LEG ROOM (in.)	39.9/41.3	Average
CARGO SPACE (cu. ft.)	150	Very Large
PAYLOAD	2200	Average
TOW RATING (lbs.)	6500	High
SEATING	9	
WHEEL SIZE (in.)	15/16	

Specifications may vary.

Competition	POOR — GOOD	Pg.
Chevy Suburban		105
Ford Bronco		113
Ford Explorer		115
GMC Yukon		125
Mits. Montero		143

Chevrolet Tahoe

Large Sport Utility

Formerly called the Blazer, the Tahoe is Chevrolet's large sport utility vehicle and has little in common with this year's smaller Blazer. Despite the new name, the Tahoe is essentially unchanged, with the exception of a standard driver's side airbag. The Tahoe is available as a 2-door and a 4-door vehicle. ABS is standard and daytime running lamps are new.

Though the Tahoe shares its chassis with the C/K pickups, its engine choices and options list are quite limited. New for '96, the 2-door model is now available in 2-wheel drive as well as 4. The 4-door model will also offer 2- or 4-wheel drive. Your only engine choices are a 5.7-liter V8 or a weaker 6.5-liter turbo-diesel. Fuel economy is quite poor. Room is good in front, but it may be a squeeze in the back. In the rear, you'll have the choice of van-type panel doors or a pickup-like liftgate.

General Information

FUEL ECONOMY	14/17	Very Poor
DRIVING RANGE	450	Long
PARKING INDEX	Very Hard	
THEFT RATING		
CORPORATE TWINS	GMC Yukon	
WHERE MADE	U.S.	
YEAR OF PRODUCTION	Fifth	

Prices

Model	Retail	Mkup
Tahoe 2-door (2WD)	23,501	14%
Tahoe 2-door (4WD)	25,751	14%
Tahoe 4-door (2WD)	28,879	14%
Tahoe 4-door (4WD)	31,079	14%

The Ratings

	POOR — GOOD
COMPARATIVE RATING	
CRASH TEST	
SAFETY FEATURES	
FUEL ECONOMY	
PM COST	
REPAIR COST	
WARRANTY	
COMPLAINTS	
INSURANCE COST	

Safety

CRASH TEST	Average
SIDE CRASH PROTECT.	Weak
AIRBAGS	Driver
ANTI-LOCK BRAKES	4-wheel
BELT ADJUSTORS	Standard
BUILT-IN CHILD SEAT	None
OCCUPANT INJURY	

Specifications

LENGTH (in.)	199.1	Long
HEAD/LEG ROOM (in.)	39.9/41.7	Roomy
CARGO SPACE (cu. ft.)	123	Large
PAYLOAD	1650	Low
TOW RATING (lbs.)	7000	Very High
SEATING	6	
WHEEL SIZE (in.)	15/16	

Specifications may vary.

Competition

	POOR — GOOD	Pg.
Chevrolet Tahoe		106
Chevy Suburban		105
Ford Bronco		113
Ford Explorer		115
Mits. Montero		143

Chrysler Town and Country

Minivan

The Town and Country, all-new for 1996, is the luxury version of the new Dodge and Plymouth Grand minivans. This new design is likely to attract many luxury-oriented minivan buyers. For the extra money, you get lots of power equipment and the option of leather upholstery. The Town & Country seats seven, with four in captain's chairs. Dual airbags and ABS are standard and it also meets 1999 side impact protection standards.

The Town & Country offers a 3.8-liter V6 to go with the standard automatic overdrive, and gas mileage is among the lowest for minivans. All-wheel drive is optional. You can't get the "sport handling" package that's optional on the Grand Voyager, but if you want a firmer suspension, check out the trailer-towing package. Ride is comfortable on smooth roads. The built-in child restraints are an excellent option, but not available when you order leather seats.

The Ratings	POOR — GOOD
COMPARATIVE RATING*	
CRASH TEST	
SAFETY FEATURES	
FUEL ECONOMY	
PM COST	
REPAIR COST	
WARRANTY	
COMPLAINTS	
INSURANCE COST	

Safety	
CRASH TEST	No government results
SIDE CRASH PROTECT.	Strong
AIRBAGS	Dual
ANTI-LOCK BRAKES	4-wheel
BELT ADJUSTORS	Standard
BUILT-IN CHILD SEAT	Optional (two)
OCCUPANT INJURY	Very Good

General Information		
FUEL ECONOMY	17/24	Poor
DRIVING RANGE	400	Average
PARKING INDEX	Hard	
THEFT RATING		
CORPORATE TWINS	Gr. Caravan, Gr. Voyager	
WHERE MADE	U.S.	
YEAR OF PRODUCTION	First	

Specifications		
LENGTH (in.)	199.7	Long
HEAD/LEG ROOM (in.)	39.8/41.2	Average
CARGO SPACE (cu. ft.)	167	Very Large
PAYLOAD	1200	Low
TOW RATING (lbs.)	2000	Very Low
SEATING	7	
WHEEL SIZE (in.)	15	

Specifications may vary.

Prices

Model	Retail	Mkup
Town and Country LX (SWB)	23,905	10%
Town and Country (LWB)	23,960	10%
Town and Country LXi	29,420	11%

Competition

	POOR — GOOD	Pg.
Chrys. T and C		107
Chevy Lumina		103
Ford Windstar		118
Olds Silhouette		148
Toyota Previa		155

* Due to the importance of crash tests, vehicles with no results as of publication date cannot be given an overall rating.

Dodge Caravan

Minivan

The Caravan, all-new for 1996, will gain much deserved attention from minivan buyers. The new look still maintains much of the original feel, while bringing fresh new styling to a crowded minivan market. For '96, the Caravan comes with standard dual airbags, 4-wheel ABS and also meets 1999 government side impact standards. These safety features make the Caravan one of the safest minivans on the road.

The longer wheelbase and length of the Grand Caravan translates into more cargo room. The 4-cylinder engine is really not adequate—go for one of the three V6 engines to get more power with only a small sacrifice in fuel efficiency. Order the heavy duty suspension or "sport handling group" for improved cornering ability. The built-in child restraints are a great option. With its new design and added features, the Caravan is likely to remain at the top of the sales list for 1996.

General Information

FUEL ECONOMY	20/26	Average
DRIVING RANGE	440	Long
PARKING INDEX	Average	
THEFT RATING		
CORPORATE TWINS	Voyager, Town & Country	
WHERE MADE	U.S./Canada	
YEAR OF PRODUCTION	First	

Prices

Model	Retail	Mkup
Caravan Base	16,575	10%
Caravan SE	18,855	10%
Grand Caravan Base	17,825	10%
Grand Caravan SE	19,595	10%
Grand Caravan ES	24,205	11%

The Ratings

	POOR □□□ GOOD
COMPARATIVE RATING*	□□□□□□□□□□
CRASH TEST	□□□□□□□□□□
SAFETY FEATURES	□□□□□□□□□■
FUEL ECONOMY	□□□□■□□□□□
PM COST	□□□□□□□□■□
REPAIR COST	□□□□□□□■□□
WARRANTY	□■□□□□□□□□
COMPLAINTS	□□□□□□□□□□
INSURANCE COST	□□□□■□□□□□

Safety

CRASH TEST	No government results
SIDE CRASH PROTECT.	Strong
AIRBAGS	Dual
ANTI-LOCK BRAKES	4-wheel
BELT ADJUSTORS	Standard
BUILT-IN CHILD SEAT	Optional (two)
OCCUPANT INJURY	Good (4WD=Very Good)

Specifications

LENGTH (in.)	186.3	Average
HEAD/LEG ROOM (in.)	39.8/41.2	Average
CARGO SPACE (cu. ft.)	172	Very Large
PAYLOAD	1200	Low
TOW RATING (lbs.)	2000	Very Low
SEATING	7	
WHEEL SIZE (in.)	14/15	

Specifications may vary.

Competition

	POOR □□□ GOOD	Pg.
Dodge Caravan	□□□□□□□□□□	108
Chevy Lumina	□□□□□■□□□□	103
Ford Windstar	□□□□□□□□□■	118
Olds. Silhouette	□□□□□□□□■□	148
Toyota Previa	□□□□□□□■□□	155

* Due to the importance of crash tests, vehicles with no results as of publication date cannot be given an overall rating.

Dodge Dakota

Compact Pickup

The mid-size Dakota, which changes very little for 1996, bridges the gap between compact pickups like the Chevrolet S-10 and traditional large pickups like the Ford F-series. A driver's side airbag is still standard, dramatically improving driver protection. However, the standard ABS is only 2-wheel, not 4-wheel.

A weak 2.5-liter 4-cylinder is the standard engine. For heavier work, you'll be happier with the optional 3.9-liter V6 or Chrysler's 5.2-liter V8. You'll get average fuel economy with all of them. You'll have to choose between two- or four-wheel drive, short or long bed, manual or automatic transmission, regular or club cab, and several option packages. Ride is smoother than compact trucks, and handling is more responsive than larger pickups. Pay the extra money for 4-wheel ABS and you will have a much safer vehicle.

General Information

FUEL ECONOMY	21/25	Average
DRIVING RANGE	345	Very Short
PARKING INDEX	Hard	
THEFT RATING	Very Good	
CORPORATE TWINS		
WHERE MADE	U.S.	
YEAR OF PRODUCTION	Tenth	

Prices

Model	Retail	Mkup
Dakota WS 112 (2WD)	11,075	5%
Dakota WS 112 (4WD)	16,114	6%
Dakota WS 124 (4WD)	16,762	6%
Dakota Base Club Cab 131 (2WD)	16,251	6%
Dakota Base Club Cab 131 (4WD)	19,713	11%

The Ratings

	POOR → GOOD
COMPARATIVE RATING	□□□□□□□□■□
CRASH TEST	□□□□□□□□■□
SAFETY FEATURES	□□□■□□□□□□
FUEL ECONOMY	□□□□■□□□□□
PM COST	□□□□□■□□□□
REPAIR COST	□□□□□□□□□■
WARRANTY	□■□□□□□□□□
COMPLAINTS	□□□□□■□□□□
INSURANCE COST	□□□□■□□□□□

Safety

CRASH TEST	Very Good
SIDE CRASH PROTECT.	Weak
AIRBAGS	Driver
ANTI-LOCK BRAKES	2-whl. (4-whl.opt.)
BELT ADJUSTORS	None
BUILT-IN CHILD SEAT	None
OCCUPANT INJURY	Average

Specifications

LENGTH (in.)	189.0	Average
HEAD/LEG ROOM (in.)	39.5/41.8	Average
CARGO SPACE (cu. ft.)		
PAYLOAD	1250	Low
TOW RATING (lbs.)	2400	Low
SEATING	3	
WHEEL SIZE (in.)	15	

Specifications may vary.

Competition

	POOR → GOOD	Pg.
Dodge Dakota	□□□□□□□□■□	109
Chevrolet S-Series	□□□□□□■□□□	104
Ford Ranger	□□□□□□■□□□	117
GMC Sonoma	□■□□□□□□□□	123
Mazda B-Series	□□□■□□□□□□	139

Dodge Ram Pickup

Standard Pickup

The Ram pickup still has a very distinctive front end that sets it apart from the competition. It may, however, be this look that hurts it in sales when compared to its competition. A driver's side airbag is standard. ABS is standard only on the rear wheels, optional on all four wheels.

Engines range from a 3.9-liter V6, two V8's, a turbo diesel V6, and a thirsty 8.0-liter V10 which is a heavier version of the Dodge Viper's engine. All of these engines get poor gas mileage. An extended cab version is a new option which increases seating to six. Other choices to make include two other cab configurations, three trim levels, manual or automatic transmission, and two- or four-wheel drive. Both the payload and tow rating are average for this big pickup. Sit down before you scan the option list—it's expensive. The Ram has a hard time competing with the C/K Series and F-Series due to their excellent safety ratings.

General Information

FUEL ECONOMY	16/20	Poor
DRIVING RANGE	468	Long
PARKING INDEX	Hard	
THEFT RATING	Good	
CORPORATE TWINS		
WHERE MADE	U.S.	
YEAR OF PRODUCTION	Third	

Prices

Model	Retail	Mkup
1500 Reg. Cab SWB (2WD)	13,741	9%
1500 Reg. Cab SWB (4WD)	18,492	14%
2500 (2WD)	18,198	14%
2500 (4WD)	20,714	14%
3500 Club Cab LWB (4WD)	24,963	15%

The Ratings

	POOR — GOOD
COMPARATIVE RATING*	
CRASH TEST	
SAFETY FEATURES	
FUEL ECONOMY	
PM COST	
REPAIR COST	
WARRANTY	
COMPLAINTS	
INSURANCE COST	

Safety

CRASH TEST	No government results
SIDE CRASH PROTECT.	Weak
AIRBAGS	Driver
ANTI-LOCK BRAKES	2-whl. (4-whl.opt.)
BELT ADJUSTORS	None
BUILT-IN CHILD SEAT	None
OCCUPANT INJURY	Good (4WD=Vry. Gd.)

Specifications

LENGTH (in.)	204.1	Very Long
HEAD/LEG ROOM (in.)	40.2/41.0	Average
CARGO SPACE (cu. ft.)		
PAYLOAD	1900	Average
TOW RATING (lbs.)	4700	Average
SEATING	3/6	
WHEEL SIZE (in.)	16	

Specifications may vary.

Competition

	POOR — GOOD	Pg.
Dodge Ram Pickup		110
Chevy C/K Series		102
Ford F-Series		116
GMC Sierra		122
Toyota T100		157

* Due to the importance of crash tests, vehicles with no results as of publication date cannot be given an overall rating.

Dodge Ram Van/Ram Wagon

Full Size Van

Though its body has not changed significantly since its introduction in 1971, the Ram Van and Ram Wagon have a standard driver's airbag which Dodge hopes will improve their previously poor showing in the government crash tests. Also, 4-wheel ABS is optional on all vans and wagons. Both safety features help make these vehicles very attractive.

You can select from three payload options, three engines, and manual or automatic transmissions. Even on the highway, gas mileage will be poor; the 4-speed automatic is a little more efficient than the 3-speed. Ride on the shortest wheelbase models tends to be bouncy and uncomfortable. Chrysler has improved the van's instrument panel and controls over the years, but they're not up to today's best designs. You will find the cargo space to be very large at the expense of head and leg room. Check out the Ford Aerostar or Windstar before buying.

General Information		
FUEL ECONOMY	15/17	Poor
DRIVING RANGE	560	Very Long
PARKING INDEX	Hard	
THEFT RATING	Average	
CORPORATE TWINS		
WHERE MADE	Canada	
YEAR OF PRODUCTION	Twenty-sixth	

Prices		
Model	**Retail**	**Mkup**
Van 1500	16,253	10%
Van 2500	16,951	14%
Wagon 1500	18,738	10%
Wagon 2500	20,779	14%
Wagon 3500	21,980	15%

The Ratings	POOR — GOOD
COMPARATIVE RATING*	
CRASH TEST	
SAFETY FEATURES	
FUEL ECONOMY	
PM COST	
REPAIR COST	
WARRANTY	
COMPLAINTS	
INSURANCE COST	

Safety	
CRASH TEST	No government results
SIDE CRASH PROTECT.	Weak
AIRBAGS	Driver
ANTI-LOCK BRAKES	2-whl. (4-whl.opt.)
BELT ADJUSTORS	None
BUILT-IN CHILD SEAT	None
OCCUPANT INJURY	

Specifications		
LENGTH (in.)	187.2	Average
HEAD/LEG ROOM (in.)	40.5/39.0	Cramped
CARGO SPACE (cu. ft.)	207	Very Large
PAYLOAD	2550	High
TOW RATING (lbs.)	3500	Low
SEATING	8	
WHEEL SIZE (in.)	15/16	

Specifications may vary.

Competition	POOR — GOOD	Pg.
Dodge Ram Van/Wgn		111
Ford Aerostar		112
Ford Econoline		114
Ford Windstar		118
GMC Savana		121

* Due to the importance of crash tests, vehicles with no results as of publication date cannot be given an overall rating.

The Aerostar was scheduled to cease production in 1994, with the introduction of the Windstar, but it has been carried over into 1996 buoyed by continued steady sales. The Aerostar only comes with a driver airbag and rear-wheel ABS, two huge strikes against it.

The passenger van is actually called a wagon, while the cargo van is called a van. The wagon is available in rear-wheel drive regular- and extended-length, or 4WD extended-length. The 3-liter V6, standard on the rear-wheel drive models, is adequate. The 4-liter V6, standard on 4WD models and available on the rear-wheel-drive extended-length model, is slightly more powerful. Handling improves with 4WD, and ride is fairly good. Built-in child restraints are a noteworthy option. Watch out for the brakes, especially on wet roads. The Aerostar drives more like a van than a car, unlike most of its competition.

The Ratings	POOR — GOOD
COMPARATIVE RATING	□□□□□□□■□□
CRASH TEST	□□□□□■□□□□
SAFETY FEATURES	□□□■□□□□□□
FUEL ECONOMY	□□□■□□□□□□
PM COST	□□□□□□□□□■
REPAIR COST	□□□□□□□■□□
WARRANTY	□■□□□□□□□□
COMPLAINTS	□□□□□■□□□□
INSURANCE COST	□□□□□□□□□■

Safety	
CRASH TEST	Average
SIDE CRASH PROTECT.	Weak
AIRBAGS	Driver
ANTI-LOCK BRAKES	2-wheel
BELT ADJUSTORS	None
BUILT-IN CHILD SEAT	Optional
OCCUPANT INJURY	Average (4WD=Good)

General Information		
FUEL ECONOMY	18/24	Poor
DRIVING RANGE	420	Average
PARKING INDEX	Hard	
THEFT RATING	Very Good	
CORPORATE TWINS		
WHERE MADE	U.S.	
YEAR OF PRODUCTION	Twelfth	

Specifications		
LENGTH (in.)	174.9	Short
HEAD/LEG ROOM (in.)	39.5/41.4	Average
CARGO SPACE (cu. ft.)	141	Large
PAYLOAD	1850	Average
TOW RATING (lbs.)	4400	Average
SEATING	2/7	
WHEEL SIZE (in.)	14/15	

Specifications may vary.

Prices

Model	Retail	Mkup
Aerostar Van Regular (2WD)	17,190	10%
Aerostar Wgn Regular (2WD)	17,820	10%
Aerostar Wgn Extended (2WD)	21,120	11%
Aerostar Wgn Extended (4WD)	23,445	11%

Competition

	POOR — GOOD	Pg.
Ford Aerostar	□□□□□□□■□□	112
Chevy Lumina	□□□□□■□□□□	103
Ford Windstar	□□□□□□□□□■	118
Honda Odyssey	□□□□□■□□□□	127
Toyota Previa	□□□□□□□■□□	155

Ford Bronco

Large Sport Utility

The Bronco hasn't changed much since its last revision in 1980. A driver's airbag was added last year, improving the Bronco's already good driver protection in the government crash test program. Ford is introducing new technology this year as it replaces the conventional turn signals on the Bronco with "signal mirrors." These mirrors allow following drivers to see the turn indicator in the Bronco's side-view mirror, at the same time being invisible to the driver. Also, 4-wheel ABS comes standard.

Ford offers a 5-liter V8 and an optional 5.8-liter V8, both with plenty of power. Acceleration is peppier with the big engine; gas mileage with either V8 on this heavy vehicle is very poor. Handling, like the big Ford pickup's, is cumbersome, and the Bronco's relatively short wheelbase gives it a choppy ride. The Bronco only comes in a two door model.

The Ratings	POOR — GOOD
COMPARATIVE RATING	□□□□□□■□□□
CRASH TEST	□□□□□□□□□■
SAFETY FEATURES	□□□□□■□□□□
FUEL ECONOMY	□■□□□□□□□□
PM COST	□□□□□□□■□□
REPAIR COST	□■□□□□□□□□
WARRANTY	□■□□□□□□□□
COMPLAINTS	□□□□□■□□□□
INSURANCE COST	□□□□□□□□□■

Safety	
CRASH TEST	Very Good
SIDE CRASH PROTECT.	Strong
AIRBAGS	Driver
ANTI-LOCK BRAKES	4-wheel
BELT ADJUSTORS	None
BUILT-IN CHILD SEAT	None
OCCUPANT INJURY	

General Information		
FUEL ECONOMY	14/17	Very Poor
DRIVING RANGE	480	Very Long
PARKING INDEX	Easy	
THEFT RATING	Poor	
CORPORATE TWINS		
WHERE MADE	U.S.	
YEAR OF PRODUCTION	Seventeenth	

Specifications		
LENGTH (in.)	183.6	Average
HEAD/LEG ROOM (in.)	41.2/41.1	Roomy
CARGO SPACE (cu. ft.)	101	Large
PAYLOAD	1050	Very Low
TOW RATING (lbs.)	7000	Very High
SEATING	5/6	
WHEEL SIZE (in.)	15	

Specifications may vary.

Prices

Model	Retail	Mkup
Bronco XL	22,715	14%
Bronco XLT	25,470	14%
Bronco Eddie Bauer	28,540	15%

Competition	POOR — GOOD	Pg.
Ford Bronco	□□□□□□■□□□	113
Chevy Suburban	□□■□□□□□□□	105
Chevrolet Tahoe	□□□□■□□□□□	106
GMC Yukon	□□■□□□□□□□	125
Mits. Montero	□□□□□■□□□□	143

Ford Econoline/Club Wagon

Full Size Van

Although Ford restyled the Econoline and Club Wagon several years ago, the vehicles have not changed much since their introduction in 1974. The Econoline is for hauling cargo, and the Club Wagon is for carrying people. Ford led all van-makers with the addition of a driver's airbag in 1993, but still hasn't protected the passenger. The standard ABS operates on all four wheels.

Ford offers three payload options and four engines. The standard 6-cylinder has enough power for average use; but, for heavier duty, you may want one of the optional V8s. All come with automatic transmission. Though a bit more aerodynamic than its competitors, the Ford van is on the heavy side and thus not very fuel efficient. The Regular van seats 8, the Heavy Duty seats 12, and the Super seats 15. Ride is decent, but handling is cumbersome, though the optional handling package may help.

General Information

FUEL ECONOMY	14/15	Very Poor
DRIVING RANGE	490	Very Long
PARKING INDEX	Very Hard	
THEFT RATING	Very Good	
CORPORATE TWINS		
WHERE MADE	U.S.	
YEAR OF PRODUCTION	Twenty-second	

Prices

Model	Retail	Mkup
Econo. Van E-150 Reg. Cargo	17,545	14%
Econo. Van E-250 Reg. Cargo	17,970	14%
Club Wagon XL Base	19,695	14%
Club Wagon XLT Base	22,600	15%
Club Wagon Chateau Base	25,915	15%

The Ratings

	POOR — GOOD
COMPARATIVE RATING	
CRASH TEST	
SAFETY FEATURES	
FUEL ECONOMY	
PM COST	
REPAIR COST	
WARRANTY	
COMPLAINTS	
INSURANCE COST	

Safety

CRASH TEST	Average
SIDE CRASH PROTECT.	Weak
AIRBAGS	Driver
ANTI-LOCK BRAKES	4-wheel
BELT ADJUSTORS	None
BUILT-IN CHILD SEAT	None
OCCUPANT INJURY	

Specifications

LENGTH (in.)	211.8	Very Long
HEAD/LEG ROOM (in.)	42.3/40.3	Very Roomy
CARGO SPACE (cu. ft.)	255	Very Large
PAYLOAD	1350	Low
TOW RATING (lbs.)	6400	High
SEATING	7/8/12/15	
WHEEL SIZE (in.)	15/16	

Specifications may vary.

Competition

	POOR — GOOD	Pg.
Ford Econo./Club Wgn		114
Dodge Ram Van		111
Ford Aerostar		112
Ford Windstar		118
GMC Savana		121

Ford Explorer

Mid-Size Sport Utility

Little has changed on the exterior of the 1996 Ford Explorer; but, for the first time, a V8 engine is being offered that Ford hopes will keep the Explorer above the competition. The Explorer, all- new last year, has a contemporary front end, similar to the F-Series pickups. Most importantly, dual airbags and 4-wheel ABS are standard equipment.

The Explorer's standard engine is a 4-liter V6 with 5-speed manual or automatic overdrive, and 2- or part-time 4-wheel drive. New for this year is an optional 5.0-liter V8 which is available on 4-door models. This new V8 will add much more power with only a slight decrease in gas mileage. Gas mileage on the standard engine is better than larger utility vehicles. There are two body styles, 2- or 4-door; the 4-door has more room for adults in back. With the addition of the new engine, the Explorer is a great choice.

The Ratings

	POOR — GOOD
COMPARATIVE RATING	
CRASH TEST	
SAFETY FEATURES	
FUEL ECONOMY	
PM COST	
REPAIR COST	
WARRANTY	
COMPLAINTS	
INSURANCE COST	

Safety

CRASH TEST	Good
SIDE CRASH PROTECT.	Weak
AIRBAGS	Dual
ANTI-LOCK BRAKES	4-wheel
BELT ADJUSTORS	Standard
BUILT-IN CHILD SEAT	Optional
OCCUPANT INJURY	Very Good (2dr=Avg.)

General Information

FUEL ECONOMY	18/23	Poor
DRIVING RANGE	420	Average
PARKING INDEX	Average	
THEFT RATING		
CORPORATE TWINS		
WHERE MADE	U.S.	
YEAR OF PRODUCTION	Second	

Specifications

LENGTH (in.)	188.5	Average
HEAD/LEG ROOM (in.)	39.8/42.4	Roomy
CARGO SPACE (cu. ft.)	82	Average
PAYLOAD	950	Very Low
TOW RATING (lbs.)	5300	High
SEATING	5	
WHEEL SIZE (in.)	15/16	

Specifications may vary.

Prices

Model	Retail	Mkup
Explorer XL 2-door (2WD)	19,570	10%
Explorer XL 4-door (2WD)	20,970	10%
Explorer XL 2-door (4WD)	21,535	10%
Explorer XL 4-door (4WD)	22,890	10%
Explorer Eddie Bauer 4-dr. (4WD)	30,100	11%

Competition

	POOR — GOOD	Pg.
Ford Explorer		115
Chevrolet Blazer		100
GMC Jimmy		119
Mits. Montero		143
Olds Bravada		147

Ford F-Series Pickup

Standard Pickup

The F-Series pickup has not changed much since 1980, and it does not need to. For the past 13 years, it has been the highest selling vehicle—car or truck—in the country. A driver's airbag is standard, but there is still no passenger protection and ABS is inexplicably not available on the front wheels. But it does meet 1999 side impact protection standards.

Ford offers a 4.9-liter 6-cylinder, 3 gasoline V8s, and a beefed-up diesel V8 - all of which can be coupled with automatic or manual transmissions. The standard 6-cylinder is fairly powerful, and the electronic automatic is a good choice with any engine. Two- or four-wheel drive is available, as is a stretched "super cab" and a 4-door "crew cab" (F-350 only). Handling is typical for a large pickup: sluggish and cumbersome. Ride isn't bad on the F-150. The dashboard and controls are worse than on GM's trucks; they're illogical and old-fashioned. Otherwise, a good choice.

The Ratings

	POOR — GOOD
COMPARATIVE RATING	
CRASH TEST	
SAFETY FEATURES	
FUEL ECONOMY	
PM COST	
REPAIR COST	
WARRANTY	
COMPLAINTS	
INSURANCE COST	

Safety

CRASH TEST	Very Good
SIDE CRASH PROTECT.	Strong
AIRBAGS	Driver
ANTI-LOCK BRAKES	2-wheel
BELT ADJUSTORS	None
BUILT-IN CHILD SEAT	None
OCCUPANT INJURY	Vry. Gd. (1500 4WD=Gd.)

General Information

FUEL ECONOMY	15/19	Poor
DRIVING RANGE	309	Very Short
PARKING INDEX	Easy	
THEFT RATING	Average	
CORPORATE TWINS		
WHERE MADE	U.S./Canada	
YEAR OF PRODUCTION	Seventeenth	

Specifications

LENGTH (in.)	197.1	Long
HEAD/LEG ROOM (in.)	40.3/41.1	Average
CARGO SPACE (cu. ft.)		
PAYLOAD	2050	Average
TOW RATING (lbs.)	1900	Very Low
SEATING	3/5/6	
WHEEL SIZE (in.)	15/16	

Specifications may vary.

Prices

Model	Retail	Mkup
F-150 Reg. Cab (2WD)	14,075	9%
F-150 Reg. Cab (4WD)	16,890	10%
F-250 Reg.Cab Base (2WD)	15,685	14%
F-350 Reg. Cab Base (2WD)	17,810	14%
F-350 Crew Cab Base (2WD)	20,735	15%

Competition

	POOR — GOOD	Pg.
Ford F-Series		116
Chevy C/K Series		102
Dodge Ram Pickup		110
GMC Sierra		122
Toyota T100		157

Ford Ranger

Compact Pickup

The Ford Ranger enters its fourth year with some significant changes, the most important of which is an optional passenger side airbag to go along with its standard driver side airbag. The optional airbag has an added child-safety feature (first in U.S. auto history) which allows the airbag to be turned off when a rear-facing infant seat is in place. 4-wheel ABS is available and standard on 4x2 models with the optional 4-liter engine and on all 4x4 models.

The Ranger comes with a relatively weak 2.3-liter 4-cylinder engine. The available 3- or 4-liter V6s are better for serious load carrying. Inside you'll find a roomy interior but a low payload rating. To save some money, get the options you want in a complete package. The Splash has a "step-side" pickup box, but nothing useful you can't order on cheaper Rangers. The Super Cab is a longer version of the Ranger. Handling is typical of small pickups.

General Information

FUEL ECONOMY	22/27	Average
DRIVING RANGE	391	Average
PARKING INDEX	Hard	
THEFT RATING	Good	
CORPORATE TWINS	Mazda B-Series	
WHERE MADE	U.S.	
YEAR OF PRODUCTION	Fourth	

Prices

Model	Retail	Mkup
Ranger XL Reg. Cab (2WD)	10,555	5%
Ranger XL Reg. Cab (4WD)	15,695	6%
Ranger XL Supercab (2WD)	13,125	10%
Ranger XL Supercab (4WD)	17,570	11%
Ranger STX Supercab (4WD)	18,870	11%

The Ratings

	POOR — GOOD
COMPARATIVE RATING	
CRASH TEST	
SAFETY FEATURES	
FUEL ECONOMY	
PM COST	
REPAIR COST	
WARRANTY	
COMPLAINTS	
INSURANCE COST	

Safety

CRASH TEST	Good
SIDE CRASH PROTECT.	Weak
AIRBAGS	Dual (optional)
ANTI-LOCK BRAKES	2-whl. (4-whl.opt.)
BELT ADJUSTORS	Standard
BUILT-IN CHILD SEAT	None
OCCUPANT INJURY	Average

Specifications

LENGTH (in.)	184.3	Average
HEAD/LEG ROOM (in.)	39.1/42.4	Roomy
CARGO SPACE (cu. ft.)		
PAYLOAD	1550	Low
TOW RATING (lbs.)	1850	Very Low
SEATING	3	
WHEEL SIZE (in.)	14/15	

Specifications may vary.

Competition

	POOR — GOOD	Pg.
Ford Ranger		117
Chevrolet S-Series		104
Dodge Dakota		109
GMC Sonoma		123
Mazda B-Series		139

Ford Windstar

Minivan

Little has changed for 1996 on Ford's latest entry into the minivan market. Unfortunately for Ford, Chrysler is unveiling a new minivan this year and Ford will have its work cut out in order to keep sales up. The Windstar offers optional built-in child restraints; dual airbags and 4-wheel ABS are both standard and the Windstar meets 1999 government side impact protection standards.

The base GL comes standard with the same 3-liter V6 as is available on the Aerostar and Ranger. A 3.8-liter V6 is optional on the GL and standard on the LX, and it provides much more power. At over 200 inches, the Windstar is the longest minivan you can buy, and it has more interior room than a Grand Caravan, but not quite as much as a Toyota Previa. Most of that room is given to rear seat passengers. With its contemporary styling and decent handling, the Windstar provides a good challenge to the current generation of Chrysler minivans.

General Information		
FUEL ECONOMY	17/23	Poor
DRIVING RANGE	400	Average
PARKING INDEX	Hard	
THEFT RATING		
CORPORATE TWINS		
WHERE MADE	U.S.	
YEAR OF PRODUCTION	Second	

Prices		
Model	**Retail**	**Mkup**
Windstar Standard Van	18,270	10%
Windstar GL Wagon	19,590	10%
Windstar LX Wagon	24,465	11%

The Ratings	POOR □□□□□□□□□□ GOOD
COMPARATIVE RATING	□□□□□□□□□■
CRASH TEST	□□□□□□□□□■
SAFETY FEATURES	□□□□□□□□□■
FUEL ECONOMY	□□□■□□□□□□
PM COST	□□□□□□□□□■
REPAIR COST	□□□□■□□□□□
WARRANTY	□■□□□□□□□□
COMPLAINTS	□□□□□□□□□□
INSURANCE COST	□□□□■□□□□□

Safety	
CRASH TEST	Very Good
SIDE CRASH PROTECT.	Strong
AIRBAGS	Dual
ANTI-LOCK BRAKES	4-wheel
BELT ADJUSTORS	Standard
BUILT-IN CHILD SEAT	Optional
OCCUPANT INJURY	

Specifications		
LENGTH (in.)	201.2	Long
HEAD/LEG ROOM (in.)	39.3/41.8	Average
CARGO SPACE (cu. ft.)	144	Large
PAYLOAD	1800	Average
TOW RATING (lbs.)	3500	Low
SEATING	7	
WHEEL SIZE (in.)	15	

Specifications may vary.

Competition	POOR □□□□□□□□□□ GOOD	Pg.
Ford Windstar	□□□□□□□□□■	118
Chevy Lumina	□□□□□■□□□□	103
Honda Odyssey	□□□□□■□□□□	127
Olds Silhouette	□□□□□□□□■□	148
Toyota Previa	□□□□□□□■□□	155

GMC Jimmy

Mid-Size Sport Utility

The Jimmy, like its twin the Chevrolet Blazer, was all-new last year, and receives very few changes for 1996. Its similarity to the industry-leading Ford Explorer is no coincidence, although GMC considers the Jimmy to be a cleaner, more modern version of the Explorer. ABS is standard, and a driver's side airbag is finally available. It also now comes with optional daytime running lamps.

The Jimmy's 4.3-liter V6 is powerful enough. You'll have to choose between 2- and 4-door models, four different suspensions, and 2- or 4-wheel drive. The suspension packages go a long way towards tailoring the ride and handling to the customer's preference, one shortcoming of the previous Jimmy. There is plenty of room inside—it seats four comfortably, and you can squeeze up to six with the optional bench seat in front. With a very poor crash test, the Jimmy does not compete well with the Explorer.

General Information		
FUEL ECONOMY	17/22	Poor
DRIVING RANGE	361	Short
PARKING INDEX	Easy	
THEFT RATING		
CORPORATE TWINS	Blazer, Bravada	
WHERE MADE	U.S.	
YEAR OF PRODUCTION	Second	

Prices

Model	Retail	Mkup
Jimmy 2-door (2WD)	19,573	10%
Jimmy 4-door (2WD)	21,279	10%
Jimmy 2-door (4WD)	21,456	10%
Jimmy 4-door (4WD)	23,504	10%

The Ratings

	POOR ... GOOD (1–10)
COMPARATIVE RATING	1
CRASH TEST	2
SAFETY FEATURES	4
FUEL ECONOMY	4
PM COST	5
REPAIR COST	8
WARRANTY	2
COMPLAINTS	
INSURANCE COST	1

Safety	
CRASH TEST	Very Poor
SIDE CRASH PROTECT.	Weak
AIRBAGS	Driver
ANTI-LOCK BRAKES	4-wheel
BELT ADJUSTORS	None
BUILT-IN CHILD SEAT	None
OCCUPANT INJURY	Average

Specifications		
LENGTH (in.)	175.1	Short
HEAD/LEG ROOM (in.)	69.6/42.5	Very Roomy
CARGO SPACE (cu. ft.)	67	Small
PAYLOAD	1050	Very Low
TOW RATING (lbs.)	5000	Average
SEATING	4/6	
WHEEL SIZE (in.)	15	

Specifications may vary.

Competition

	POOR ... GOOD (1–10)	Pg.
GMC Jimmy	1	119
Chevrolet Blazer	1	100
Ford Explorer	10	115
Mits. Montero	6	143
Olds Bravada	2	147

GMC Safari

Minivan

With a completely refurbished interior the GMC Safari and its twin, the Chevrolet Astro, look and fell more like the more modern GM minivans: the Lumina, Oldsmobile Silhouette and Pontiac Trans Sport. The Safari now has dual airbags, which should greatly help its previously poor government crash test results, and integrated child safety seats are now optional.

The standard 4.3-liter V6 and automatic overdrive provide ample power, but gas mileage is poor, even for a minivan. Handling is sloppy, although the optional touring suspension will help. Ride is unsettling once you get off the highway. Like the Astro, the seats are reasonably comfortable, but make sure you have enough leg room in the front. Cargo space in the Safari competes well with other minivans. Even with its interior changes, this vehicle is greatly outclassed by its rivals.

The Ratings	POOR □□□□□□□□□□ GOOD
COMPARATIVE RATING*	□□□□□□□□□□
CRASH TEST	□□□□□□□□□□
SAFETY FEATURES	□□□□□□□■□□
FUEL ECONOMY	□□■□□□□□□□
PM COST	□□□□□□□■□□
REPAIR COST	□□□□□□□■□□
WARRANTY	□■□□□□□□□□
COMPLAINTS	□□□□□■□□□□
INSURANCE COST	□□□□□□□□□■

Safety	
CRASH TEST	No government results
SIDE CRASH PROTECT.	Weak
AIRBAGS	Dual
ANTI-LOCK BRAKES	4-wheel
BELT ADJUSTORS	Standard
BUILT-IN CHILD SEAT	Optional
OCCUPANT INJURY	Average

General Information		
FUEL ECONOMY	16/21	Poor
DRIVING RANGE	486	Very Long
PARKING INDEX	Hard	
THEFT RATING	Average	
CORPORATE TWINS	Chevrolet Astro	
WHERE MADE	U.S.	
YEAR OF PRODUCTION	Twelfth	

Specifications		
LENGTH (in.)	189.8	Average
HEAD/LEG ROOM (in.)	39.2/41.6	Average
CARGO SPACE (cu. ft.)	152	Very Large
PAYLOAD	1900	Average
TOW RATING (lbs.)	5500	High
SEATING	5/8	
WHEEL SIZE (in.)	15	

Specifications may vary.

Prices

Model	Retail	Mkup
Safari Cargo Base	18,405	10%
Safari Passenger Base	19,246	10%

Competition	POOR □□□□□□□□□□ GOOD	Pg.
GMC Safari	□□□□□□□□□□	120
Ford Aerostar	□□□□□□□■□□	112
Ford Windstar	□□□□□□□□□■	118
Honda Odyssey	□□□□□■□□□□	127
Toyota Previa	□□□□□□□■□□	155

* Due to the importance of crash tests, vehicles with no results as of publication date cannot be given an overall rating.

GMC Savana

Full Size Van

For 1996, GMC decided to change the name of the Vandura/Rally, a name that has been around for 15 years, to the Savana. The twin of the Chevy Van, the new Savana comes with a redesigned interior and exterior which gives it a freshened, more up-to-date appearance. Dual airbags are now standard, along with 4-wheel ABS, making this big van very attractive to consumers.

Much like the old Vandura/Rally, the Savana has many options, so be careful that you get only what you want. You can choose between five engines, two lengths, and two trim levels. The engines get typical gas mileage for a large van—very poor. Additionally, you have your choice of two different types of doors. The interior is comfortable and the passengers have good head and leg room. This all-new van should give the Chevy Van and Dodge Ram Van some competition.

The Ratings

	POOR — GOOD
COMPARATIVE RATING*	
CRASH TEST	
SAFETY FEATURES	
FUEL ECONOMY	
PM COST	
REPAIR COST	
WARRANTY	
COMPLAINTS	
INSURANCE COST	

Safety

CRASH TEST	No government results
SIDE CRASH PROTECT.	Weak
AIRBAGS	Dual
ANTI-LOCK BRAKES	4-wheel
BELT ADJUSTORS	Standard
BUILT-IN CHILD SEAT	None
OCCUPANT INJURY	

General Information

FUEL ECONOMY	13/17	Very Poor
DRIVING RANGE	465	Long
PARKING INDEX	Very Hard	
THEFT RATING		
CORPORATE TWINS	Chevy Van/Express Van	
WHERE MADE	U.S./Canada	
YEAR OF PRODUCTION	First	

Specifications

LENGTH (in.)	238.8	Very Long
HEAD/LEG ROOM (in.)	40.6/41.2	Roomy
CARGO SPACE (cu. ft.)	267	Very Large
PAYLOAD	3200	Very High
TOW RATING (lbs.)	8000	Very High
SEATING	15	
WHEEL SIZE (in.)	15/16	

Specifications may vary.

Prices

Model	Retail	Mkup
Savana Special	18,969	14%
Savana 3500	21,951	14%

Competition

	POOR — GOOD	Pg.
GMC Savana		121
Dodge Ram Van		111
Ford Aerostar		112
Ford Econoline		114
Pontiac Tr. Sport		150

* Due to the importance of crash tests, vehicles with no results as of publication date cannot be given an overall rating.

GMC Sierra

Standard Pickup

The Sierra gets some significant changes for 1996 that will make it a much more competitive standard size pickup. A driver airbag is standard, and the standard ABS is now on all four wheels. Also, daytime running lamps are now an option. The Sierra's performance in government crash tests will make it a more attractive choice.

With the addition of a side-access-panel for the extended cab models, the typical 2-door truck now has 3, making getting in and out easier. You'll have plenty of choices when buying a Sierra. You can choose between eight engines (a V6, three gasoline V8s and four diesel V8s), manual or automatic transmission, 2-or 4-wheel drive, three cab sizes, two box lengths, three trim levels and five stereos. Ride and handling are going to vary with the suspension choice. If you have the patience to wade carefully through the options list to personalize your Sierra, you should find something that meets your needs well.

The Ratings	POOR — GOOD
COMPARATIVE RATING	
CRASH TEST	
SAFETY FEATURES	
FUEL ECONOMY	
PM COST	
REPAIR COST	
WARRANTY	
COMPLAINTS	
INSURANCE COST	

Safety	
CRASH TEST	Very Good
SIDE CRASH PROTECT.	Weak
AIRBAGS	Driver
ANTI-LOCK BRAKES	4-wheel
BELT ADJUSTORS	Standard
BUILT-IN CHILD SEAT	None
OCCUPANT INJURY	Very Good

General Information		
FUEL ECONOMY	17/22	Poor
DRIVING RANGE	646	Very Long
PARKING INDEX	Very Hard	
THEFT RATING	Average	
CORPORATE TWINS	Chevrolet C/K Series	
WHERE MADE	U.S./Canada	
YEAR OF PRODUCTION	Ninth	

Specifications		
LENGTH (in.)	213.4	Very Long
HEAD/LEG ROOM (in.)	39.9/41.7	Roomy
CARGO SPACE (cu. ft.)		
PAYLOAD	1950	Average
TOW RATING (lbs.)	7500	Very High
SEATING	3	
WHEEL SIZE (in.)	15/16	

Specifications may vary.

Prices

Model	Retail	Mkup
Sierra 1500 Reg. Cab Base (2WD)	14,086	10%
Sierra 2500 Reg. Cab Base (2WD)	16,953	14%
Sierra 3500 Reg. Cab Base (2WD)	18,156	14%
Sierra Crew Cab Base (2WD)	21,290	14%
Sierra Chassis Cab Base (2WD)	17,638	14%

Competition

	POOR — GOOD	Pg.
GMC Sierra		122
Chevy C/K Series		102
Dodge Ram Pickup		110
Ford F-Series		116
Toyota T100		157

GMC Sonoma

Compact Pickup

The Sonoma, GM's entrant into the compact pickup class, comes with minor changes in 1996. It now has an optional side-access-panel which will make getting in and out of the small back seats easier. This panel acts as a third door, however, it can only be opened when the passenger door is open. A driver's side airbag is standard as is 4-wheel ABS.

The Sonoma's 2.2-liter 4-cylinder engine, which is only available on the 2-wheel drive models, may be OK for some buyers. Head and leg room is good. You should consider one of two 4.3-liter V6 engine options if you anticipate doing much hauling, although your gas mileage will suffer if you choose the large engines. You'll have to choose between manual or automatic transmission, two cab sizes, two box sizes, three wheelbases, 2- or 4-wheel drive and seven suspension packages. Many of the option packages offer significant discounts, so make sure you look at everything.

General Information

FUEL ECONOMY	18/25	Poor
DRIVING RANGE	399	Average
PARKING INDEX	Hard	
THEFT RATING		
CORPORATE TWINS	Chevrolet S-Series	
WHERE MADE	U.S.	
YEAR OF PRODUCTION	Third	

Prices

Model	Retail	Mkup
Sonoma Reg. Cab Base (2WD)	11,090	6%
Sonoma Reg. Cab Base (4WD)	15,730	6%
Sonoma Club Coupe (2WD)	13,852	10%
Sonoma Club Coupe (4WD)	18,482	10%

The Ratings

	POOR — GOOD
COMPARATIVE RATING	
CRASH TEST	
SAFETY FEATURES	
FUEL ECONOMY	
PM COST	
REPAIR COST	
WARRANTY	
COMPLAINTS	
INSURANCE COST	

Safety

CRASH TEST	Poor
SIDE CRASH PROTECT.	Weak
AIRBAGS	Driver
ANTI-LOCK BRAKES	4-wheel
BELT ADJUSTORS	None
BUILT-IN CHILD SEAT	None
OCCUPANT INJURY	Average (4WD=Good)

Specifications

LENGTH (in.)	205.0	Very Long
HEAD/LEG ROOM (in.)	39.5/42.4	Roomy
CARGO SPACE (cu. ft.)		
PAYLOAD	1600	Low
TOW RATING (lbs.)	5500	High
SEATING	3	
WHEEL SIZE (in.)	15	

Specifications may vary.

Competition

	POOR — GOOD	Pg.
GMC Sonoma		123
Chevrolet S-Series		104
Dodge Dakota		109
Ford Ranger		117
Mazda B-Series		139

GMC Suburban

Large Sport Utility

The Suburban is a 4-door station wagon version of the GMC Sierra Pickup, and no other manufacturer offers anything quite like it. It is the twin of the Chevrolet Suburban, which is based on the Chevrolet C/K Series Pickup. Daytime running lamps have been added to the already standard ABS and driver airbag.

Since an unloaded Suburban weighs close to 5,000 pounds, the standard 5.7-liter V8 has a lot of work to do. Optional engines include a 7.4-liter V8 and a 6.5-liter turbo-diesel V8; all engines come with 4-speed automatic overdrive. Gas mileage is dreary with the 5.7-liter, abysmal with the 7.4-liter. 4-wheel drive is available. The Suburban is becoming more popular with the car pool set and offers a variety of seating options. You can tow more than three tons. Handling is sluggish, but you don't buy a Suburban for its handling—you buy it for its sheer size.

The Ratings	POOR ← → GOOD
COMPARATIVE RATING	□□□■□□□□□□
CRASH TEST	□□□□□□□□■□
SAFETY FEATURES	□□□□■□□□□□
FUEL ECONOMY	□□■□□□□□□□
PM COST	□□□□■□□□□□
REPAIR COST	□□□□□□□□□■
WARRANTY	□■□□□□□□□□
COMPLAINTS	■□□□□□□□□□
INSURANCE COST	□□□□□□□□□■

Safety	
CRASH TEST	Very Good
SIDE CRASH PROTECT.	Weak
AIRBAGS	Driver
ANTI-LOCK BRAKES	4-wheel
BELT ADJUSTORS	Standard
BUILT-IN CHILD SEAT	None
OCCUPANT INJURY	Very Good

General Information		
FUEL ECONOMY	13/18	Poor
DRIVING RANGE	672	Very Long
PARKING INDEX	Very Hard	
THEFT RATING	Very Poor	
CORPORATE TWINS	Chevrolet Suburban	
WHERE MADE	U.S.	
YEAR OF PRODUCTION	Fifth	

Specifications		
LENGTH (in.)	220.0	Very Long
HEAD/LEG ROOM (in.)	39.9/41.3	Average
CARGO SPACE (cu. ft.)	150	Very Large
PAYLOAD	2200	Average
TOW RATING (lbs.)	6600	High
SEATING	9	
WHEEL SIZE (in.)	15/16	

Specifications may vary.

Prices		
Model	**Retail**	**Mkup**
Suburban 1500 (2WD)	24,027	14%
Suburban 2500 (2WD)	25,259	14%
Suburban 1500 (4WD)	26,337	14%
Suburban 2500 (4WD)	27,487	14%

Competition	POOR ← → GOOD	Pg.
GMC Suburban	□□□■□□□□□□	124
Ford Bronco	□□□□□□■□□□	113
Isuzu Trooper	□□□□□□□□□□	132
Jeep Gr. Cherokee	□□□□□□□□□□	134
Mits. Montero	□□□□□■□□□□	143

GMC Yukon

Large Sport Utility

The Yukon, the upscale twin of the full-size Chevrolet Tahoe, has minor changes for 1996. The Yukon is designed to be a smaller version of the large Suburban. Daytime running lamps are now standard, along with 4-wheel ABS and a driver's side airbag.

Like the Tahoe, the Yukon has a shorter list of engines and options than the full-size pickups they share a chassis with. Choose between a 5.7-liter V8 and a 6.5-liter turbo-diesel V8, with either a manual or automatic transmission. Ride is rough on anything but smooth roads. Handling is more responsive than many smaller utility vehicles, but it's certainly no sports car. Comfort inside is average and you should have plenty of head and leg room. Choose between two or four doors and 2- or 4-wheel drive. The Yukon does not compete very well with the Ford Bronco.

General Information

FUEL ECONOMY	14/17	Very Poor
DRIVING RANGE	450	Long
PARKING INDEX	Average	
THEFT RATING	Very Poor	
CORPORATE TWINS	Chevrolet Tahoe	
WHERE MADE	U.S.	
YEAR OF PRODUCTION	Fifth	

Prices

Model	Retail	Mkup
Yukon 2-door (2WD)	19,573	14%
Yukon 4-door (2WD)	21,279	14%
Yukon 2-door (4WD)	21,456	14%
Yukon 4-door (4WD)	23,504	14%

The Ratings

	POOR — GOOD
COMPARATIVE RATING	
CRASH TEST	
SAFETY FEATURES	
FUEL ECONOMY	
PM COST	
REPAIR COST	
WARRANTY	
COMPLAINTS	
INSURANCE COST	

Safety

CRASH TEST	Average
SIDE CRASH PROTECT.	Weak
AIRBAGS	Driver
ANTI-LOCK BRAKES	4-wheel
BELT ADJUSTORS	Standard
BUILT-IN CHILD SEAT	None
OCCUPANT INJURY	Very Good

Specifications

LENGTH (in.)	188.5	Average
HEAD/LEG ROOM (in.)	39.9/41.9	Roomy
CARGO SPACE (cu. ft.)	99	Average
PAYLOAD	1500	Low
TOW RATING (lbs.)	7000	Very High
SEATING	6	
WHEEL SIZE (in.)	16	

Specifications may vary.

Competition

	POOR — GOOD	Pg.
GMC Yukon		125
Chevy Suburban		105
Ford Bronco		113
Ford Explorer		115
Mits. Montero		143

The Tracker, only available as a 2-door, is almost identical to the Suzuki Sidekick. Unlike the Sidekick, which only comes with a soft top, the Tracker is available either as a hardtop or a convertible. For 1996, new safety features include dual airbags and optional 4-wheel ABS.

The only two-wheel drive model is a base convertible; four-wheel drive models are available as convertibles or hardtops. All Trackers get a 1.6-liter 4-cylinder engine, although there is a peppier version on four-wheel drive models and on two-wheel drive models in states with relaxed emissions standards. The ride is on the stiff side, but tolerable on smooth roads. Accommodations are okay up front, but it is a tight squeeze for two in the back and you'll find the cargo space skimpy. Don't take turns too tightly in this vehicle—it's too narrow and high off the ground to handle sudden movements.

The Ratings

	POOR ... GOOD
COMPARATIVE RATING	□□□□■□□□□□
CRASH TEST	□□■□□□□□□□
SAFETY FEATURES	□□□□□■□□□□
FUEL ECONOMY	□□□□□■□□□□
PM COST	□□□□□□□□■□
REPAIR COST	□■□□□□□□□□
WARRANTY	□■□□□□□□□□
COMPLAINTS	□□□□□□□□■□
INSURANCE COST	■□□□□□□□□□

Safety

CRASH TEST	Poor
SIDE CRASH PROTECT.	Weak
AIRBAGS	Dual
ANTI-LOCK BRAKES	4-wheel (optional)
BELT ADJUSTORS	None
BUILT-IN CHILD SEAT	None
OCCUPANT INJURY	Very Poor

General Information

FUEL ECONOMY	24/26	Average
DRIVING RANGE	278	Very Short
PARKING INDEX	Very Easy	
THEFT RATING	Very Poor (4WD=Poor)	
CORPORATE TWINS	Suzuki Sidekick	
WHERE MADE	Canada	
YEAR OF PRODUCTION	Eighth	

Specifications

LENGTH (in.)	142.5	Very Short
HEAD/LEG ROOM (in.)	39.5/42.1	Roomy
CARGO SPACE (cu. ft.)	33	Very Small
PAYLOAD	850	Very Low
TOW RATING (lbs.)	1000	Very Low
SEATING	4	
WHEEL SIZE (in.)	15	

Specifications may vary.

Prices

Model	Retail	Mkup
Tracker Hardtop Base (2WD)	14,570	5%
Tracker Hardtop Base (4WD)	15,320	5%
Tracker LSi Hardtop (2WD)	14,970	5%
Tracker Conv. Base (2WD)	13,870	5%
Tracker Conv. Base (4WD)	14,450	5%

Competition

	POOR ... GOOD	Pg.
Geo Tracker	□□□□■□□□□□	126
Jeep Cherokee	□□□■□□□□□□	133
Kia Sportage	□□□□□□□□□□	136
Suzuki X-90	□□□□□□□□□□	152
Toyota RAV4	□□□□□□□□□□	156

Honda Odyssey

Minivan

The Odyssey enters '96 with no major changes. This front-wheel drive vehicle is different than most other minivans in many respects. It is lower than, but not as wide as, other minivans, making it easier to maneuver. The most striking feature about the Odyssey is that it has two sedan-type doors for access to the rear seats, while most minivans have only one sliding door. Dual airbags and ABS are standard. The Odyssey meets 1999 side impact standards for trucks and vans.

Honda is rumored to be introducing a V6 on the Odyssey for next year's model, but for now, it gets the same 2.2-liter 4-cylinder engine found on the Accord. The middle bench seat doesn't come out, and the rear seat, which cleverly folds into the floor of the cargo bay, doesn't quite become flush with the floor, making the loading surface uneven. As a result, cargo space is not quite as generous as the competition.

General Information		
FUEL ECONOMY	20/24	Average
DRIVING RANGE	378	Short
PARKING INDEX	Average	
THEFT RATING		
CORPORATE TWINS		
WHERE MADE	Japan	
YEAR OF PRODUCTION	Second	

Prices		
Model	**Retail**	**Mkup**
Odyssey LX 7 passenger	23,560	15%
Odyssey LX 6 passenger	23,970	13%
Odyssey EX	25,550	13%

The Ratings	POOR → GOOD
COMPARATIVE RATING	□□□□□■□□□□
CRASH TEST	□□□□□□□■□□
SAFETY FEATURES	□□□□□□□□■□
FUEL ECONOMY	□□□□■□□□□□
PM COST	□□■□□□□□□□
REPAIR COST	□□□□■□□□□□
WARRANTY	■□□□□□□□□□
COMPLAINTS	□□□□□□□□□□
INSURANCE COST	□□□□■□□□□□

Safety	
CRASH TEST	Good
SIDE CRASH PROTECT.	Strong
AIRBAGS	Dual
ANTI-LOCK BRAKES	4-wheel
BELT ADJUSTORS	Standard
BUILT-IN CHILD SEAT	None
OCCUPANT INJURY	

Specifications		
LENGTH (in.)	187.2	Average
HEAD/LEG ROOM (in.)	40.1/40.7	Average
CARGO SPACE (cu. ft.)	103	Large
PAYLOAD		
TOW RATING (lbs.)	2000	Very Low
SEATING	7	
WHEEL SIZE (in.)	15	

Specifications may vary.

Competition	POOR → GOOD	Pg.
Honda Odyssey	□□□□□■□□□□	127
Chevy Lumina	□□□□□■□□□□	103
Ford Windstar	□□□□□□□□□■	118
Olds Sihouette	□□□□□□□□■□	148
Toyota Previa	□□□□□□□■□□	155

Honda Passport

Mid-Size Sport Utility

The 1996 Passport, which is basically an Isuzu Rodeo with the Honda name, will not be released until early 1996. Until then, the '95 (pictured) will continue to be sold. The Passport represents Honda's first U.S. light truck entry in this country. Airbags are not available in the 1995 model, but are expected for 1996. ABS only operated on the rear wheels in 1995 and is also expected to be improved.

The base DX is only available with two-wheel drive, a manual transmission, and a weak 2.6-liter 4-cylinder engine. The mid-level LX comes with a more powerful 3.2-liter V6 and offers two- or four-wheel drive, and manual or automatic transmission. The up-level EX comes with the larger engine, but only with four-wheel drive. One would hope that Honda will pick a better vehicle to market, or build a better one themselves, next time.

The Ratings

	POOR — GOOD (scale of 10)
COMPARATIVE RATING*	
CRASH TEST	
SAFETY FEATURES	6
FUEL ECONOMY	3
PM COST	5
REPAIR COST	9
WARRANTY	1
COMPLAINTS	3
INSURANCE COST	5

Safety

CRASH TEST	No government results
SIDE CRASH PROTECT.	Weak
AIRBAGS	Dual
ANTI-LOCK BRAKES	2-whl. (4-whl.opt.)
BELT ADJUSTORS	None
BUILT-IN CHILD SEAT	None
OCCUPANT INJURY	

General Information

FUEL ECONOMY	16/19	Poor
DRIVING RANGE	372	Short
PARKING INDEX	Average	
THEFT RATING		
CORPORATE TWINS	Isuzu Rodeo	
WHERE MADE	U.S.	
YEAR OF PRODUCTION	Third	

Specifications

LENGTH (in.)	176.5	Short
HEAD/LEG ROOM (in.)	38.0/42.5	Average
CARGO SPACE (cu. ft.)	75	Small
PAYLOAD	2000	Average
TOW RATING (lbs.)	2000	Very Low
SEATING	6	
WHEEL SIZE (in.)	15/16	

Specifications may vary.

Prices**

Model	Retail	Mkup
Passport DX (2WD)	16,610	15%
Passport LX (2WD)	20,015	15%
Passport LX (4WD)	22,680	15%
Passport EX (4WD)	25,780	15%

Competition

	POOR — GOOD (scale of 10)	Pg.
Honda Passport		128
Chevrolet Blazer	1	100
Ford Explorer	10	115
Jeep Cherokee	4	133
Mits. Montero	6	143

** 1996 prices not available at press time. Prices based on 1995 data.

* Due to the importance of crash tests, vehicles with no results as of publication date cannot be given an overall rating.

Isuzu Hombre

Compact Pickup

Because of slumping sales and an outdated look, Isuzu has decided to redesign its Pickup and name it, the Hombre. The Hombre will come with much fewer options than the Pickup did—at least in its first year of production. It finally comes with an airbag, but only on the driver's side, and an optional ABS system.

There is only one engine choice: a 2.2-liter 4-cylinder, which will not allow you to do much towing or hauling of heavy payloads. The seats are not that comfortable and the ride is only good on smooth roads. Payload and tow ratings are low compared to other compact pickups. The only notable options include air conditioning and a better radio. It looks as though the replacement of the Pickup may not be much of an improvement and will not offer substantial competition to the Ford Ranger, Dodge Dakota, or the Chevy S-Series.

The Ratings	POOR — GOOD
COMPARATIVE RATING*	
CRASH TEST	
SAFETY FEATURES	
FUEL ECONOMY	
PM COST	
REPAIR COST	
WARRANTY	
COMPLAINTS	
INSURANCE COST	

Safety	
CRASH TEST	No government results
SIDE CRASH PROTECT.	Weak
AIRBAGS	Driver
ANTI-LOCK BRAKES	4-wheel (optional)
BELT ADJUSTORS	None
BUILT-IN CHILD SEAT	None
OCCUPANT INJURY	Average

General Information		
FUEL ECONOMY	23/30	Average
DRIVING RANGE	494	Very Long
PARKING INDEX	Average	
THEFT RATING		
CORPORATE TWINS		
WHERE MADE	Japan	
YEAR OF PRODUCTION	First	

Specifications		
LENGTH (in.)	189.0	Average
HEAD/LEG ROOM (in.)	39.5/42.4	Roomy
CARGO SPACE (cu. ft.)		
PAYLOAD	1650	Low
TOW RATING (lbs.)	2000	Very Low
SEATING	2	
WHEEL SIZE (in.)	14/15	

Specifications may vary.

Prices

Model	Retail	Mkup
Prices unavailable at press time.		
Expected range: $10-16,000		

Competition

	POOR — GOOD	Pg.
Isuzu Hombre		129
Chevrolet S-Series		104
Dodge Dakota		109
Ford Ranger		117
Mazda B-Series		139

* Due to the importance of crash tests, vehicles with no results as of publication date cannot be given an overall rating.

Isuzu Oasis

Minivan

The first minivan entrant for Isuzu is not really Isuzu's creation, but Honda's. Just as Honda sells Isuzu's Rodeo as the Passport, Isuzu now sells Honda's Odyssey as the Oasis. Like the Odyssey, the Oasis is designed to be more like a car than a minivan. With a wide stance and low ground clearance, the Oasis drives much like a car and also has conventional doors instead of a sliding door like the rest of its minivan competition. Dual airbags and ABS are standard.

The power comes from a 2.2-liter 4-cylinder engine which delivers only adequate power, but unfortunately, there are no other engine choices. The middle seat in the Oasis does not come out, and the rear seat cleverly folds into the floor, but not quite flush, making the loading surface uneven. As a result, cargo space is not as generous as the competition.

The Ratings	
	POOR □□□□□□□□ GOOD
COMPARATIVE RATING*	□□□□□□□□□□
CRASH TEST	□□□□□□□□□□
SAFETY FEATURES	□□□□□□■□□□
FUEL ECONOMY	□□□□■□□□□□
PM COST	□□■□□□□□□□
REPAIR COST	□□□□■□□□□□
WARRANTY	□□□□□□■□□□
COMPLAINTS	□□□□□□□□□□
INSURANCE COST	□□□□■□□□□□

Safety	
CRASH TEST	No government results
SIDE CRASH PROTECT.	Weak
AIRBAGS	Dual
ANTI-LOCK BRAKES	4-wheel
BELT ADJUSTORS	Standard
BUILT-IN CHILD SEAT	None
OCCUPANT INJURY	

General Information		
FUEL ECONOMY	20/24	Average
DRIVING RANGE	378	Short
PARKING INDEX	Average	
THEFT RATING		
CORPORATE TWINS		
WHERE MADE	Japan	
YEAR OF PRODUCTION	First	

Specifications		
LENGTH (in.)	187.2	Average
HEAD/LEG ROOM (in.)	40.1/40.7	Average
CARGO SPACE (cu. ft.)	103	Large
PAYLOAD		
TOW RATING (lbs.)	2000	Very Low
SEATING	7	
WHEEL SIZE (in.)	14/15	

Specifications may vary.

Prices		
Model	**Retail**	**Mkup**
Prices unavailable at press time.		
Expected range: $25-28,000		

Competition		
	POOR □□□□□□□□ GOOD	**Pg.**
Isuzu Oasis	□□□□□□□□□□	130
Chevy Lumina	□□□□□■□□□□	103
Ford Windstar	□□□□□□□□□■	118
Honda Odyssey	□□□□□■□□□□	127
Toyota Previa	□□□□□□□■□□	155

* Due to the importance of crash tests, vehicles with no results as of publication date cannot be given an overall rating.

The Rodeo, built on the Isuzu pickup's body and chassis, is basically a four-door Amigo station wagon. New for 1996 are standard dual airbags, which should help it score well in future government crash tests. It comes standard with 2-wheel ABS, 4-wheel is optional.

The 2.6-liter, 120-hp 4-cylinder engine, available only on manual transmission two-wheel drive Rodeos, is completely inadequate. The optional 3.2-liter, 190-hp V6 is more powerful. Fuel economy with both engines is poor. There is a lot of racket inside and handling is also poor. If you need to carry four people, you'll find more room inside the Rodeo than in the past Amigo; however, head and leg room will still be tight. The sloping roof cuts rear cargo space and the instrument panel has some weird buttons for the lights and wipers. A new improved suspension should help improve the ride.

The Ratings	POOR □□□□□□□□ GOOD
COMPARATIVE RATING*	□□□□□□□□□□
CRASH TEST	□□□□□□□□□□
SAFETY FEATURES	□□□□□■□□□□
FUEL ECONOMY	□□■□□□□□□□
PM COST	□□□□■□□□□□
REPAIR COST	□□□□□□□□■□
WARRANTY	□□□□□□■□□□
COMPLAINTS	□□□□■□□□□□
INSURANCE COST	□□□□■□□□□□

Safety	
CRASH TEST	No government results
SIDE CRASH PROTECT.	Weak
AIRBAGS	Dual
ANTI-LOCK BRAKES	2-whl. (4-whl.opt.)
BELT ADJUSTORS	None
BUILT-IN CHILD SEAT	None
OCCUPANT INJURY	Average

General Information		
FUEL ECONOMY	15/18	Poor
DRIVING RANGE	350	Very Short
PARKING INDEX	Average	
THEFT RATING	Average	
CORPORATE TWINS	Honda Passport	
WHERE MADE	U.S.	
YEAR OF PRODUCTION	Sixth	

Specifications		
LENGTH (in.)	176.5	Short
HEAD/LEG ROOM (in.)	38.6/41.2	Cramped
CARGO SPACE (cu. ft.)	75	Small
PAYLOAD	900	Very Low
TOW RATING (lbs.)	4500	Average
SEATING	5	
WHEEL SIZE (in.)	15/16	

Specifications may vary.

Prices

Model	Retail	Mkup
Rodeo S 4-cylinder Man. (2WD)	16,990	11%
Rodeo S V6 Auto. (2WD)	20,820	14%
Rodeo S V6 Man. (4WD)	21,740	15%
Rodeo S V6 Auto. (4WD)	22,890	15%
Rodeo LS V6 Man. (4WD)	26,310	15%

Competition

	POOR □□□□□□□□ GOOD	Pg.
Isuzu Rodeo	□□□□□□□□□□	131
Chevrolet Blazer	■□□□□□□□□□	100
Ford Explorer	□□□□□□□□□■	115
Jeep Cherokee	□□□■□□□□□□	133
Mits. Montero	□□□□□■□□□□	143

* Due to the importance of crash tests, vehicles with no results as of publication date cannot be given an overall rating.

Isuzu Trooper

Mid-Size Sport Utility

The Trooper, which comes as a 2- or 4-door, four-wheel drive model, is the only Isuzu product that isn't based on the Isuzu pickup's chassis and body. The 1996 model has dual airbags which will help improve previously abysmal occupant protection. Also, 4-wheel ABS is standard.

The 3.2-liter V6 comes in single or twin-cam form, and the twin cam has been upgraded for '96 to deliver more power. The Trooper's gas mileage is near the bottom of the list. Ride is poor, but at least it's not as noisy as the Rodeo. Handling is inferior to most other utility vehicles. It's roomy and comfortable with a nicely shaped cargo area, though you won't be able to carry as much as other sport utilities. The dashboard is better than on other Isuzu models. The Trooper will benefit from its dual airbags, but it could use a bigger, more economical engine.

The Ratings

	POOR — GOOD
COMPARATIVE RATING*	
CRASH TEST	
SAFETY FEATURES	
FUEL ECONOMY	
PM COST	
REPAIR COST	
WARRANTY	
COMPLAINTS	
INSURANCE COST	

Safety

CRASH TEST	No government results
SIDE CRASH PROTECT.	Weak
AIRBAGS	Dual
ANTI-LOCK BRAKES	4-wheel
BELT ADJUSTORS	Standard
BUILT-IN CHILD SEAT	None
OCCUPANT INJURY	Good

General Information

FUEL ECONOMY	16/18	Poor
DRIVING RANGE	383	Short
PARKING INDEX	Average	
THEFT RATING	Average	
CORPORATE TWINS		
WHERE MADE	Japan	
YEAR OF PRODUCTION	Fifth	

Specifications

LENGTH (in.)	178.9	Short
HEAD/LEG ROOM (in.)	39.8/40.8	Average
CARGO SPACE (cu. ft.)	90	Average
PAYLOAD	1200	Low
TOW RATING (lbs.)	5000	Average
SEATING	6	
WHEEL SIZE (in.)	15/16	

Specifications may vary.

Prices**

Model	Retail	Mkup
Trooper S 4-door	24,350	16%
Trooper RS 2-door	25,950	14%
Trooper LS 4-door	27,700	18%
Trooper SE 4-door	33,450	18%

Competition

	POOR — GOOD	Pg.
Isuzu Trooper		132
Chevrolet Blazer		100
Ford Explorer		115
GMC Jimmy		119
Mits. Montero		143

**1996 prices not available at press time. Prices based on 1995 data.

* Due to the importance of crash tests, vehicles with no results as of publication date cannot be given an overall rating.

Jeep Cherokee

The Cherokee, pioneer of the four-door sport utility market, has a list of offerings for 1996 and comes in two- or four-door models. To get ABS, you must pay extra and buy a model with a 4-liter engine; however, a driver's side airbag is standard with all models.

The standard engine on the base SE is an anemic 2.5-liter 4-cylinder. A 4-liter V6 with automatic overdrive is optional on the SE and standard on the Sport and Country models. You have the choice of two-wheel drive or one of two four-wheel drive systems. Handling is among the best of utility vehicles. Ride is rough on all but smooth roads. The front seat, the same one used in the Grand Cherokee, is roomy and comfortable, but the rear seat is cramped for adults. The dashboard has a dated look and feel. One virtue is its low price, but fancy Cherokees approach the price of a Grand Cherokee, a better vehicle.

General Information

FUEL ECONOMY	19/23 Poor
DRIVING RANGE	424 Average
PARKING INDEX	Easy
THEFT RATING	Very Poor (2-dr.=Poor)
CORPORATE TWINS	
WHERE MADE	U.S.
YEAR OF PRODUCTION	Thirteenth

Prices

Model	Retail	Mkup
Cherokee SE 2-dr. (2WD)	14,645	6%
Cherokee SE 2-dr. (4WD)	16,160	6%
Cherokee Sport 4-dr. (2WD)	18,033	10%
Cherokee Sport 4-dr. (4WD)	19,545	10%
Cherokee Country 4-dr. (4WD)	21,976	11%

The Ratings

	POOR — GOOD
COMPARATIVE RATING	□□□■□□□□□□
CRASH TEST	□□□□□□■□□□
SAFETY FEATURES	□□□■□□□□□□
FUEL ECONOMY	□□□■□□□□□□
PM COST	□□□□□□■□□□
REPAIR COST	□□□□□□□□□■
WARRANTY	□■□□□□□□□□
COMPLAINTS	□□□■□□□□□□
INSURANCE COST	□□□□■□□□□□

Safety

CRASH TEST	Good
SIDE CRASH PROTECT.	Weak
AIRBAGS	Driver
ANTI-LOCK BRAKES	4-wheel (optional)
BELT ADJUSTORS	None
BUILT-IN CHILD SEAT	None
OCCUPANT INJURY	Average (4WD=Good)

Specifications

LENGTH (in.)	166.9	Very Short
HEAD/LEG ROOM (in.)	38.3/41.4	Cramped
CARGO SPACE (cu. ft.)	72	Small
PAYLOAD	1150	Very Low
TOW RATING (lbs.)	5000	Average
SEATING	5	
WHEEL SIZE (in.)	15	

Specifications may vary.

Competition

	POOR — GOOD	Pg.
Jeep Cherokee	□□□■□□□□□□	133
Chevy Blazer	■□□□□□□□□□	100
Ford Explorer	□□□□□□□□□■	115
GMC Jimmy	■□□□□□□□□□	119
Mits. Montero	□□□□□■□□□□	143

The Grand Cherokee is the best of what sport utilities can be, and with new additions for 1996, it becomes even better. It now has standard dual airbags to go along with its 4-wheel ABS. Speed sensitive steering and an upgraded front suspension make for a better ride and control. It also meets 1999 government side impact protection standards.

The Grand Cherokee comes with a powerful 4-liter V6 or a more powerful 5.2-liter V8. You can choose two-wheel drive, or one of three four-wheel drive systems; "Quadra-Trac" is the easiest to use. A built-in foldout child safety seat is a great option. Handling is quite good for a sport-utility vehicle, and it improves with the optional Up Country suspension. The Grand Cherokee has only a little more room inside than the Cherokee. Front seats are comfortable, but the rear seat isn't as pleasant or spacious. Cargo room is adequate.

The Ratings

	POOR □□□□□□□□ GOOD
COMPARATIVE RATING*	□□□□□□□□□□
CRASH TEST	□□□□□□□□□□
SAFETY FEATURES	□□□□□□□□□■
FUEL ECONOMY	□□■□□□□□□□
PM COST	□□□□□□■□□□
REPAIR COST	□□□□□□□□□■
WARRANTY	□■□□□□□□□□
COMPLAINTS	□■□□□□□□□□
INSURANCE COST	□□□□■□□□□□

Safety

CRASH TEST	No government results
SIDE CRASH PROTECT.	Strong
AIRBAGS	Dual
ANTI-LOCK BRAKES	4-wheel
BELT ADJUSTORS	Standard
BUILT-IN CHILD SEAT	Optional
OCCUPANT INJURY	Good (4WD=Vry. Gd.)

General Information

FUEL ECONOMY	15/21	Poor
DRIVING RANGE	391	Average
PARKING INDEX	Easy	
THEFT RATING	Very Poor	
CORPORATE TWINS		
WHERE MADE	U.S.	
YEAR OF PRODUCTION	Fourth	

Specifications

LENGTH (in.)	177.1	Short
HEAD/LEG ROOM (in.)	38.9/40.9	Cramped
CARGO SPACE (cu. ft.)	79	Average
PAYLOAD	1150	Very Low
TOW RATING (lbs.)	5000	Average
SEATING	6	
WHEEL SIZE (in.)	15	

Specifications may vary.

Prices

Model	Retail	Mkup
Grand Cherokee Laredo (2WD)	24,603	10%
Grand Cherokee Laredo (4WD)	26,571	10%
Grand Cherokee Limited (2WD)	30,479	11%
Grand Cherokee Limited (4WD)	32,906	11%

Competition

	POOR □□□□□□□□ GOOD	Pg.
Jeep Gr. Cherokee	□□□□□□□□□□	134
Ford Bronco	□□□□□□■□□□	113
Ford Explorer	□□□□□□□□□■	115
GMC Jimmy	■□□□□□□□□□	119
Mits. Montero	□□□□□■□□□□	143

* Due to the importance of crash tests, vehicles with no results as of publication date cannot be given an overall rating.

Jeep Wrangler

Small Sport Utility

The Wrangler changes little this year. In fact, with the exception of improved safety, its roots as a World War II-era vehicle are clearly visible. A driver's side airbag is standard and 4-wheel ABS is now optional on all models. The Wrangler will be all-new for 1997 so you may want to consider waiting to buy.

The 2.5-liter 4-cylinder engine found on the S offers adequate power in the relatively light Wrangler; the 4-liter V6 found on the SE and Sahara models is much better. Transmission choices are 5-speed manual or 3-speed automatic, and all Wranglers come with part-time 4-wheel drive. Handling is about average for sport-utility vehicles, but notably worse than any car. The Wrangler's element is really off the road. Ride is harsh on any surface, and the rear seat is cramped and uncomfortable for adults. Comfort and weather sealing are minimal with the soft top, but the heater is powerful.

General Information

FUEL ECONOMY	19/20 Poor
DRIVING RANGE	285 Very Short
PARKING INDEX	Very Easy
THEFT RATING	Very Poor
CORPORATE TWINS	
WHERE MADE	U.S.
YEAR OF PRODUCTION	Tenth

Prices

Model	Retail	Mkup
Wrangler S	12,290	4%
Wrangler SE	15,983	10%

The Ratings

	POOR — GOOD
COMPARATIVE RATING*	
CRASH TEST	
SAFETY FEATURES	
FUEL ECONOMY	
PM COST	
REPAIR COST	
WARRANTY	
COMPLAINTS	
INSURANCE COST	

Safety

CRASH TEST	No government results
SIDE CRASH PROTECT.	Weak
AIRBAGS	Driver
ANTI-LOCK BRAKES	4-wheel (optional)
BELT ADJUSTORS	Standard
BUILT-IN CHILD SEAT	None
OCCUPANT INJURY	Average

Specifications

LENGTH (in.)	151.9	Very Short
HEAD/LEG ROOM (in.)	41.4/39.4	Average
CARGO SPACE (cu. ft.)	22	Very Small
PAYLOAD	2000	Average
TOW RATING (lbs.)	2000	Very Low
SEATING	4	
WHEEL SIZE (in.)	15	

Specifications may vary.

Competition

	POOR — GOOD	Pg.
Jeep Wrangler		135
Geo Tracker		126
Jeep Cherokee		133
Kia Sportage		136
Suzuki Sidekick		151

* Due to the importance of crash tests, vehicles with no results as of publication date cannot be given an overall rating.

Kia Sportage

Small Sport Utility

Though Kia has been manufacturing vehicles for Ford since the mid-80s, the Sportage is only the second U.S. model Kia has offered under its own nameplate. The Sportage (pronounced SPOR-tedge), was designed for the growing U.S. sport utility market. New for 1996 is the addition of a much needed driver's side airbag as standard equipment and ABS, though it only operates on the rear wheels.

The 2-liter 4-cylinder engine is adequate, and fuel economy is average for this segment of vehicles. A more powerful engine would be nice; unfortunately, none is offered. Don't expect to haul anything as both the payload and tow ratings are very low. The model lineup is fairly simple, with only a base model and an optional EX package that comes with some luxury amenities. Four-wheel drive is standard, and only one body style (4-door) is available.

General Information

FUEL ECONOMY	19/23	Poor
DRIVING RANGE	332	Very Short
PARKING INDEX	Very Easy	
THEFT RATING		
CORPORATE TWINS		
WHERE MADE	Japan /South Korea	
YEAR OF PRODUCTION	Second	

Prices

Model	Retail	Mkup
Sportage (2WD)	13,495	
Sportage (4WD)	15,295	
Sportage EX (4WD)	16,195	

The Ratings

	POOR — GOOD
COMPARATIVE RATING*	
CRASH TEST	
SAFETY FEATURES	
FUEL ECONOMY	
PM COST	
REPAIR COST	
WARRANTY	
COMPLAINTS	
INSURANCE COST	

Safety

CRASH TEST	No government results
SIDE CRASH PROTECT.	Weak
AIRBAGS	Driver
ANTI-LOCK BRAKES	2-wheel
BELT ADJUSTORS	None
BUILT-IN CHILD SEAT	None
OCCUPANT INJURY	

Specifications

LENGTH (in.)	159.4	Very Short
HEAD/LEG ROOM (in.)	39.6/44.5	Very Roomy
CARGO SPACE (cu. ft.)	55	Small
PAYLOAD	850	Very Low
TOW RATING (lbs.)	2000	Very Low
SEATING	4	
WHEEL SIZE (in.)	15	

Specifications may vary.

Competition

	POOR — GOOD	Pg.
Kia Sportage		136
Geo Tracker		126
Jeep Cherokee		133
Jeep Wrangler		135
Suzuki Sidekick		151

* Due to the importance of crash tests, vehicles with no results as of publication date cannot be given an overall rating.

Land Rover Discovery

Mid-Size Sport Utility

Like its close sibling the Range Rover, the Discovery comes standard with dual airbags and is geared toward the wealthier and more rugged sport utility buyer. It's slightly smaller than the Range Rover, but you should have no problem doing any necessary suburban hauling in comfort. 4-wheel ABS is standard and it meets 1999 side impact protection standards.

A revamped 3.9-liter V8 is fairly powerful, but with the vehicle alone weighing over two tons, it may strain under heavy loads. Though it officially seats seven, the two seats in the rear are uncomfortable and only for children. 4-wheel drive is standard, as is just about anything else you could possibly want. Options include fog lights and a CD-player. Room inside for passengers and luggage is cramped; make sure you are comfortable before you buy. The new Land Rover Discovery will make you feel like you're on a safari when all you're doing is the carpool and grocery shopping.

General Information

FUEL ECONOMY	13/16	Very Poor
DRIVING RANGE	328	Very Short
PARKING INDEX	Average	
THEFT RATING		
CORPORATE TWINS		
WHERE MADE	Great Britain	
YEAR OF PRODUCTION	Second	

Prices

Model	Retail	Mkup
Discovery Base	29,950	

The Ratings

	POOR — GOOD (box 1–10)
COMPARATIVE RATING	
CRASH TEST	
SAFETY FEATURES	9
FUEL ECONOMY	2
PM COST	1
REPAIR COST	2
WARRANTY	4
COMPLAINTS	
INSURANCE COST	5

Safety

CRASH TEST	No government results
SIDE CRASH PROTECT.	Strong
AIRBAGS	Dual
ANTI-LOCK BRAKES	4-wheel
BELT ADJUSTORS	Standard
BUILT-IN CHILD SEAT	None
OCCUPANT INJURY	

Specifications

LENGTH (in.)	178.7	Short
HEAD/LEG ROOM (in.)	37.4/38.5	Vry. Cramped
CARGO SPACE (cu. ft.)	70	Small
PAYLOAD	1650	Low
TOW RATING (lbs.)	7700	Very High
SEATING	5/7	
WHEEL SIZE (in.)	16	

Specifications may vary.

Competition

	POOR — GOOD (box 1–10)	Pg.
Lnd Rvr Discovery		137
Chevy Blazer	1	100
Ford Explorer	10	115
GMC Jimmy	1	119
Mits. Montero	6	143

Land Rover Range Rover

Large Sport Utility

There are only minor changes in the 1996 edition of the Range Rover, whose design dates back to 1970. For the second straight year, dual airbags are standard. While other manufacturers seemed to be adding them only one at a time, Land Rover added two at once. Also, 4-wheel ABS continues to be standard, and it meets 1999 side impact standards.

The naming has changed slightly on these large sport utility vehicles. You can now buy a 4.0SE or a 4.6HSE, with the numbers corresponding to their engine sizes. As expected, the 4.6HSE will allow you to tow almost four tons. Four-wheel drive and an automatic transmission are standard. A Range Rover weighs roughly 4,500 pounds, so acceleration is fairly slow and fuel economy is dismal. Typical of this class of vehicles, handling is on the sluggish side, though the ride is comfortable. Cargo space is small so don't expect to pack as much as you can in other sport utilities.

The Ratings	POOR — GOOD
COMPARATIVE RATING*	
CRASH TEST	
SAFETY FEATURES	
FUEL ECONOMY	
PM COST	
REPAIR COST	
WARRANTY	
COMPLAINTS	
INSURANCE COST	

Safety	
CRASH TEST	No government results
SIDE CRASH PROTECT.	Strong
AIRBAGS	Dual
ANTI-LOCK BRAKES	4-wheel
BELT ADJUSTORS	Standard
BUILT-IN CHILD SEAT	None
OCCUPANT INJURY	

General Information		
FUEL ECONOMY	12/15	Very Poor
DRIVING RANGE	320	Very Short
PARKING INDEX	Average	
THEFT RATING		
CORPORATE TWINS		
WHERE MADE	Great Britain	
YEAR OF PRODUCTION	Tenth	

Specifications		
LENGTH (in.)	185.5	Average
HEAD/LEG ROOM (in.)	38.1/42.6	Average
CARGO SPACE (cu. ft.)	58	Small
PAYLOAD	1200	Low
TOW RATING (lbs.)	6500	High
SEATING	5	
WHEEL SIZE (in.)	16	

Specifications may vary.

Prices		
Model	**Retail**	**Mkup**
Range Rover Base	55,000	

Competition	POOR — GOOD	Pg.
Lnd Rvr Range Rvr		138
Chevy Suburban		105
Ford Bronco		113
GMC Yukon		125
Mits. Montero		143

* Due to the importance of crash tests, vehicles with no results as of publication date cannot be given an overall rating.

Mazda B-Series Pickup

Compact Pickup

The B-Series, which was all-new in '94, receives no major changes for 1996. The greatest addition since 1994 has been the standard driver's side airbag. The B-Series is a clone of the Ford Ranger, whose introduction preceded that of the B-Series by one year. The Ranger has optional ABS and an optional passenger airbag this year; with luck, the passenger side airbag will also appear on the B-Series soon. 4-wheel ABS does come optional.

The standard 2.3-liter 4-cylinder engine (on the B2300) is OK for light duty use, but if you plan on carrying a significant load, or simply want more power, consider the 3- or 4-liter V6 options (on the B3000 or B4000, respectively); the 4x4 version only comes with the 4-liter engine. Option choices aren't quite as extensive as they are for the Ranger; most are grouped in packages. An extended cab is available. The instrument panel features functional design and well-placed controls.

General Information

FUEL ECONOMY	22/27	Average
DRIVING RANGE	408	Average
PARKING INDEX	Easy	
THEFT RATING	Very Good	
CORPORATE TWINS	Ford Ranger	
WHERE MADE	Japan	
YEAR OF PRODUCTION	Third	

Prices

Model	Retail	Mkup
B2300 Short Bed Base (2WD)	10,055	8%
B2300 Short Bed Base (4WD)	15,100	8%
B3000 Cab Plus SE (2WD)	14,560	12%
B4000 Cab Plus LE (2WD)	16,480	12%
B4000 Cab Plus LE (4WD)	20,510	12%

The Ratings

	POOR … GOOD
COMPARATIVE RATING	□□□■□□□□□□
CRASH TEST	□□□□□□□■□□
SAFETY FEATURES	□□□■□□□□□□
FUEL ECONOMY	□□□□■□□□□□
PM COST	□□□□□□□■□□
REPAIR COST	□□□□□□■□□□
WARRANTY	□□□■□□□□□□
COMPLAINTS	□□■□□□□□□□
INSURANCE COST	■□□□□□□□□□

Safety

CRASH TEST	Good
SIDE CRASH PROTECT.	Weak
AIRBAGS	Driver
ANTI-LOCK BRAKES	2-whl. (4-whl.opt.)
BELT ADJUSTORS	None
BUILT-IN CHILD SEAT	None
OCCUPANT INJURY	Average

Specifications

LENGTH (in.)	184.5	Average
HEAD/LEG ROOM (in.)	39.1/42.4	Roomy
CARGO SPACE (cu. ft.)		
PAYLOAD	1250	Low
TOW RATING (lbs.)	4800	Average
SEATING	2	
WHEEL SIZE (in.)	14/15	

Specifications may vary.

Competition

	POOR … GOOD	Pg.
Mazda B-Series	□□□■□□□□□□	139
Chevrolet S-Series	□□□□□□■□□□	104
Dodge Dakota	□□□□□□□□■□	109
Ford Ranger	□□□□□□■□□□	117
GMC Sonoma	□■□□□□□□□□	123

Mazda MPV

Minivan

The Mazda MPV, or multipurpose passenger vehicle, which was unchanged for seven years, finally receives an overhaul for 1996. Among the many changes is the addition of a rear door on the driver's side and a freshened look. Also new this year is the addition of standard dual airbags and 4-wheel ABS.

The MPV offers 3 trim levels: DX, LX, or ES. Among the many options is the choice of four captain's chairs or a bench seat, which will raise the seating to eight. Fuel economy is poor; it gets even worse with the optional 4-wheel drive, which is otherwise a fine choice. Brakes, handling and ride are inferior to most minivans. Interior room and cargo space are inferior to other minivans. With the new revisions, the MPV moves competitively up in the crowded minivan market, although other models like the Ford Windstar, Chevy Lumina, and Honda Odyssey offer much more.

The Ratings	POOR — GOOD
COMPARATIVE RATING*	
CRASH TEST	
SAFETY FEATURES	□□□□□□■□□□
FUEL ECONOMY	□□■□□□□□□□
PM COST	□□□■□□□□□□
REPAIR COST	□□■□□□□□□□
WARRANTY	□□□■□□□□□□
COMPLAINTS	□□□■□□□□□□
INSURANCE COST	□□□□■□□□□□

Safety	
CRASH TEST	No government results
SIDE CRASH PROTECT.	Weak
AIRBAGS	Dual
ANTI-LOCK BRAKES	4-wheel
BELT ADJUSTORS	None
BUILT-IN CHILD SEAT	None
OCCUPANT INJURY	Poor

General Information		
FUEL ECONOMY	16/22	Poor
DRIVING RANGE	353	Short
PARKING INDEX	Easy	
THEFT RATING	Average	
CORPORATE TWINS		
WHERE MADE	Japan	
YEAR OF PRODUCTION	First	

Specifications		
LENGTH (in.)	183.5	Average
HEAD/LEG ROOM (in.)	40.0/40.4	Average
CARGO SPACE (cu. ft.)	38	Very Small
PAYLOAD	1000	Very Low
TOW RATING (lbs.)	4800	Average
SEATING	4/8	
WHEEL SIZE (in.)	15	

Specifications may vary.

Prices**

Model	Retail	Mkup
MPV L (2WD)	21,495	11%
MPV LX (2WD)	22,375	11%
MPV LX (4WD)	25,770	11%
MPV LXE (2WD)	24,765	11%
MPV LXE (4WD)	27,995	11%

Competition	POOR — GOOD	Pg.
Mazda MPV		140
Chevy Lumina	□□□□□■□□□□	103
Ford Aerostar	□□□□□□□■□□	112
Honda Odyssey	□□□□□■□□□□	127
Toyota Previa	□□□□□□□■□□	155

**1996 prices not available at press time. Prices based on 1995 data.

* Due to the importance of crash tests, vehicles with no results as of publication date cannot be given an overall rating.

Mercury Villager

Minivan

The Villager minivan, a near-twin of the Nissan Quest, receives fresh styling for 1996, including new nose, tail and side moldings. The interior is also freshened, creating a nicer looking minivan. The Villager is available in three trim levels—base GS, luxury LS, and sport-luxury Nautica. The Villager's resemblance to the Dodge Caravan is no coincidence; Mercury is trying to emulate Chrysler's minivan success. ABS and dual airbags are standard, but the Villager keeps awkward motorized shoulder belts and separate lap belts.

The ride is a bit soft, very much like a regular passenger car's, with standard suspension. Handling is competent, but can be firmed up with the optional handling package. The 3-liter V6, with automatic overdrive, is acceptably responsive. Go for the towing package if you'll be hauling anything at all. The integrated child seats are excellent options.

General Information

FUEL ECONOMY	17/23 Poor
DRIVING RANGE	400 Average
PARKING INDEX	Average
THEFT RATING	Very Good
CORPORATE TWINS	Nissan Quest
WHERE MADE	U.S.
YEAR OF PRODUCTION	Fourth

Prices

Model	Retail	Mkup
Villager GS Cargo Van	19,385	10%
Villager GS	19,940	10%
Villager LS	24,300	11%
Villager Nautica	26,390	11%

The Ratings

	POOR — GOOD
COMPARATIVE RATING*	
CRASH TEST	
SAFETY FEATURES	
FUEL ECONOMY	
PM COST	
REPAIR COST	
WARRANTY	
COMPLAINTS	
INSURANCE COST	

Safety

CRASH TEST	No government results
SIDE CRASH PROTECT.	Weak
AIRBAGS	Dual
ANTI-LOCK BRAKES	4-wheel
BELT ADJUSTORS	Standard
BUILT-IN CHILD SEAT	Optional
OCCUPANT INJURY	Very Good

Specifications

LENGTH (in.)	189.9	Average
HEAD/LEG ROOM (in.)	39.4/39.9	Cramped
CARGO SPACE (cu. ft.)	126	Large
PAYLOAD	1200	Low
TOW RATING (lbs.)	3500	Low
SEATING	7	
WHEEL SIZE (in.)	15	

Specifications may vary.

Competition

	POOR — GOOD	Pg.
Mercury Villager		141
Chevy Lumina		103
Ford Aerostar		112
Pontiac Tr. Sport		150
Toyota Previa		155

* Due to the importance of crash tests, vehicles with no results as of publication date cannot be given an overall rating.

Mitsubishi Mighty Max

Compact Pickup

The Mighty Max has not changed much since the mid-80s, and is showing its age. For 1996, Mitsubishi has dropped the four-wheel drive model, losing its more-powerful engine. The styling on the available two-wheel drive model is outdated. There are no airbags offered for 1996, and the lack of ABS makes the Mighty Max a poor choice.

The 2.4-liter 4-cylinder engine will most likely not be powerful enough for carrying loads. Ride, handling, and accommodations are comparable to other small pickups. The options list is fairly short; one of the most desirable is power steering. Like other compact pickups, don't expect to be able to haul or tow very much. Basic controls and gauges are well laid out. The Mighty Max is a holdover from the 80s, and unfortunately, Mitsubishi has no immediate plans to give it an overhaul. Skip the Mighty Max and look at the Dodge Dakota, Chevy S-Series or Ford Ranger.

General Information

FUEL ECONOMY	21/25	Average
DRIVING RANGE	301	Very Short
PARKING INDEX	Hard	
THEFT RATING	Average	
CORPORATE TWINS		
WHERE MADE	Japan	
YEAR OF PRODUCTION	Tenth	

Prices

Model	Retail	Mkup
Mighty Max Man.	11,170	
Mighty Max Auto.	12,460	

The Ratings

	POOR … GOOD
COMPARATIVE RATING*	□□□□□□□□□□
CRASH TEST	□□□□□□□□□□
SAFETY FEATURES	■□□□□□□□□□
FUEL ECONOMY	□□□□■□□□□□
PM COST	□□■□□□□□□□
REPAIR COST	□□■□□□□□□□
WARRANTY	□□□□■□□□□□
COMPLAINTS	□□□□□□□□□■
INSURANCE COST	■□□□□□□□□□

Safety

CRASH TEST	No government results
SIDE CRASH PROTECT.	Weak
AIRBAGS	None
ANTI-LOCK BRAKES	None
BELT ADJUSTORS	None
BUILT-IN CHILD SEAT	None
OCCUPANT INJURY	Average

Specifications

LENGTH (in.)	177.2	Short
HEAD/LEG ROOM (in.)	38.8/41.9	Average
CARGO SPACE (cu. ft.)		
PAYLOAD	1600	Low
TOW RATING (lbs.)	3500	Low
SEATING	2	
WHEEL SIZE (in.)	14/15	

Specifications may vary.

Competition

	POOR … GOOD	Pg.
Mits. Mighty Max	□□□□□□□□□□	142
Chevy S-Series	□□□□□□■□□□	104
Dodge Dakota	□□□□□□□□■□	109
Ford Ranger	□□□□□□■□□□	117
GMC Sonoma	□■□□□□□□□□	123

* Due to the importance of crash tests, vehicles with no results as of publication date cannot be given an overall rating.

Mitsubishi Montero

Mid-Size Sport Utility

The Montero receives slight refinements as it enters 1996. Monteros come in two trim levels this year, either LS or SR. New for '96 are dual airbags; the ABS system, optional on LS and standard on SR, operates on all four wheels.

The 3-liter V6 on the LS should do an okay job at accelerating this 2-ton behemoth when empty, but with a load, you'll likely find it a bit lacking. The 3.5-liter V6 on the SR is much more powerful. Gas mileage with either engine is abysmal. Automatic overdrive is standard on the SR, optional on the LS. If you like real wood and leather, Mitsubishi will tack them on to the SR for about $2,200. Ride is smoother and quieter than most utility vehicles, but handling is very clumsy. Comfort inside is good, but the cargo area is skimpy. With a very good crash test rating, the Montero competes well with other mid-to-large size sport utilities.

The Ratings	POOR ... GOOD (1–10)
COMPARATIVE RATING	6
CRASH TEST	9
SAFETY FEATURES	7
FUEL ECONOMY	3
PM COST	3
REPAIR COST	4
WARRANTY	5
COMPLAINTS	7
INSURANCE COST	1

Safety	
CRASH TEST	Very Good
SIDE CRASH PROTECT.	Weak
AIRBAGS	Dual
ANTI-LOCK BRAKES	4-wheel (optional)
BELT ADJUSTORS	Standard
BUILT-IN CHILD SEAT	None
OCCUPANT INJURY	

General Information		
FUEL ECONOMY	15/18	Poor
DRIVING RANGE	413	Average
PARKING INDEX	Average	
THEFT RATING	Very Poor	
CORPORATE TWINS		
WHERE MADE	Japan	
YEAR OF PRODUCTION	Fifth	

Specifications		
LENGTH (in.)	185.2	Average
HEAD/LEG ROOM (in.)	40.9/40.3	Average
CARGO SPACE (cu. ft.)	39	Very Small
PAYLOAD	1400	Low
TOW RATING (lbs.)	5000	Average
SEATING	7	
WHEEL SIZE (in.)	15	

Specifications may vary.

Prices

Model	Retail	Mkup
Montero LS man.	28,470	17%
Montero LS auto.	29,350	17%
Montero SR auto.	37,740	20%

Competition

	POOR ... GOOD (1–10)	Pg.
Mits. Montero	6	143
Chevy Blazer	1	100
Ford Bronco	7	113
GMC Jimmy	1	119
Olds Bravada	2	147

Nissan Pathfinder

Mid-Size Sport Utility

The Nissan Pathfinder is scheduled to be all-new in 1996, but will not debut until early in the year. In the meantime, we have included the picture for the 1995 model which will continue to be sold until the '96 is available. Airbags are not available on the '95, but are expected on the '96, and ABS is standard on both the '95 and '96 models.

A 3-liter V6 is the only engine choice on the Pathfinder. Base XE and mid-level SE models come with either manual or automatic transmission; the up-level LE comes only with automatic. A more powerful V6 is rumored to be included in the options list when the '96 debuts. Handling, like the Jeep Cherokee's, is about as good as it gets for a utility vehicle, but short of the mark set by the better cars. It's a bit tight inside, and not too comfortable in back; however, the '96 will be slightly larger, giving riders more room.

The Ratings

	POOR — GOOD (1–10)
COMPARATIVE RATING*	
CRASH TEST	
SAFETY FEATURES	6
FUEL ECONOMY	3
PM COST	4
REPAIR COST	9
WARRANTY	3
COMPLAINTS	
INSURANCE COST	5

Safety

CRASH TEST	No government results
SIDE CRASH PROTECT.	Weak
AIRBAGS	Dual
ANTI-LOCK BRAKES	2-wheel
BELT ADJUSTORS	Standard
BUILT-IN CHILD SEAT	None
OCCUPANT INJURY	Average

General Information

FUEL ECONOMY	17/20	Poor
DRIVING RANGE	367	Short
PARKING INDEX	Easy	
THEFT RATING		
CORPORATE TWINS		
WHERE MADE	Japan	
YEAR OF PRODUCTION	First	

Specifications

LENGTH (in.)	171.9	Very Short
HEAD/LEG ROOM (in.)	39.3/42.6	Roomy
CARGO SPACE (cu. ft.)	80	Average
PAYLOAD		
TOW RATING (lbs.)	3500	Low
SEATING	5	
WHEEL SIZE (in.)	15	

Specifications may vary.

Prices

Model	Retail	Mkup
Pathfinder XE-V6 (4x2)	21,549	13%
Pathfinder LE-V6 auto. (4x2)	28,849	13%
Pathfinder XE-V6 (4x4)	23,149	13%
Pathfinder SE-V6 (4x4)	27,549	13%
Pathfinder LE-V6 auto. (4x4)	31,249	13%

Competition

	POOR — GOOD (1–10)	Pg.
Nissan Pathfinder		144
Chevy Blazer	1	100
Ford Explorer	10	115
Jeep Cherokee	4	133
Mits. Montero	6	143

* Due to the importance of crash tests, vehicles with no results as of publication date cannot be given an overall rating.

The Nissan pickup has not changed much since the mid-80s, but a new lineup is scheduled to be released in early 1996. For now, Nissan is continuing to sell the 1995's at least through the end of the year. Nissan has not released many details on the new '96 model, so the picture above is from 1995. You won't find airbags on the '95's; a drivers airbag should be present for '96. ABS is standard on the rear wheels.

The 2.4-liter 4-cylinder engine provides adequate power for most uses; a more powerful 3-liter V6, better suited for any heavier hauling, is available on both 4x2 and 4x4 models. The King Cab has extra interior room. If you're familiar with Japanese pickups, the Nissan won't surprise you in ride, handling, or interior comfort; all are worse than on typical cars. Options are minimal; power steering makes handling more enjoyable. Basic controls and gauges are easy to use.

General Information

FUEL ECONOMY	18/20	Poor
DRIVING RANGE	302	Very Short
PARKING INDEX	Easy	
THEFT RATING	Average	
CORPORATE TWINS		
WHERE MADE	U.S./Japan	
YEAR OF PRODUCTION	Eleventh	

Prices

Model	Retail	Mkup
Standard (4x2)	10,394	6%
XE Regular Cab (4x2)	11,780	10%
XE-V6 King Cab (4x2)	14,639	12%
XE Regular Cab (4x4)	15,489	10%
XE-V6 King Cab (4x4)	18,500	13%

The Ratings

	POOR … GOOD (1–10)
COMPARATIVE RATING*	
CRASH TEST	
SAFETY FEATURES	3
FUEL ECONOMY	4
PM COST	4
REPAIR COST	9
WARRANTY	3
COMPLAINTS	10
INSURANCE COST	1

Safety

CRASH TEST	No government results
SIDE CRASH PROTECT.	Weak
AIRBAGS	Driver
ANTI-LOCK BRAKES	2-wheel
BELT ADJUSTORS	None
BUILT-IN CHILD SEAT	None
OCCUPANT INJURY	Average

Specifications

LENGTH (in.)	174.6	Short
HEAD/LEG ROOM (in.)	39.3/42.2	Roomy
CARGO SPACE (cu. ft.)		
PAYLOAD	1400	Low
TOW RATING (lbs.)	3500	Low
SEATING	3	
WHEEL SIZE (in.)	14/15	

Specifications may vary.

Competition

	POOR … GOOD (1–10)	Pg.
Nissan Pickup		145
Chevrolet S-Series	7	104
Dodge Dakota	9	109
Ford Ranger	7	117
Mazda B-Series	4	139

* Due to the importance of crash tests, vehicles with no results as of publication date cannot be given an overall rating.

With the Quest and its look-alike twin the Villager, Nissan and Mercury have tried to catch up with Chrysler's successful minivans. They've been successful on many fronts, and with several new changes for 1996, they move one step closer. New for '96 are updated grilles, bumpers and tail-lamps, and, most importantly, dual airbags. ABS is optional.

The only available engine is a 3-liter V6, but acceleration and power are good. Fuel economy is poor. Ride and handling are good by minivan standards. On the interior, seating is comfortable and now the Quest comes with integrated child safety seats which is an excellent option. The cargo space is competitive with other minivans, too. With these new additions, the Quest is sure to attract more attention. However, the Chrysler minivans are all-new this year; so the Quest may still be left behind.

The Ratings

	POOR ⟶ GOOD
COMPARATIVE RATING*	□□□□□□□□□□
CRASH TEST	□□□□□□□□□□
SAFETY FEATURES	□□□□□□□■□□
FUEL ECONOMY	□□□■□□□□□□
PM COST	□□□□□□□□■□
REPAIR COST	□□□□□□■□□□
WARRANTY	□□■□□□□□□□
COMPLAINTS	□■□□□□□□□□
INSURANCE COST	□□□□□□□□□■

Safety

CRASH TEST	No government results
SIDE CRASH PROTECT.	Weak
AIRBAGS	Dual
ANTI-LOCK BRAKES	4-wheel (optional)
BELT ADJUSTORS	Standard
BUILT-IN CHILD SEAT	Optional
OCCUPANT INJURY	Good

General Information

FUEL ECONOMY	17/23	Poor
DRIVING RANGE	400	Average
PARKING INDEX	Hard	
THEFT RATING	Very Good	
CORPORATE TWINS	Mercury Villager	
WHERE MADE	U.S./Japan	
YEAR OF PRODUCTION	Fourth	

Specifications

LENGTH (in.)	189.9	Average
HEAD/LEG ROOM (in.)	39.5/39.9	Cramped
CARGO SPACE (cu. ft.)	125	Large
PAYLOAD	1600	Low
TOW RATING (lbs.)	3500	Low
SEATING	7	
WHEEL SIZE (in.)	15	

Specifications may vary.

Prices

Model	Retail	Mkup
Quest XE	20,899	14%
Quest GXE	25,699	14%

Competition

	POOR ⟶ GOOD	Pg.
Nissan Quest	□□□□□□□□□□	146
Ford Windstar	□□□□□□□□□■	118
Honda Odyssey	□□□□□■□□□□	127
Pontiac Tr. Sport	□□□□□□□□■□	150
Toyota Previa	□□□□□□□■□□	155

* Due to the importance of crash tests, vehicles with no results as of publication date cannot be given an overall rating.

Oldsmobile Bravada

Mid-Size Sport Utility

Oldsmobile finally joins the sport utility parade in 1996 with its introduction of the Bravada, the twin of the Chevy Blazer and the GMC Jimmy. The Bravada is designed to be the upscale version of the three and appeal to luxury sedan owners looking for the off-road feel. Driver's side airbags and ABS are standard, but it performed badly in government crash tests.

Like the Blazer and Jimmy, the Bravada is powered by a 4.3-liter V6 engine that produces adequate power for this mid-sized sport utility. The Bravada only comes in a 4-door model which is designed to seat six. The optional towing package goes a long way towards tailoring the ride and handling to the customer's preference. With full-time, all-wheel drive, you should have little trouble getting around on slick roads. If you can live without the name plate, choose the less expensive Blazer, though neither match up very well against the Ford Explorer.

General Information		
FUEL ECONOMY	16/21	Poor
DRIVING RANGE	342	Very Short
PARKING INDEX	Average	
THEFT RATING		
CORPORATE TWINS	Chevy Blazer, GMC Jimmy	
WHERE MADE	U.S.	
YEAR OF PRODUCTION	First	

Prices		
Model	**Retail**	**Mkup**
Bravada	29,505	

The Ratings	POOR ... GOOD
COMPARATIVE RATING	□■□□□□□□□□
CRASH TEST	□■□□□□□□□□
SAFETY FEATURES	□□□□□■□□□□
FUEL ECONOMY	□□■□□□□□□□
PM COST	□□□□■□□□□□
REPAIR COST	□□□□□□□■□□
WARRANTY	□□■□□□□□□□
COMPLAINTS	□□□□□□□□□□
INSURANCE COST	□□□□■□□□□□

Safety	
CRASH TEST	Very Poor
SIDE CRASH PROTECT.	Strong
AIRBAGS	Driver
ANTI-LOCK BRAKES	4-wheel
BELT ADJUSTORS	None
BUILT-IN CHILD SEAT	None
OCCUPANT INJURY	Average

Specifications		
LENGTH (in.)	180.9	Short
HEAD/LEG ROOM (in.)	39.7/42.4	Roomy
CARGO SPACE (cu. ft.)	74	Small
PAYLOAD	1100	Very Low
TOW RATING (lbs.)	5000	Average
SEATING	6	
WHEEL SIZE (in.)	15	

Specifications may vary.

Competition	POOR ... GOOD	Pg.
Olds Bravada	□■□□□□□□□□	147
Chevy Blazer	■□□□□□□□□□	100
Ford Explorer	□□□□□□□□□■	115
GMC Jimmy	■□□□□□□□□□	119
Mits. Montero	□□□□□■□□□□	143

Oldsmobile Silhouette

Minivan

The Oldsmobile Silhouette and its twins, the Pontiac Trans Sport and the Chevy Lumina Minivan, have been good competition for the Chrysler minivans. Although the Silhouette performs well in the government's frontal impact crash test, a second airbag is sorely missed in this family vehicle. It is scheduled to be all-new in '97.

There is only one engine choice this year—a powerful 3.4-liter V6 which out performs the past engines Olds has offered. You have your choice of one or two built-in child restraints, an excellent option. Ride is competent on good roads, but handling is unresponsive at highway speeds. The optional touring suspension and traction control, which you have to buy together, improve handling. You'll need some time to get used to the driving position and visibility. The Silhouette will have a tough time competing with the new Chrysler minivan, especially with only one airbag.

The Ratings

	POOR — GOOD
COMPARATIVE RATING	□□□□□□□□■□
CRASH TEST	□□□□□□■□□□
SAFETY FEATURES	□□□□■□□□□□
FUEL ECONOMY	□□□■□□□□□□
PM COST	□□□□□□□■□□
REPAIR COST	□□□□□□□□■□
WARRANTY	□□■□□□□□□□
COMPLAINTS	□□□□□■□□□□
INSURANCE COST	□□□□□□□□□■

Safety

CRASH TEST	Good
SIDE CRASH PROTECT.	Weak
AIRBAGS	Driver
ANTI-LOCK BRAKES	4-wheel
BELT ADJUSTORS	None
BUILT-IN CHILD SEAT	Optional (two)
OCCUPANT INJURY	

General Information

FUEL ECONOMY	19/26	Poor
DRIVING RANGE	420	Average
PARKING INDEX	Hard	
THEFT RATING	Average	
CORPORATE TWINS	Lumina Minivan, Tr. Sport	
WHERE MADE	U.S.	
YEAR OF PRODUCTION	Seventh	

Specifications

LENGTH (in.)	194.7	Long
HEAD/LEG ROOM (in.)	39.2/40.0	Cramped
CARGO SPACE (cu. ft.)	113	Large
PAYLOAD	1400	Low
TOW RATING (lbs.)	3000	Low
SEATING	7	
WHEEL SIZE (in.)	15	

Specifications may vary.

Prices

Model	Retail	Mkup
Silhouette Series I	21,355	11%
Silhouette Series II	22,655	11%

Competition

	POOR — GOOD	Pg.
Olds Silhouette	□□□□□□□□■□	148
Chevy Lumina	□□□□□■□□□□	113
Ford Windstar	□□□□□□□□□■	118
Honda Odyssey	□□□□□■□□□□	127
Toyota Previa	□□□□□□□■□□	155

Plymouth Voyager

Minivan

The Voyager, along with the other Chrysler minivans, is totally redesigned for 1996. These industry leaders carry on with standard dual airbags and a body that meets 1999 government side impact standards. ABS is now standard. This new look should help keep the Voyager ahead of its competition.

You get to choose between four engines: an inadequate 2.5-liter 4-cylinder, an adequate 3-liter V6, or the more powerful 3.3-liter or 3.8-liter V6s. All except the 3.8-liter are equally efficient. Since Grand Voyagers have a longer wheelbase and a body with more room, the 3.3-liter is worth the extra money. Handling improves with the heavy duty suspension, and the ride remains good. The built-in child restraints are an excellent option. The new Voyager should serve many needs while still being fun to drive.

The Ratings	POOR — GOOD
COMPARATIVE RATING*	
CRASH TEST	
SAFETY FEATURES	
FUEL ECONOMY	
PM COST	
REPAIR COST	
WARRANTY	
COMPLAINTS	
INSURANCE COST	

Safety	
CRASH TEST	No government results
SIDE CRASH PROTECT.	Strong
AIRBAGS	Dual
ANTI-LOCK BRAKES	4-wheel
BELT ADJUSTORS	Standard
BUILT-IN CHILD SEAT	Optional (two)
OCCUPANT INJURY	Good

General Information		
FUEL ECONOMY	20/26	Average
DRIVING RANGE	440	Long
PARKING INDEX	Average	
THEFT RATING		
CORPORATE TWINS	Caravan, Town & Country	
WHERE MADE	U.S./Canada	
YEAR OF PRODUCTION	First	

Specifications		
LENGTH (in.)	186.3	Average
HEAD/LEG ROOM (in.)	39.8/41.2	Average
CARGO SPACE (cu. ft.)	146	Very Large
PAYLOAD	1200	Low
TOW RATING (lbs.)	2000	Very Low
SEATING	7	
WHEEL SIZE (in.)	14/15	

Specifications may vary.

Prices

Model	Retail	Mkup
Voyager Base	16,160	10%
Voyager SE	18,855	10%
Grand Voyager Base	17,410	10%
Grand Voyager SE	19,595	10%

Competition

	POOR — GOOD	Pg.
Plymouth Voyager		149
Chevy Lumina		103
Ford Windstar		118
Honda Odyssey		127
Toyota Previa		155

* Due to the importance of crash tests, vehicles with no results as of publication date cannot be given an overall rating.

Pontiac Trans Sport

Minivan

The Trans Sport receives only minor changes as it prepares to be totally redesigned in 1997. Like its twins, the Chevrolet Lumina and Oldsmobile Silhouette, the Trans Sport offers reliable family transportation. Traction control is now optional, and a driver's airbag and ABS remain standard.

The only engine offered is a more powerful 3.4-liter V6 with automatic overdrive. It provides plenty of power and even gets better gas mileage than the old engines Pontiac offered. You have the choice of one or two fold-out child safety restraints, which is an excellent option. Ride is generally smooth, but handling is sluggish on the open road. The windshield posts are distracting. The Trans Sport has much less cargo space than other minivans. One fancy option is the new power sliding door, designed to overcome the traditional difficulties with heavy minivan side doors.

The Ratings	POOR — GOOD
COMPARATIVE RATING	□□□□□□□□■□
CRASH TEST	□□□□□□■□□□
SAFETY FEATURES	□□□□■□□□□□
FUEL ECONOMY	□□□■□□□□□□
PM COST	□□□□□□□■□□
REPAIR COST	□□□□□□□□■□
WARRANTY	□■□□□□□□□□
COMPLAINTS	□□□□■□□□□□
INSURANCE COST	□□□□□□□□□■

Safety	
CRASH TEST	Good
SIDE CRASH PROTECT.	Weak
AIRBAGS	Driver
ANTI-LOCK BRAKES	4-wheel
BELT ADJUSTORS	None
BUILT-IN CHILD SEAT	Optional (two)
OCCUPANT INJURY	Very Good

General Information		
FUEL ECONOMY	19/26	Poor
DRIVING RANGE	420	Average
PARKING INDEX	Hard	
THEFT RATING	Average	
CORPORATE TWINS	Lumina, Silhouette	
WHERE MADE	U.S.	
YEAR OF PRODUCTION	Seventh	

Specifications		
LENGTH (in.)	192.2	Long
HEAD/LEG ROOM (in.)	39.2/40.0	Cramped
CARGO SPACE (cu. ft.)	113	Large
PAYLOAD	1400	Low
TOW RATING (lbs.)	3000	Low
SEATING	7	
WHEEL SIZE (in.)	15	

Specifications may vary.

Prices*

Model	Retail	Mkup
Trans Sport SE	17,889	11%

Competition

	POOR — GOOD	Pg.
Pontiac Tr. Sport	□□□□□□□□■□	150
Ford Aerostar	□□□□□□□■□□	112
Ford Windstar	□□□□□□□□□■	118
Honda Odyssey	□□□□□■□□□□	127
Toyota Previa	□□□□□□□■□□	155

*1996 pirces not available at press time. Prices based on 1995 data.

Suzuki Sidekick

Small Sport Utility

The Sidekick, all-new for 1996, has many new refinements that are sure to make this a more competitive vehicle. The Sidekick is designed to be a fun, affordable sport utility vehicle which is comfortable enough for everyday use and rugged enough for weekend off-roading. Standard safety features include dual airbags and 2-wheel ABS, 4-wheel is optional.

A new 1.8-liter 4-cylinder engine is standard this year. It has decent power, but acceleration will not be as fast as some of its competition. The width of the Sidekick has been extended to improve handling and responsiveness. You'll find ample interior space, but not much room for luggage. With large tires, traction and cornering have improved over last year, but be warned, the Sidekick still has a high rollover risk. It comes in two trim levels, JX and HLX, and offers just a few options.

General Information

FUEL ECONOMY	23/26 Average
DRIVING RANGE	348 Very Short
PARKING INDEX	Very Easy
THEFT RATING	Very Poor (4-dr.=Avg.)
CORPORATE TWINS	Geo Tracker
WHERE MADE	Canada/Japan
YEAR OF PRODUCTION	Eighth

Prices

Model	Retail	Mkup
Sidekick JS 2-dr. man. (2WD)	12,899	6%
Sidekick JS 4-dr. man. (2WD)	14,399	6%
Sidekick JX 4-dr. man. (4WD)	15,999	9%
Sidekick Sport JX man.	17,999	9%
Sidekick Sport JLX man.	18,999	12%

The Ratings

	POOR — GOOD
COMPARATIVE RATING *	
CRASH TEST	
SAFETY FEATURES	
FUEL ECONOMY	
PM COST	
REPAIR COST	
WARRANTY	
COMPLAINTS	
INSURANCE COST	

Safety

CRASH TEST	No government results
SIDE CRASH PROTECT.	Weak
AIRBAGS	Dual
ANTI-LOCK BRAKES	2-whl. (4-whl.opt.)
BELT ADJUSTORS	None
BUILT-IN CHILD SEAT	None
OCCUPANT INJURY	Average

Specifications

LENGTH (in.)	158.7	Very Short
HEAD/LEG ROOM (in.)	40.6/42.1	Very Roomy
CARGO SPACE (cu. ft.)	45	Very Small
PAYLOAD	850	Very Low
TOW RATING (lbs.)	1000	Very Low
SEATING	4	
WHEEL SIZE (in.)	15	

Specifications may vary.

Competition

	POOR — GOOD	Pg.
Suzuki Sidekick		151
Geo Tracker		126
Jeep Cherokee		133
Jeep Wrangler		135
Kia Sportage		136

* Due to the importance of crash tests, vehicles with no results as of publication date cannot be given an overall rating.

Suzuki X-90

Small Sport Utility

All-new this year, Suzuki takes aim at the young and the young-at-heart with their new two seat sport utility. It comes with many standard features such as power windows and door locks, and most importantly, dual airbags and 4-wheel ABS. Also standard are daytime running lamps which improve the visibility of the X-90.

The X-90 is powered by a small 1.6-liter 4-cylinder engine which will deliver adequate power and gas mileage, but don't expect it to out-power its competition. There are two models to choose from: X-90 2WD or X-90 4WD; the 4WD really comes in handy if you plan to go off-roading. This is a very small vehicle, so don't expect to be able to carry or tow much of anything. Ride will be good on smooth roads, but will be much like a Jeep Wrangler on bumpy ones. Make sure you test drive the X-90 before you buy.

The Ratings	POOR □□□□□□□□□□ GOOD
COMPARATIVE RATING*	□□□□□□□□□□
CRASH TEST	□□□□□□□□□□
SAFETY FEATURES	□□□□□□■□□□
FUEL ECONOMY	□□□□□■□□□□
PM COST	□□□□□□□□■□
REPAIR COST	□□■□□□□□□□
WARRANTY	■□□□□□□□□□
COMPLAINTS	□□□□□□□□□□
INSURANCE COST	□□□□■□□□□□

Safety	
CRASH TEST	No government results
SIDE CRASH PROTECT.	Weak
AIRBAGS	Dual
ANTI-LOCK BRAKES	4-wheel
BELT ADJUSTORS	None
BUILT-IN CHILD SEAT	None
OCCUPANT INJURY	

General Information		
FUEL ECONOMY	25/28	Average
DRIVING RANGE	289	Very Short
PARKING INDEX	Very Easy	
THEFT RATING		
CORPORATE TWINS		
WHERE MADE	Japan	
YEAR OF PRODUCTION	First	

Specifications		
LENGTH (in.)	146.1	Very Short
HEAD/LEG ROOM (in.)	34.2/41.5	Vry. Cramped
CARGO SPACE (cu. ft.)	8	Very Small
PAYLOAD	400	Very Low
TOW RATING (lbs.)	1000	Very Low
SEATING	2	
WHEEL SIZE (in.)	15	

Specifications may vary.

Prices

Model	Retail	Mkup
X-90 5-speed man. (2WD)	13,499	
X-90 5-speed man. (4WD)	14,999	
X-90 4-speed auto. (4WD)	15,949	

Competition

	POOR □□□□□□□□□□ GOOD	Pg.
Suzuki X-90	□□□□□□□□□□	152
Geo Tracker	□□□□■□□□□□	126
Jeep Cherokee	□□□■□□□□□□	133
Jeep Wrangler	□□□□□□□□□□	135
Suzuki Sidekick	□□□□□□□□□□	151

* Due to the importance of crash tests, vehicles with no results as of publication date cannot be given an overall rating.

Toyota 4Runner

Mid-Size Sport Utility

The Toyota 4Runner enters 1996 with a new body, a redesigned interior and many new safety features which make it one of the most attractive and safe vehicles in the sport utility class. The 4Runner is trying to distance itself from the pack with its looks and versatility. Dual airbags and 2-wheel ABS come standard, 4-wheel optional.

The engines for '96 are more powerful and fuel efficient than last year's choices. But beware, this is a very heavy vehicle and acceleration will be anything but fast. Ride, handling, rear-seat room and comfort have all improved over last year's disappointing model. With an extended wheelbase and width, the interior is more spacious and comfortable for 5 adults though head and leg room is still cramped. The dashboard is better than most of the competition and visibility is good. With the addition of dual airbags, the 4Runner is a good, but expensive, choice.

General Information		
FUEL ECONOMY	19/21	Poor
DRIVING RANGE	344	Very Short
PARKING INDEX	Easy	
THEFT RATING	Very Poor	
CORPORATE TWINS		
WHERE MADE	Australia	
YEAR OF PRODUCTION	Seventh	

Prices		
Model	**Retail**	**Mkup**
4Runner V6 auto. (2WD)	22,508	18%
4Runner 4-cylinder man. (4WD)	21,838	18%
4Runner V6 man. (4WD)	23,958	18%
4Runner V6 auto. (4WD)	25,008	18%

The Ratings	POOR □□□□ GOOD
COMPARATIVE RATING*	□□□□□□□□□□
CRASH TEST	□□□□□□□□□□
SAFETY FEATURES	□□□■□□□□□□
FUEL ECONOMY	□□□■□□□□□□
PM COST	□□□■□□□□□□
REPAIR COST	□□□□□■□□□□
WARRANTY	□■□□□□□□□□
COMPLAINTS	□□□□□□□■□□
INSURANCE COST	■□□□□□□□□□

Safety	
CRASH TEST	No government results
SIDE CRASH PROTECT.	Weak
AIRBAGS	Driver
ANTI-LOCK BRAKES	2-whl. (4-whl.opt.)
BELT ADJUSTORS	Standard
BUILT-IN CHILD SEAT	None
OCCUPANT INJURY	Average

Specifications		
LENGTH (in.)	176.0	Short
HEAD/LEG ROOM (in.)	38.7/41.5	Cramped
CARGO SPACE (cu. ft.)	78	Average
PAYLOAD	300	Very Low
TOW RATING (lbs.)	3500	Low
SEATING	5	
WHEEL SIZE (in.)	15	

Specifications may vary.

Competition	POOR □□□□ GOOD	Pg.
Toyota 4Runner	□□□□□□□□□□	153
Chevrolet Blazer	■□□□□□□□□□	100
Ford Explorer	□□□□□□□□□■	115
GMC Jimmy	■□□□□□□□□□	119
Mits. Montero	□□□□□■□□□□	143

* Due to the importance of crash tests, vehicles with no results as of publication date cannot be given an overall rating.

Toyota Land Cruiser

Large Sport Utility

The Land Cruiser has been around in various forms since the 1960's; the latest version does battle with the Jeep Grand Cherokee. For '96, there is a new exterior package and, most importantly, dual airbags and ABS are both standard equipment.

The engine is a hefty, gas-guzzling 4.5-liter 6-cylinder with automatic transmission and all-wheel drive. Because the Land Cruiser tips the scales at 4,700 pounds, don't expect stunning acceleration or decent fuel economy. The ride is fairly comfortable, but handling is sluggish. Seats are roomy, as is the cargo area. Controls are competent, nothing fancy. The differential-locks package may be useful for foul-weather driving. You'll also find an average tow rating, but payload is low. With the addition of dual airbags, this year's Land Cruiser competes well with the Jeep Grand Cherokee and the Ford Bronco.

General Information		
FUEL ECONOMY	13/15	Very Poor
DRIVING RANGE	351	Short
PARKING INDEX	Hard	
THEFT RATING	Very Poor	
CORPORATE TWINS		
WHERE MADE	Japan	
YEAR OF PRODUCTION	Sixth	

Prices

Model	Retail	Mkup
Land Cruiser Base	40,258	20%

The Ratings

	POOR — GOOD
COMPARATIVE RATING*	
CRASH TEST	
SAFETY FEATURES	
FUEL ECONOMY	
PM COST	
REPAIR COST	
WARRANTY	
COMPLAINTS	
INSURANCE COST	

Safety

CRASH TEST	No government results
SIDE CRASH PROTECT.	Weak
AIRBAGS	Dual
ANTI-LOCK BRAKES	4-wheel
BELT ADJUSTORS	Standard
BUILT-IN CHILD SEAT	None
OCCUPANT INJURY	Very Good

Specifications

LENGTH (in.)	189.8	Average
HEAD/LEG ROOM (in.)	40.3/42.2	Roomy
CARGO SPACE (cu. ft.)	91	Average
PAYLOAD	1650	Low
TOW RATING (lbs.)	5000	Average
SEATING	5/7	
WHEEL SIZE (in.)	16	

Specifications may vary.

Competition

	POOR — GOOD	Pg.
Toy. Land Cruiser		154
Chevy Blazer		100
Ford Bronco		113
GMC Jimmy		119
Mits. Montero		143

* Due to the importance of crash tests, vehicles with no results as of publication date cannot be given an overall rating.

Toyota Previa

Minivan

The Previa enters '96 with no exterior changes, but does improve under the hood. It comes in two trim levels, DX or LE. Dual airbags are standard, and ABS is optional on all models.

The Previa is offered in rear- or four-wheel drive. They all seat seven people. Automatic overdrive is standard except on the rear-drive DX. The standard, and only engine, is a 2.4-liter supercharged engine which was optional last year, and is much more adept at carrying this big vehicle. Handling and ride are about the best you can get in a minivan, especially if you buy an All-Trac version. The interior is comfortable and cargo space is even greater than in the Chrysler "Grand" models. With side impact protection that meets 1999 government standards, the Previa is one of the safest minivans on the maket. However, the Previa may have a difficult time keeping up with the all-new Chrysler minivans.

General Information		
FUEL ECONOMY	18/22	Poor
DRIVING RANGE	376	Short
PARKING INDEX	Average	
THEFT RATING	Average	
CORPORATE TWINS		
WHERE MADE	Japan	
YEAR OF PRODUCTION	Sixth	

Prices		
Model	**Retail**	**Mkup**
Previa DX (2WD)	24,318	17%
Previa DX (All-Trac)	27,858	17%
Previa LE (2WD)	28,858	18%
Previa LE (All-Trac)	32,198	18%

The Ratings	
	POOR … GOOD
COMPARATIVE RATING	□□□□□□□■□□
CRASH TEST	□□□□□■□□□□
SAFETY FEATURES	□□□□□□□■□□
FUEL ECONOMY	□□□■□□□□□□
PM COST	□□□■□□□□□□
REPAIR COST	□□□■□□□□□□
WARRANTY	□■□□□□□□□□
COMPLAINTS	□□□□□□■□□□
INSURANCE COST	□□□□□□□□□■

Safety	
CRASH TEST	Average
SIDE CRASH PROTECT.	Strong
AIRBAGS	Dual
ANTI-LOCK BRAKES	4-wheel (optional)
BELT ADJUSTORS	Standard
BUILT-IN CHILD SEAT	None
OCCUPANT INJURY	Average (4WD=Vry. Gd.)

Specifications		
LENGTH (in.)	187.0	Average
HEAD/LEG ROOM (in.)	39.4/40.1	Cramped
CARGO SPACE (cu. ft.)	152	Very Large
PAYLOAD	1650	Low
TOW RATING (lbs.)	3500	Low
SEATING	7	
WHEEL SIZE (in.)	15	

Specifications may vary.

Competition		
	POOR … GOOD	**Pg.**
Toyota Previa	□□□□□□□■□□	155
Ford Windstar	□□□□□□□□□■	118
Ford Aerostar	□□□□□□□■□□	112
Honda Odyssey	□□□□□■□□□□	127
Pontiac Tr. Sport	□□□□□□□□■□	150

Toyota adds yet another car to its lineup this year as it introduces the RAV4 (Recreational Active Vehicle with 4WD) to the sport utility market. It is designed to be a light off-road vehicle. Toyota has equipped this new vehicle well with standard dual airbags and optional 4-wheel ABS.

The RAV4 is powered by an average 2-liter 4-cylinder engine, which can beat out many sporty coupes and sedans, but is unable to compete with some of the other small sport utilities. It has a wide stance, which gives it decent room inside for four, but five is a squeeze. You have your choice between a 2- or 4-door model, and many different appearance packages. This vehicle was not designed to handle heavy off-road use, or to tow anything more than 1500 lbs. in weight. Part of a new generation of small sport utilities, the RAV4, with its dual airbags and looks, should have little trouble competing with competitors like the X-90.

The Ratings

	POOR ... GOOD
COMPARATIVE RATING*	□□□□□□□□□□
CRASH TEST	□□□□□□□□□□
SAFETY FEATURES	□□□□□□■□□□
FUEL ECONOMY	□□□□□■□□□□
PM COST	□□□■□□□□□□
REPAIR COST	□□□□■□□□□□
WARRANTY	□■□□□□□□□□
COMPLAINTS	□□□□□□□□□□
INSURANCE COST	□□□□■□□□□□

Safety

CRASH TEST	No government results
SIDE CRASH PROTECT.	Weak
AIRBAGS	Dual
ANTI-LOCK BRAKES	4-wheel (optional)
BELT ADJUSTORS	Standard
BUILT-IN CHILD SEAT	None
OCCUPANT INJURY	

General Information

FUEL ECONOMY	24/29	Average
DRIVING RANGE	398	Average
PARKING INDEX	Very Easy	
THEFT RATING		
CORPORATE TWINS		
WHERE MADE	Japan	
YEAR OF PRODUCTION	First	

Specifications

LENGTH (in.)	145.9	Very Short
HEAD/LEG ROOM (in.)	40.0/40.4	Average
CARGO SPACE (cu. ft.)	27	Very Small
PAYLOAD	800	Very Low
TOW RATING (lbs.)	1500	Very Low
SEATING	4	
WHEEL SIZE (in.)	16	

Specifications may vary.

Prices

Model	Retail	Mkup
Prices unavailable at press time.		
Expected range: $16-18,000		

Competition

	POOR ... GOOD	Pg.
Toyota RAV4	□□□□□□□□□□	156
Geo Tracker	□□□□■□□□□□	126
Jeep Cherokee	□□□■□□□□□□	133
Jeep Wrangler	□□□□□□□□□□	135
Suzuki Sidekick	□□□□□□□□□□	151

* Due to the importance of crash tests, vehicles with no results as of publication date cannot be given an overall rating.

Toyota T100

Standard Pickup

The T100 Pickup is the first Japanese truck to compete with larger domestic pickups like the Dodge Ram, Ford F-Series, and Chevrolet C/K Series. It receives few changes from 1995 for the '96 model year. Engine options aren't quite as broad as with the domestics, but a driver's side airbag is standard. Four-wheel ABS is only available on the DX V6.

The standard 2.7-liter 4-cylinder engine is not nearly powerful enough and the 3.4-liter V6 optional engine provides decent power, but doesn't match the power of the V8s in most large U.S. pickups. Neither will give you good fuel economy. You have your choice of two- and four-wheel drive models, and you can pick from automatic overdrive or 5-speed manual. Ride, comfort, inside room and handling present no surprises. Like most Toyotas, the Pickup has a nicely laid-out dashboard and controls.

General Information

FUEL ECONOMY	17/21 Poor
DRIVING RANGE	456 Long
PARKING INDEX	Hard
THEFT RATING	Average
CORPORATE TWINS	
WHERE MADE	Japan
YEAR OF PRODUCTION	Fourth

Prices

Model	Retail	Mkup
T100 Reg. Cab 4-cyl. man. (4x2)	14,448	
T100 Reg. Cab 4-cyl. auto. (4x2)	15,348	
T100 Xtracab V6 man. (4x2)	18,018	
T100 SR5 Xtracab V6 auto. (4x2)	19,738	
T100 Xtracab V6 Base (4x4)	21,908	

The Ratings

	POOR — GOOD (1–10)
COMPARATIVE RATING	5
CRASH TEST	9
SAFETY FEATURES	4
FUEL ECONOMY	4
PM COST	4
REPAIR COST	5
WARRANTY	2
COMPLAINTS	10
INSURANCE COST	1

Safety

CRASH TEST	Very Good
SIDE CRASH PROTECT.	Weak
AIRBAGS	Driver
ANTI-LOCK BRAKES	4-wheel (optional)
BELT ADJUSTORS	Standard
BUILT-IN CHILD SEAT	None
OCCUPANT INJURY	

Specifications

LENGTH (in.)	209.1 Very Long
HEAD/LEG ROOM (in.)	39.6/42.9 Roomy
CARGO SPACE (cu. ft.)	
PAYLOAD	1700 Average
TOW RATING (lbs.)	4000 Average
SEATING	3
WHEEL SIZE (in.)	15

Specifications may vary.

Competition

	POOR — GOOD (1–10)	Pg.
Toyota T100	5	157
Chevy C/K Series	10	102
Dodge Ram Pickup		110
Ford F-Series	9	116
GMC Sierra	10	122

Toyota Tacoma

Compact Pickup

The Tacoma, a compact pickup, replaces the outdated Toyota Pickup for 1996. The Tacoma comes with new engines, a new body, and a new frame and chassis. You can choose between 2WD and 4WD, and regular and extended-cab models. A driver's side airbag is standard equipment; 4-wheel ABS is optional.

Toyota offers a wide variety of engine choices. For starters, there is the standard 2.4-liter 4-cyl. which will provide adequate power, or you can choose a more powerful 2.7-liter, or an even bigger 3.4-liter V6. Seating inside is comfortable and the ride is like most compact pickups, smooth on smooth roads. A new off-road package is available that allows you to shift into 4-wheel-drive on the go. With its many changes, this new compact pickup should present some competition for the Ford Ranger, Chevy S-Series, and Dodge Dakota pickups.

General Information		
FUEL ECONOMY	23/28	Average
DRIVING RANGE	378	Short
PARKING INDEX	Easy	
THEFT RATING	Average (4WD=Poor)	
CORPORATE TWINS		
WHERE MADE	U.S./Canada/Japan	
YEAR OF PRODUCTION	Second	

Prices		
Model	**Retail**	**Mkup**
Tacoma Base (4x2)	12,028	
Tacoma Reg. Cab 4-cyl. Base (4x4)	16,908	
Tacoma Xtracab 4-cyl. Base (4x4)	18,338	
Tacoma Reg. Cab V6 Base (4x4)	18,028	
Tacoma Xtracab V6 Base (4x4)	19,418	

The Ratings	POOR □□□□□□□□ GOOD
COMPARATIVE RATING*	□□□□□□□□□□
CRASH TEST	□□□□□□□□□□
SAFETY FEATURES	□□□■□□□□□□
FUEL ECONOMY	□□□□□■□□□□
PM COST	□□□■□□□□□□
REPAIR COST	□□□■□□□□□□
WARRANTY	□■□□□□□□□□
COMPLAINTS	□□□□□□□□□□
INSURANCE COST	□□□□■□□□□□

Safety	
CRASH TEST	No government results
SIDE CRASH PROTECT.	Weak
AIRBAGS	Driver
ANTI-LOCK BRAKES	4-wheel (optional)
BELT ADJUSTORS	Standard
BUILT-IN CHILD SEAT	None
OCCUPANT INJURY	Average

Specifications		
LENGTH (in.)	180.5	Short
HEAD/LEG ROOM (in.)	38.2/41.7	Cramped
CARGO SPACE (cu. ft.)		
PAYLOAD	1650	Low
TOW RATING (lbs.)	3500	Low
SEATING	3	
WHEEL SIZE (in.)	14/15	

Specifications may vary.

Competition	POOR □□□□□□□□ GOOD	Pg.
Toyota Tacoma	□□□□□□□□□□	158
Chevrolet S-Series	□□□□□□■□□□	104
Dodge Dakota	□□□□□□□□■□	109
GMC Sonoma	□■□□□□□□□□	123
Mazda B-Series	□□□■□□□□□□	139

* Due to the importance of crash tests, vehicles with no results as of publication date cannot be given an overall rating.

Index

Wanted: Complaints and Questions

One of the most valuable, but little used, services of the government is the Auto Safety Hotline. By calling the toll-free Hotline to report safety problems, your particular concern or problem will become part of the National Highway Transportation Safety Administration's (NHTSA) complaint database. This complaint database is extraordinarily important to government decision makers who often take action based on this information. In addition, it provides consumer groups, like the Center for Auto Safety, with the evidence they need to force the government to act. Unless government engineers or safety advocates have evidence of a wide-scale problem, little can be done to get manufacturers to correct the defect.

Few government services have the potential to do so much for the consumer as this complaint database. NHTSA also offers a Vehicle Owner's Questionnaire which allows you to present your complaint to the government in writing. To receive a copy, call the Auto Safety Hotline at 800-424-9393 (or 202-366-0123 in Washington, DC).

The questionnaire asks for information that the agency's technical staff will need to evaluate the problem. This information also gives the government an indication of which vehicles are causing consumers the most problems. After you fill out and return the questionnaire, a few things will happen. First, a copy will go to NHTSA's safety defect investigators. Then, a copy will be sent to the manufacturer of the vehicle, with a request for help in resolving the problem. You will also be notified that your questionnaire has been received.

You can also use the questionnaire to report defects in tires and child safety seats. In fact, we strongly encourage you to report any problems with child safety seats. Now that child safety seats are required by law in all fifty states, we have noticed that numerous design and safety problems have surfaced. If the government knows about these problems, they will be more likely to take action so that modifications are made in these life-saving devices.

By calling the Auto Safety Hotline and filling out the Vehicle Owner's Questionnaire, you are not only making your voice heard to the government and the manufacturers but also helping regulate and police the automobile industry.